THE GREAT MISS DRIVER

"*By Heaven, the girl on the mantelpiece at Hatcham Ford!*"

[Page 270.]

THE
GREAT MISS DRIVER

BY

ANTHONY HOPE

AUTHOR OF

TRISTRAM OF BLENT, DOUBLE HARNESS,
HELENA'S PATH, LOVE'S LOGIC

Copyright, 1908, by Anthony Hope Hawkins

THE GREAT MISS DRIVER

CHAPTER I

WHAT IS SHE LIKE?

"PERHAPS you won't believe me," said I, "but till yesterday I never so much as heard of her existence."

"I've not the least difficulty in believing you. That was old Nick's way. It wasn't your business—was it?—so he didn't talk to you about it. On the other hand, when a thing was your business—that's to say, when he wanted your services—he told you all about it. But I believe I'm the only person he did tell. I'm sure he didn't tell a soul down in Catsford. Finely put about they'll be!"

Mr. Cartmell, of Fisher, Son, & Cartmell (he was the only surviving representative of the firm), broke off to hide a portion of his round red face in a silver tankard; Loft, the butler, had brought it to him on his arrival without express orders given; I had often seen the same vessel going into Mr. Driver's study on the occasion of the lawyer's calls.

He set the tankard—much lightened it must have been—on the mantelpiece and walked to the window, taking a pull at his cigar. We were in my room—my "office" it was generally called in the household. He stood looking out, talking to me half over his shoulder.

"A man's mind turns back at times like these. I remember him hard on forty years ago. I was a lad then, just gone into the business. Mr. Fisher was alive —not the one you remember—not poor Nat—but the old gentleman. Nat was the junior, and I was in the last year of my articles. Well, Nick Driver came to the old gentleman one morning and asked him to act for him—said he thought he was big enough by now. The old gentleman didn't want to, but poor Nat had an eye for a man and saw that Driver meant to get on. So they took him, and we've acted for him ever since. It wasn't many years before he—" Cartmell paused a moment, laying the finger-tips of his right hand against the finger-tips of his left, and straightening his arms from the elbow like a swimmer —" before he began to drive his wedge into the county."

The good man was fairly launched on his subject; much of it was new to me, in detail if not in broad outline, and I listened with interest. Besides, there was nothing else to do until the time came to start. But the story will bear a little summarizing, like a great many other stories; Cartmell was too fond of anecdotes. Thus summarized then:

Nicholas Driver began life as a tanner in Catsford. He was thrifty and saved money. With the money he bought land and built some villas; with the rent of the villas—more land. He had faith in the development of Catsford. He got early news of the coming of the railway; he pledged every house and every inch of land—and bought more land. So the process went on—detailed by Mr. Cartmell, indicated here. Nich-

WHAT IS SHE LIKE?

olas Driver became moderately rich—and, by the way, his Catsford property had never ceased to rise in value and was rising still. Then, as it seemed (even Mr. Cartmell spoke conjecturally), an era of speculation followed—first in England, then in America. "That," Cartmell interjected, "was when he picked up this girl's mother, not that she was American, but he met her about that time." He must have speculated largely and successfully, or he could not have made all that money—so stood the case. The money made, the process of " driving his wedge into the county" began. "The county" must, here and henceforward, be carefully distinguished from "the town." Geographical contiguity does not bridge a social chasm.

First he bought Hatcham Ford, a small but beautiful Jacobean house lying on the banks of the river, some mile and a half out of Catsford at that time, now caught in the lengthening fringe of the town. While in residence there, he spread his territory to the north and west, acquiring all the outlying farms which the Lord Fillingford of the day was free to sell; then, too, he made his first audacious bid for Fillingford Manor itself—the first of many, it appeared. Though the later no longer seemed audacious, all had been fruitless; Lord Fillingford could not sell without his son's consent, and that was withheld. The family struggled on in perpetual financial straits, hating Nicholas Driver, but envying him his money, never coming to an open rupture with him for fear of his power or apprehension of its own necessities; never sparing a sneer or a secret thrust when either was safe. For his part, baffled in that quarter, he turned to the east and approached Mr. Dormer of Breysgate Priory. It was a beautiful place. Down by the lake lay the old Cistercian monastery; the original building was in ruins, but a small house had been built on in the days of Elizabeth, and this was still habitable. High on the hill stood the big, solidly handsome, Georgian mansion, erected by the Dormer of the day when the estate came into the hands of the family. From the hilltop the park rolled out and out in undulating curves of rich grass-land and spreading woods. To Nicholas Driver's joy and surprise—he had anticipated another struggle and feared another rebuff—Mr. Dormer was ready to sell—for a price. He was elderly, his wife middle-aged, his only heir a cousin toward whom he was indifferent and who, though heir of entail to the property, would be unable to keep it up, unless his predecessor left him money for the purpose. In these circumstances matters were soon arranged. The cousin was bought off, his consent given, and the Dormers retired to a smaller place, properly the dower house—Hingston Hall, situated fifteen miles from Catsford. Behold Nicholas Driver a country gentleman on a distinctly large scale!

"And with how much ready money to his name besides you'll get some idea about when the will is proved," Mr. Cartmell ended impressively.

His impressiveness impressed me; I do not know why I should be ashamed to confess it. A great deal of anything impresses ordinary people; a great deal of hill is a mountain, a great deal of water is an ocean, a great deal of brain is a genius; and so on. Similarly, a great deal of money has its grandeur—for ordinary people.

"It might be a million and a half—a million and a half sovereigns, Austin!—and it's growing every night while you sleep! And now—he's dead!"

"You do die just the same—that's the worst of it."

"And not an old man either!"

"Sixty-three!"

"Tut—I shall be that myself in three years—and you can't tire me yet!"

"Perhaps making millions and driving wedges is—rather exhausting, Cartmell. You split the tree; don't you blunt the wedge in time, too?"

"The end came easy, did it?"

"Oh, yes, in his sleep. So the nurse tells me. I wasn't there myself."

"I'm glad it was easy. After all, he was a very old friend of mine—and a very valuable client. Let's see, how long have you been with him?"

"Four years."

"Going to stay?"

I rose and began to brush my hat. "If you come to that," said I, "are you going to stay either, Cartmell? I gather that she can do as she pleases about that?"

"Every rod of ground and every farthing of money—bating decent charities! It's a great position."

"It's a very unexplored one so far as we're concerned," I made bold to remark.

"Have you seen him since—since the end, Austin?"

"Yes. Would you like to?"

"No, I shouldn't," he answered bluntly. "Perhaps it's brutal. I know it's cowardly. But I don't like death."

"Nonsense! You make half your income out of it. I say, I suppose we might as well start?"

"Yes," he assented absently. "I wonder how she's turned out!"

I looked at him with quickened interest. "Turned out? That sounds almost as if you'd seen her."

"I have seen her. Come along. I'll tell you about it as we drive down."

We traversed the long corridor which leads from my office to the hall. Loft was waiting for us, with an attendant footman. Loft addressed me in a muffled voice; his demeanor might always be relied on for perfection—he would not once unmuffle his voice till his master was buried.

"The landau is waiting, sir. The omnibus for Miss Driver's maid and the luggage has gone on." Wonderful man! He spoke of "Miss Driver" as if she had lived for years in the house.

Cartmell gave him a queer look and emitted a low chuckle as we got into the landau, behind the big grays. Mr. Driver always drove grays, and he liked them big, so that he could rattle up the hill to his house.

"Maid! Luggage!" muttered Cartmell. "The bus'll hold 'em, I think, with a bit to spare! By his orders I sent her twenty pounds on Tuesday; that's all she's had as yet. I only had time to telegraph about—the rest."

WHAT IS SHE LIKE?

"Interesting wire to get! But about your seeing her, Cartmell?"

In honor of the occasion Cartmell, like myself, had put on a black frock coat and a silk hat, properly equipped with a mourning band of respectful width. But he wore the coat with a jaunty air, and the hat slightly but effectively cocked on one side, so that the quiet yet ingrained horsiness of his aspect suffered little from the unwonted attire. The confidential wink with which he now turned his plump rubicund face toward me preserved his general harmony. With the mournful atmosphere of Breysgate Priory, however, I could not help feeling that my own lank jaws and more precisely poised head-gear consorted better.

"You can hold your tongue, Austin?"

"A very shrewd man has paid me four hundred a year for four years past on that understanding."

"Then what happened at the Smalls, at Cheltenham?"

"Isn't that beginning the story at the wrong end?" I asked.

"That was where she was"—he searched for a word—"where she was planted. She lived at three or four different places altogether, you know."

"And the mother?"

"Mother died—vanished anyhow—early in the proceedings. Well, word came of trouble at Cheltenham. Small, though of my own profession, was an ass. He wrote a bleating letter—yes, he was more like a sheep, really—to old Nick. Nick told me I must go and put it to rights. So I went."

"Why didn't he go himself?"

"I think," said Cartmell cautiously, "that he had some kind of a feeling against seeing the girl. Really that's the only thing that accounts for his behavior all through."

"Did he never see her?"

"Never—since she was quite a child. So he told me. But let me finish the story—if you want to hear it. Being ordered, I went. They lived in a beastly villa and were, to speak generally, a disgrace to humanity by their utter flabbiness. But there was a flashy sort of a gentleman, by the name of Powers." He stopped and looked at me for a minute. "A married flashy gentleman named Nelson Powers. She was sixteen —and she wrote to Powers. A good many letters she'd written to Powers. Small was such a fool that Powers guessed there was money in it. And she, of course, had never thought of a Mrs. Powers. How should she? Sixteen and——"

"Hopelessly innocent?"

"I really think so," he answered with an air, rather odd, of advancing a paradox. "She let him worm out of her all that she knew about her father—which was that he paid the bills for her and that Small had told her that he was rich. She didn't know where he lived, but Powers got that out of Small without much trouble, and then it was blackmail on Mr. Driver, of course."

"Did you get at Powers? Had to pay him something, I suppose?"

"I got at Mrs. Powers—and paid her. Much better! We had the letters in twenty-four hours. Powers really repented that time, I think! But I had orders to take her away from the Smalls. The same man never failed Nick Driver twice! I sent her under escort to Dawlish—at least near there—to a clergyman's family, where she's been ever since. But it can't be denied that she left Cheltenham rather—well, rather under a cloud. If you ask me what I think about it——"

I had been growing interested—yet not interested in precisely the point about which Mr. Cartmell conjectured that I might be about to inquire.

" Did she say anything about it herself? " I interrupted.

He stroked his chin. " She said rather a curious thing—she was only sixteen, you know. She said that we might have given her credit for being able to take just a little care of herself."

" That sounds like underrating your diplomacy, Cartmell."

" I thought myself that it reflected on the bill I proposed to send in! Funny, wasn't it? From a chit like that! "

" What did you say? "

" Asked her if she'd like a foot-warmer for the journey to Dawlish."

" Capital! You were about to tell me what you thought about it? "

" The folly of a young ignorant girl, no doubt. Powers was an insinuating rascal—and a girl doesn't know at that age the difference between a gentleman and a cad. He moved too soon, though. We were in lots of time to prevent real mischief—and Mrs. Powers came up to the scratch! " He drummed his fingers on the window of the landau, looking thoughtful and, as it seemed to me, retrospectively puzzled.

"And did all go smoothly with the clergyman's family?"

"She's been there ever since. I've heard of no trouble. The governess's reports of her were excellent, I remember Mr. Driver telling me once."

"Well then, we can forget all about Powers."

"Yes, yes," said Cartmell, drumming his fingers still.

"And what was she like?"

Cartmell looked at me, a smile slowly breaking across his broad face. "Here's the station. Suppose you see for yourself," he suggested.

We had ten minutes to wait before Miss Driver's train was due—we had been careful to run no risk of not being on the spot to receive her. Cartmell was at no loss to employ the time. I left him plunging into an animated discussion of the points of a handsome cob which stood outside the station: on the handsome cob's back was a boy, no less handsome, fresh of color and yellow-haired. I knew him to be young Lord Lacey, heir to the Fillingford earldom, but I had at that time no acquaintance with him, and passed on into the station, where I paced up and down among a crowd of loiterers and hasteners—for Catsford was by now a bustling center whence and whither men went and came at all hours of the day and most hours of the night. Driver had foreseen that this would come about! It had come about; he had grown rich; he lay dead. It went on happening still, and thereby

WHAT IS SHE LIKE?

adding to the piles of gold which he could no longer handle.

Instead of indulging in these trite reflections—to be excused only by the equal triteness of death, which tends to evoke them—I should have done well to consider my own position. A man bred for a parson but, for reasons of his own, averse from adopting the sacred calling, is commonly not too well fitted for other avocations—unless perhaps he would be a schoolmaster, and my taste did not lie that way. In default of private means, an easy berth at four hundred pounds a year may well seem a godsend. It had assumed some such celestial guise to me when, on the casual introduction of my uncle one day in London, Mr. Driver had offered it to me. As his private secretary, I drew the aforementioned very liberal salary, I had my " office " in the big house on the hill, I dwelt in the Old Priory (that is to say, in the little dwelling house built on to the ruinous remains of the ancient foundation), I was seldom asked for more than three hours' work a day, I had a horse to ride, and plenty of leisure for the books I loved. It would be very unfortunate to have to give up all that. Verily the question " What is she like? " had a practical, an economic, importance for me which raised it far above the sphere of mere curiosity or the nonsense of irrelevant romance. Was she a sensible young woman who would know a good secretary when she saw one? Or, on the other hand, was she not? A secretary of some sort she would certainly require.

Nay, perhaps, she wouldn't. The one utterance of

hers which had been, so far, credibly reported to my ears was to the effect that she could take care—just a little care—of herself. This at sixteen! This on the top of circumstances which at first sight indicated that she had taken particularly bad care of herself! Letters to a man like Powers! My imagination, forsaking my own position and prospects, constructed a confident picture of Powers, proceeded to sketch Mrs. Powers — strong lights here! — and to outline the family of the Smalls of Cheltenham. It ended by rejoicing that she had been removed from the influence of Powers and the environment of the Smalls of Cheltenham. Because, look at the matter how one might or could, there was no denying that it was the sort of incident which might just as well—or even better—not have happened at all. At the best, it was not altogether pleasant. Surely that was the truth—and not merely the abortive parson talking again? Well, even the abortive parson was sometimes right.

Cartmell clapped me on the shoulder. The handsome boy had, it appeared, departed, after receiving from an obsequious porter the copy of *Country Life*, in quest of which he had ridden to the station from Fillingford Manor.

"Here comes the train! I wonder if I shall know her again!"

Two minutes later, that observation of Cartmell's seemed to me plainly foolish. A man might like her or dislike her, trust her or not trust her—oh, away with these fatal alternatives, antitheses, or whatever they are! They confine judgment, and often falsify it.

WHAT IS SHE LIKE?

He might do all these things at once—and I fancied that she might welcome his perplexity. He would not be very likely to forget her—nor she to be pleased if he did.

That was only a first impression of her, as she got out of the train.

CHAPTER II

MAKING AMENDS

CARTMELL'S talk, as we drove back, was calculated to give her an almost overwhelming idea of her possessions and (if her temperament set that way) of her responsibilities. Big commercial buildings, blocks of shops, whole streets of small houses, drew from the lawyer a point of the finger and a brief, " That's yours "—or sometimes he would tell how her father had bought, how built, and how profited by the venture. Every time she would turn her head to look where his finger pointed, and nod slightly, gravely, composedly. She seemed to be reserving her opinion of it all. The only time she spoke was when we were emerging from the town and he showed her Hatcham Ford, saying, as usual, " That's yours," but adding that it was let furnished to Mr. Leonard Octon, who was abroad just now. Then her nod of understanding was accompanied by a low murmur, " It's very pretty."

She said nothing when we drove into the park of Breysgate Priory itself: yet I saw her eyes fixed intently on the great house on the hill, which comes into view directly the drive is entered, and certainly looks imposing enough. After the first formal greeting she did not speak to me, nor I to her, until her reception at the house was over and we had sat down to luncheon. But she had smiled at me once—when we were still standing by the door, on the terrace at the top of the steps, and Cartmell was showing her what he called "the lie of the land." The omnibus with its pair of big horses and its pair of big men came trotting up the hill, and on its big roof lay one small battered trunk. Loft was waiting to give orders to his footmen for the disposal of her luggage: when he saw the solitary and diminutive article, he advanced and, with pronounced graciousness, received it from the omnibus himself. She watched, and then gave me the smile that I have mentioned; evidently Loft—or Loft in conjunction with that humble box—appealed to her sense of humor.

Cartmell was soon at his ease with her: he called her "My dear" twice before we got to the sweets. The second time he apologized for taking the liberty—on the first occasion, I suppose, the words slipped out unnoticed by himself.

"But I like it," she said. "My father spoke so warmly about you in his letter."

Cartmell looked at me for a moment; we neither of us knew of a letter.

"He told me never to part with Mr. Cartmell because an honest lawyer was worth his weight in gold."

"I ride fourteen-seven," said Cartmell with a chuckle.

"And he said something about you, too," she added, looking at me, "but perhaps I'd better not repeat that."

"Shall I try to guess it?" I asked. "Did he say I was a scholar?"

"Yes."

"And a gentleman?"

"Yes."

"But confoundedly conceited?"

"No—well, not quite. Something like it, Mr. Austin. How did you know?"

"It's what he use to say to me himself three times a week?"

Her face had lit up in merriment during this little talk, but now she grew thoughtful again. I might well have looked thoughtful, too; so far as had appeared at present, there was no injunction against parting with me—no worth-his-weight-in-gold appraisement of the secretary!

"I expect he liked the scholar-and-gentleman part," she reflected. "He wasn't at all a scholar himself, I suppose?"

"He'd had no time for that," said Cartmell.

"Nor a gentleman?"

It was an embarrassing question—from a daughter about her father—addressed to Cartmell who owed him much and to me who had eaten his bread. Besides—he was lying there in his room upstairs. Cartmell faced the difficulty with simple directness.

"He wasn't polished in manner; when he was opposed or got angry, he was rough. But he was honest and straight, upright and just, kind and——"

"Kind?" she interrupted, a note of indignation plain to hear in her voice. "Not to me!"

That was awkward again!

"My dear Miss Driver, for what may have been amiss he's made you the best amends he could." He waved his arm as though to take in all the great house in which we sat. "Handsome amends!"

"Yes," she assented—but her assent did not sound very hearty.

A long silence followed—an uncomfortable silence. She was looking toward the window, and I could watch her face unperceived. From our first meeting I had been haunted by a sense of having seen her before, but I soon convinced myself that this was a delusion. I had not seen her, nor anyone like her (she was not at all like her father), in the flesh, but I had seen pictures that were like her. Not modern pictures, but sixteenth- or seventeenth-century portraits. Her hair was brown with ruddy tips, her brows not arched but very straight, her nose fine-cut and high, her mouth not large but her lips very red. Her chin was rather long, and her face wore the smooth, almost waxy, pallor which the pictures I was reminded of are apt to exhibit. Her eyes were so pronounced and bright a hazel that, seeing them on a canvas, one might have suspected the painter of taking a liberty with fact for the sake of his composition.

Cartmell broke the silence. "Since he wrote you a letter, may I venture to ask—?" He stopped and glanced at me. "Perhaps you wouldn't mind giving us five minutes to ourselves, Austin?"

I thought the request not unnatural, and rose promptly from my chair. But we had reckoned without our host—our new host.

"Why do you tell him to go?" she demanded of

Cartmell with a sudden sharpness. " I don't ask him to go. I don't want him to go. Sit down, please, Mr. Austin."

Cartmell had his two elbows on the table; he bit his thumb as he glanced up at her from under raised brows. He was not often called to book so sharply as that. I thought that she would make apology, but she made none. As I obediently—and, I fear, hastily —sat down again, she took a letter from a little bag which hung at her waist.

" What did you want to ask? " she said to Cartmell in a tone which was smooth but by no means overconciliatory.

Cartmell's manner said " Have it if you want it! " as he inquired bluntly, " Does your father say anything about your mother? "

She took the letter from its envelope and unfolded it. " About my mother he says this: ' It is necessary for me to say a few words about your mother. Mr. Cartmell is in possession of all proofs necessary to establish your position as my daughter, and there is no need for you to trouble your head about that, as not the smallest difficulty can arise. The personal aspect of the case is that on which I must touch. Three years after your birth your mother left me under circumstances which made it impossible for me to have any further communication with her. She went to Australia, and died five years later in Melbourne from an attack of typhoid fever. I caused constant inquiry to be made as to her position and took measures to secure that she should suffer no hardship. The circumstances to which I have referred made it imperative that I should remove you from her charge. As she consented to give up all claim on you, I did not go to the trouble of obtaining a divorce—which she did not desire either, as matters had been kept quiet. You will ask, and with reason, why I did not bring you up myself, and why I have delayed publicly acknowledging you as my daughter till the hour of my death. I can give no reason good to the world. I can give none good to my own conscience, unless it is a good one to say that a man is what God made him and that there are some things impossible to some men. It will seem a hard saying, but I could not endure to have you with me. I know myself, and I can only assure you that, if your childhood has not been a very happy one as it is, it would have been no happier if spent under my roof. Now we have been only strangers—you would have been worse than a stranger then.' "

Miss Driver, who had read in a low but level and composed voice, paused here for a moment—perhaps in doubt whether to read more. Then she went on: " ' With that much excuse—for I have none other—I must now, my daughter, say good-by, for I am dying. Though of my own choice I have not seen you since your infancy. I have not been without thought for you. I hesitated long before throwing on your shoulders all the burden which I have created for my own and carried on them. But in the end nature has seemed to say to me—and to speak more strongly as I grow weaker—that you are the person to whom it should belong and that, if things go wrong, it will be nature's fault, not mine. Don't spend more than two-thirds of your income—the other third should go back to work and bring in more. Give handsomely when you give, but don't be always dribbling out small sums; they mount up against you without aiding the recipients. Go to church unless you really dislike it. Be independent, but not eccentric. You have a great position; make it greater. Be a power in your world. About love and marriage, remember always that being sensible in general matters is no guarantee that you will act sensibly there. So be doubly on your guard. Suspect and fear marriage, even while you seek the best alliance you can find. Be you man or woman, by marriage you give another a power over you. Suspect it—suspect your lover—suspect yourself. You need fear no man except the man to whom you have given yourself. With earnest wishes for your welfare, I remain your affectionate father—NICHOLAS DRIVER.'"

During the reading Cartmell's face had been disturbed and sad; once or twice he fidgeted restively in his chair. I had listened intently, seeming again to hear the measured full voice, the hard clean-cut counsels, to which I had listened almost daily for the last four years. Fine sense! And a heart somewhere? I was inclined to answer yes—but how deep it lay, and what a lot of digging to get there! He had never given his daughter one chance of so much as putting her hand to the spade.

She tucked the letter away in her little bag; she was smiling again by now. I had smiled myself—my memories being so acutely touched; but she must have smiled for discernment, not for memory.

MAKING AMENDS

"Now I think I should like to go and see him."

Cartmell excused himself, as I knew he would.

"I've never seen him, that I can remember, you know," she said.

The meeting of the Catsford Corporation (the town had become a borough ten years before—largely owing to Mr. Driver's efforts) could not wait. But Cartmell had one thing to say before he went; it was not on business, nor arising out of the letter; he was to have a full business discussion with her on the morrow. He took her hand in both of his and pressed it—forgetful apparently of her sharp rebuke.

"You can't live in this great house all alone," he said. "I wonder your father said nothing about that!"

"Oh, that's all right. Chat's coming in a week. She'd have come with me, but Mrs. Simpson wouldn't let her go till a new governess could be got. Four girls, you see, and Mrs. Simpson thinks she's an invalid. Besides, Chat wouldn't come without a new black silk dress. So I had to give her most of that money—and she'll be here in a week—and I haven't got a new dress."

I noticed that her black dress was far from new. It was, in fact, rather rusty. Her black straw hat, however, appeared to be new. It was a large spreading sort of hat.

"Yes, Mr. Austin, the hat's new," she remarked.

The girl seemed to have a knack of noticing where one's eyes happened to be.

"I can give you lots of money," Cartmell assured

her. "And—er—'Chat' was governess at the Simpsons', was she?"

"Yes, she's been there for years, but she's very fond of me, and agreed to come and be my companion. She taught me all I know. I'm sure you'll like Chat."

"You can only try her," said he, rather doubtfully. I think that he would have preferred, Miss Driver, to cut loose from the old days altogether. "But, you know, we can't call her just 'Chat.' It must be short for something?"

"Short for Chatters—Miss Chatters. And she says Chatters is really—or was really—Charteris. That's pronounced Charters, isn't it?" She addressed the last question to me, and I said that I believed she was right. "I shall get on very well by myself till she comes." She questioned me again. "Do you live in the house?"

"No, I live down at the Old Priory. But I have my office in the house."

"Oh, yes. Now, if Mr. Cartmell must go, will you take me up?"

She stopped a moment, though, to look at the pictures—old Mr. Driver had bought some good ones—and so gave me one word with Cartmell.

"Depend upon it," he whispered. "Chat's a fool. People who keep telling you their names ought to be spelt like better names, when they aren't, are always fools. Why don't they spell 'em that way, or else let it alone?"

There seemed to be a good deal in that.

Cartmell gone, we went together up the broad

"He might have given me a chance!"

MAKING AMENDS

staircase which sprang from the center of the hall. As we passed a chair, she took off her hat and flung it down. The rich masses old brown hair, coiled about her head, caught the sun of a bright spring afternoon; she ran swiftly and lightly up the stairs. " Nice, soft, thick, carpet!" she remarked. I began to perceive that she would enjoy the incidental luxuries of her new position—and that she did enjoy the one great luxury—life. I fancied that she enjoyed it enormously.

We trod another " nice, soft, thick, carpet " for the length of a long passage and came to his door. I opened it, let her pass in, and was about to close it after her. But as we reached his room, a sudden shadow of trouble or of fear had fallen upon her— grief it could hardly be.

" No," she said. " Come in, too. Remember—he's a stranger."

To be in the room with the dead seems to be itself a partaking of death; it is at least, for a moment, a suspension of life. Yet the still welcome is not unfriendly.

She walked toward the bed alone, but in an instant beckoned to me to follow her. She bent down and moved the covering. His broad strong face looked resolute and brave as ever. It looked—to speak truth—as hard as ever also.

Her eyes were set on him; suddenly she caught hold of my hand; " Don't go." I pressed her hand, for I heard her breathing quickly. I just caught her next words: " He might have given me a chance!"

" I believe he was sorry about that at the end."

She shook her head. " He's given you a big chance now."

She nodded, but absently. " How strange to—to be his doing—and he there! And then—all this! " She let go my hand, took a step forward, bent and kissed his brow quickly. " How cold! " she murmured and grasped my hand tightly again. To my fancy she seemed surprised—and relieved—that the sleeper did not stir.

We were—as I say—out of the world; we were just two creatures, living for a little while, by the side of a third who lived no more.

" You shouldn't kiss him unless you forgive," I said.

She kissed him again and drew the sheet over his face.

" He must have been a fine man. I forgive. Come, let's go."

Outside, the world was with us—and I wondering whether that was what I had really said.

At least she seemed to bear me no ill-will. " Are you free to come for a walk? " she asked. " I should like some fresh air."

" Would you like to see the gardens? "

" No—that means pottering. Take me for a good spin."

By a happy thought I remembered Tor Hill and took her there. The hill lies at the extremity of the Priory park, looking down on the road which separates our dominions from the Fillingford country; beyond the road the Manor itself can be seen by glimpses through the woods which surround it. Catsford lies in the valley to the left; away to the right, but not in sight, lay Oxley Lodge, and Overington Grange, the seat of Sir John Aspenick. Here she could take a bird's-eye view of her position and that of her nearest neighbors.

"I'm glad to see Fillingford," she remarked. "My father mentioned it—in the earlier part of that letter. He said that he had wanted to buy it, but Lord Fillingford couldn't or wouldn't sell."

"His son's consent was necessary—that's the present man—and he wouldn't give it. Indeed the story runs that he hated Mr. Driver for trying to buy."

She seemed to take as careful a view of Fillingford Manor as the distance and the trees allowed.

"My father seems to have been sorry he couldn't buy it. He seemed to think it might still be sold."

"Surely you've got enough! And, for my part, I should much prefer the Priory. It's muggy down there in the valley—though I believe it's a very fine house."

"You've not been there?"

"No. We of the Priory have had small dealings with Fillingford lately. We've kept up the forms of civility—but it's been very distant. Underneath, there's been a kind of silent feud—well, more or less silent; but I daresay that'll be all over now."

"My father wrote 'Possibly you in your way may succeed better than I in mine.'"

"Fillingford wouldn't sell. He's hard up, but he can get along. And there's always the chance of a rich marriage for his son—or even for himself."

I really spoke without any thought of a personal

reference, but I perceived, directly afterward, that I might well seem to have made one; a marriage with Miss Driver would be undoubtedly rich. She gave no sign, however, of taking my remark in that sense, unless any inference can be drawn from her saying, " Oh, he's a widower? "

" He's a widower of forty, or a year or two more —and he's got a son of about seventeen—a very good-looking lad. His sister, Lady Sarah Lacey, keeps house for him, and according to local gossip is a bit of a shrew."

She began to laugh as she said with a mock sigh, " One's too old for me, and the other's too young— they must look somewhere else, I'm afraid! And then —how should I get on with the shrew? I'm rather a shrew myself—at least I've been told so."

" You'd better let them alone," I counseled her with a smile.

" Oh, no, I shan't do that," she rejoined with a decisiveness which I began to recognize as an occasional feature of her speech. " It'll be more amusing to see what they're like—presently. And what of the Dormers? My father mentioned them."

" A very nice old couple—but I fear he's failing."

A slight grimace dismissed the Dormers as not holding much interest for her.

" Oh, you won't want for neighbors. There are plenty of them, and they'll all be tremendously excited about you and will flock to call as soon as you can receive them."

" It must seem funny to them. I suppose they'd never heard of me? "

MAKING AMENDS

"I don't believe any of them had. Your father had no intimates, unless Mr. Cartmell can be called one. Besides—well, I'd never heard of you myself!"

"And here we are old friends!" she said graciously.

"That's very kind—but you mustn't think yourself bound to take over the secretary with the rest of the furniture."

She looked steadily in my face for several seconds, seeming to size me up—if I may be allowed the expression. Then she smiled—not gayly, yet again by no means sadly. It was the smile which I came to call later her mystery smile; and, as a general rule, it meant—in plain language—mischief. Of course, on this first day I did not attach these associations to it. It struck me as merely rather curious; as a man talks to himself, so she seemed to smile to herself, forgetting her interlocutor.

"Oh, well—stay and see how you like me," she said.

CHAPTER III

ON THE USE OF SCRAPES

WE were settling down. It was a week since the funeral. The borough and the neighborhood had survived their first stupefaction at the apparition of Miss Driver; the local journals had achieved their articles, organs of wider circulation and greater dignity their paragraphs; the charities which received legacies had given thanks, those which did not were turning resigned but hopeful eyes to the future. The undertaker sent in his bill, and the Town Council discussed the project of a Driver Memorial Hall—with a hardly disguised anticipation of the quarter from which the bulk of the money was to come.

There was really not much more to do till Miss Driver's first days of mourning were over, and the fascinating speculations as to her personal gifts and qualities could look to find some satisfaction from her appearances on public and private occasions. Only Cartmell still was—and would be for weeks—busy on the labors attendant on the transfer of a great estate, and the rearrangements necessitated by the loss of an able and experienced man—a masterly worker—and the succession of a girl ignorant of business. For

ON THE USE OF SCRAPES

the rest we were, as I say, settling down. Even Cartmell's activity caused us at Breysgate no sense of bustle, for it took him to London the day after the funeral and kept him there for above a fortnight.

When I say that "we" were settling down I mean the trio formed by Miss Driver, myself—and Miss Emily Chatters. It is my duty to introduce Miss Chatters with proper formality, and I will introduce her presently—but let us take people in their order. Miss Driver had inspected her property (except the wine cellar which, to Loft's dismay, she declined to enter); she had chosen her own set of rooms and given orders for them to be entirely refurnished; she had announced her intention—and small blame to her—of extending the refurnishing process to all the sitting-rooms—at least to the sitting-rooms; she had chosen her own hack from the stables—and I have no doubt that she had done what was immediately requisite as regards her wardrobe. At any rate, an air of achievement dwelt about her. For my part I performed my duties, and began to find that I had less work to do—and more time occupied in doing it. In Mr. Driver's day we worked as few men except Mr. Driver understood work from ten to one; then, as a rule, I was free. Under the new *régime* we worked at a gentler pressure—a much gentler pressure—for the same morning hours; but I stayed to lunch always, I came back to tea frequently, and I returned to dinner two or three evenings in the week. My duties as secretary grew lighter, but I seemed to be assuming the functions of a companion. I may do myself the incidental justice of saying that I rather resented this tendency to transform my office; but it was not easy to resist. She was paying for my whole time as her father had paid for it; it was her right, within wide limits, to say to what uses it should be put. Or—I could go. The liberty—perhaps it is rather theoretical—of " chucking my job " remained to me as to every free-born Englishman—who sees his way to getting another whereby to live. Not that I wished to surrender mine; I was interested and—to tell the truth—I grew, within our jurisdiction, important. She approached the assumption of her power cautiously, and at first would return almost any answer to almost any letter at my suggestion. I did not expect this to last, but so it was for the moment. For instance it was I, in ultimate reality, who offered that ten thousand pounds toward the Memorial Hall. I had a great difficulty in fixing the proper figure. If I may judge from the language employed by the Mayor (Councillor Bindlecombe) in public, I exceeded all possible anticipations of munificence; in private, I am told, he confessed to having entertained a hope of fifteen thousand. I imagine that my figure was not, on a balancing of considerations, far wide of the mark. Cartmell thought five thousand would have served—but old Cartmell was a screw with other people's money. I remembered " Give handsomely when you give." So, I think, did Jenny Driver. All the same, Bindlecombe did, in my opinion, open his mouth a bit too wide.

Miss Chatters came two days after the funeral—in the new black silk dress: it rustled powerfully. She was tall, had pale-brown hair with a broad parting in

ON THE USE OF SCRAPES

the middle, a very long inquiring nose, faded blue eyes, an absolutely flat chin, and—inconceivable gentility. If we others were settling she settled far quicker. She took the bedroom next to Jenny Driver's; she annexed a small sitting-room for her own—next but one to Jenny Driver's; she had a glass of the best port every day at eleven. (" She came down to the cellar and chose the bin herself, sir," Loft informed me with a wry smile of grudge for his dearest possessions.) Yet all these acts of proprietorship—for they pretty nearly came to that —were performed with a meekness, a deprecation, a ladylikeness (I can find no other word) that made opposition seem unkind and criticism ungenerous. It was only " Poor Chat! " She had a habit of talking to Jenny in a kind of baby-language, and used to refer to herself as " Poor Chat." " Poor Chat doesn't know! " " Poor Chat's not wise! " Also she did keep talking about her name and the respectability of her descent. In fact she was a woman of a number of silly affectations and one or two exasperating foibles, and Cartmell never varied from his impromptu judgment—expressed before he had seen her—that she was a fool. It is my deliberate opinion that she wished to be thought more of a fool than she was—partly from an idea that little sillinesses and affectations were genteel, partly with the notion that they were disarming. She seemed always bent on showing you that she was not the sort of person from whom any opposition need be feared, nor any undue exercise of influence apprehended. It could only be supposed that she had found this line of conduct useful in her relations toward her employers; by contrast it flattered both their superior brains and their superior positions. I allow for her natural taste, for her standards of gentility. But she was a snob, too, "Poor Chat," and a time-server.

No harder words than those need be used about her—and they are too hard perhaps; for there is one thing to be said on the other side—and it is a thing of weight. Chat was fifty; as a governess she was hopelessly out of date; I do not suppose that she saw her daily bread secure for three months ahead. For a hundred pounds a year certain—secure from the caprice of employers or of fate—she would probably have done or been anything—even, so far as she could, honest.

But honesty alone, as she may well have reflected, does not breed security of tenure in subordinate positions. I am far from saying that it ought; on the whole I consider it to be a commoner, and therefore a cheaper and more easily obtainable—and replaceable—commodity than either a good brain or an agreeable demeanor. At any rate how easily it may come near to costing a man his place I was very soon to discover by my own experience. Well, perhaps, to honesty I ought to add a lack of diplomacy and a temper naturally hot. But I am not sure: I cannot see how any man could have done anything very different—given that he was barely honest.

"There's a person in the drawing-room with the ladies, sir," said Loft one day when I came up to tea at four o'clock.

Loft's social terminology was exact. When he said

ON THE USE OF SCRAPES

a " person " he did not mean a " gentleman "—who was a gentleman—nor a " man "—who was a member of the definitely lower orders of the community; he meant somebody in between, one of the doubtful cases.

" A Mr. Powers, sir. He's been here perhaps half an hour."

It may readily be supposed that I had not forgotten the name of Powers; the name and the incident were irrevocably—and uncomfortably—fixed in my mind. This " person " might not be the same Powers, but in overwhelming probability he was. Even if Jenny had not been in communication with him—and I did not believe that she had—the paragraphs would easily have brought about this visit—or visitation. He came scenting prey—he had read of the heiress! But why had she let him in?

" Did he give you a card, Loft? "

" Yes, sir. I took it in, and Miss Driver told me to ask the person to come in."

If it were not material, neither was it necessary to ask what Loft thought about the matter. Plainly Mr. Powers was not up to his standard for drawing-room visitors.

" Have you got the card? "

He took it from the hall table. " Mr. Nelson Powers." There was no address.

" All right, Loft. But before I join them, I want to telephone to London." Of course Mr. Driver had installed a telephone, and many a day we had kept it very busy."

By luck I got into speedy communication with

Cartmell at his hotel. He heard my news. His answer was to the point: "Kick him out."

"But if I try to do that, it gives you away. You're not supposed to have told me."

"Then give me away," came back instantly. "Only get him out. He's a dangerous rascal—and not fit for any decent man or woman to talk to. How in Heaven's name she can——"

"Perhaps she's frightened," I pleaded. He answered only "Kick him out," and cut off communication.

She did not look at all frightened when I went in. She was standing opposite Powers, smiling gayly and mischievously. Powers was apparently just taking his leave. So much gained! I determined to go to the hall with him and give him a hint, on Cartmell's behalf, that he need not come again. But things were not to be as easy as that.

"Well, then, we shall see you at eight o'clock," said Jenny, giving him her hand.

"Delighted," said he, bowing low. "Good afternoon. Good afternoon, Miss Chatters." Chat was sitting by, tatting. She habitually tatted.

"This is my old friend Mr. Nelson Powers," said Jenny. "Mr. Powers—Mr. Austin." We bowed—neither of us cordially. The man's eyes were wary and very alert; he looked at me as though I might be a policeman in plain clothes; possibly my expression gave him some excuse.

Jenny rang the bell. "Mr. Powers is coming back to dinner. You'll come, of course? We shall have a pleasant little party of four!"

ON THE USE OF SCRAPES 37

"I'm sorry, but I'm engaged to dinner to-night."

Jenny gave me a quick look, Chat gave me a long one. Loft appeared. "*Au revoir*, Mr. Powers!" With a pronounced bow over his hat Powers was out of the room. I made no effort to follow. Jenny's face told me that the battle was to be fought where we were.

She poured out a cup of tea and gave it to me. Then, as she sat down, she said, "I'm sorry you can't come to-night. Where are you going?"

I did not want Chat there—but I remembered what happened to Cartmell when he did not want me there.

"I'm not going anywhere," I said.

Her pallid face flushed a little, but she smiled. Chat looked at her and got up; no, Chat was not altogether a fool! "Yes, please, Chat," said Jenny very quietly. Chat left us. I finished my tea—it was cold, and easy to gulp down—and waited for the storm.

"You've nothing to add to your polite excuses?" she inquired.

"Does that gentleman come from Cheltenham?"

"Yes, from Cheltenham, Mr. Austin. But how did you come to know that? Did my father mention him?" She was not embarrassed—only very angry.

"No."

"It was Mr. Cartmell?"

"Yes. He had no right, I daresay, but I'm glad he did—and so will he be."

"If both my solicitor and my secretary are glad—!" She broke off with a scornful laugh. "I'm not going to discuss the matter with you, but I like people who are about me to receive my invitations with politeness."

"This isn't easy for me, Miss Driver, but—that man oughtn't to come to this house. He oughtn't to be allowed to see you."

She rose from her chair, her eyes set unmovingly on my face. Her voice was low. "How dare you say that? How dare you? Am I to take orders from you—my secretary—my servant?"

"You called me your friend the other day."

"I seem to have been hasty. A kind friend indeed to listen to stories against me!"

"The story is against the man—not against you."

"Are you dining with any other friends to-night?"

"I've told you that I'm not."

"Then I request—I desire—that you will make it convenient to give me the pleasure of your company —to meet my friend, Mr. Powers."

My temper went suddenly. "I won't sit at meat with the blackguard—above all, not in your company."

I saw her fist clench itself by her side. "I repeat my request," she said.

"I repeat my refusal, but I can do no less than offer you my resignation."

"You won't accept my offer—but I accept yours very gladly."

"It will be kind of you to relieve me from my duties as soon as possible."

"To-morrow." She turned her back on me and walked off to the window. I stood there a minute, and then went to the door. She turned round, and our eyes met. I waited for a moment, but she faced round to the window again, and I went out.

I walked quickly down the hill. I was very unhappy, but I was not remorseful. I knew that another man could have done the thing much better, but it had been the right thing to do and I had done it as well as I could. She had made no attempt to defend Powers, nor to deny what she must have known that Cartmell had said about him. Yet, while tacitly admitting that he was a most obnoxious description of blackguard, she asked him to dinner—and ordered me to sit by and see them together. If her service entailed that sort of thing, then indeed there must be an end to service with her. But grieved as I was that this must be so—and the blow to me was heavy on all grounds, whether of interest or of feeling—I grieved more that she should sit with him herself than that she bade me witness what seemed in my eyes her degradation. What was the meaning of it? I was at that time nowhere near understanding her.

My home was no more than a cottage, built against the south wall of the Old Priory. The front door opened straight into my parlor, without hall or vestibule; a steep little stair ran up from the corner of the room itself and led to my bedroom on the floor above. Behind my parlor lay the kitchen and two other rooms, occupied by my housekeeper, Mrs. Field, and her husband, who was one of the gardeners. It was all very small, but it was warm, snug, and homely. The walls were covered almost completely with my books, which overflowed on to chairs and tables, too. When fire and lamp were going in the evening, the little room seemed to glow with a studious cheerfulness, and my old leather armchair wooed me with affectionate welcome. In four years I had taken good root in my little home. I had to uproot myself—to-morrow.

With this pang, there came suddenly one deeper. I was about to lose—perforce—what was now revealed to me as a great, though a very new, interest in my life. From the first both Cartmell and I had been keenly interested in the heiress—the lonely girl who came to reign over Breysgate and to dispose of those millions of money. We had both, I think, been touched with a certain romantic, or pathetic, element in the situation. We had not talked about it, much less had we talked about what we felt ourselves or about what we meant to do; but it had grown into a tacit understanding between us that more than our mere paid services were due from us to Jenny Driver. No man had been very near her father, but we had been nearest; we did not mean that his daughter should be without friends if she would accept friendship. Nay, I think we meant a little more than that. She was young and ignorant; Nick Driver's daughter might well be willful and imperious. We meant that she should not easily escape our service and our friendship; they should be more than offered; they should be pressed; if need be, they should be secretly given. It had been an honest idea of ours—but it seemed hard to work in practice. Such service as I could give was ended well-nigh before it had begun. I thought it only too likely that Cartmell's also would soon end, save, at least, for strictly professional purposes. And I could not see how this end was to be avoided in his case any more than it had been found possible to avoid it in mine. With the best will in the world, there were limits. "Some things are impossible to some men," old Mr. Driver had said in that letter; it had been impossible to me—as it would, I think, have been to most men—to see Powers welcomed by her as a gentleman and a friend.

Yet I began almost to be sorry—almost to ask why I had not swallowed Powers and accepted the invitation to dinner. Might I, in that way, have had a better chance of getting rid of Powers in the end? It would have been a wrong thing to do—I was still quite clear about that—wrong in every way, and very disgusting, to boot; quite fatal to my self-respect, and an acquiescence in a horrible want of self-respect in Jenny. But I might have been useful to her. Now I could be of no use. That evening I first set my feet on what I may perhaps call a moral slope. It looked a very gentle slope; there did not appear to be any danger in it; it did not look as though you could slip on it or as if it would be difficult to recover yourself if slip you did. But, in fact, at the bottom of that moral slope—which grew steeper as it descended—lay a moral precipice. Nothing less can I call the conclusion that anything which might be useful to Jenny Driver became, by the mere force of that possible utility, morally right—conduct, so to speak, becoming to an officer and a gentleman. I was not, of course, at all aware that my insidious doubt—or, rather, my puzzling discontent with myself—could lead to any such chasm as that.

I ate my chop and tried to settle down to my books. First I tried theology, the study of which I had by on means abandoned. But I was not theologically inclined that night. Then I took up a magazine; politics emphatically would not do! I fell back on anthropology, and got on there considerably better. Yet presently my attention wandered even from that. I sat with the book open before me, at a page where three members of the Warramunga tribe were represented in adornments that, on an ordinary evening, would have filled me with admiration. No, I was languid about it. The last thing I remembered was hearing the back door locked—which meant that the Fields were going to bed. After that I fail to trace events, but I imagine that I speedily fell sound asleep —with the book open before me and my pipe lying by it on the table.

I awoke with a little shiver, pretended to myself that I had never stopped reading, gave up the pretence, pushed back my chair from the table, rose, and turned to the fire behind me.

In my old leather arm-chair sat Jenny Driver.

She wore a black evening dress, with a cloak of brown fur thrown open in front—both, no doubt, new acquisitions. The fire had died down to a small heap of bright red embers. When first I saw her, she was crouching close over it—the night was chilly—and her face was red with its glow.

"Miss Driver! I—I'm afraid I've been asleep," I stammered. "Have you been here long?"

She glanced at the clock; it was half-past ten. "About twenty minutes. I've had a good look round

—at your room, and your books, and that queer picture which seems to have sent you to sleep. Your room's very comfortable."

"Yes, it's a jolly little room," I agreed. "But what——?"

"And I've had a good look at you, too," she continued. "Do you know, Mr. Austin, you're really rather handsome?"

"I daresay I look my best by lamplight," I suggested, smiling.

"No, really I think you are—in the thin ascetic style. I like that—anyhow for a change. Well, I wanted a word with you, so I waited till Chat went to bed, and then slipped down."

It was on the tip of my tongue to observe that it was rather late; but a smile on Jenny's lips somehow informed me that she expected just such an objection. So I said nothing.

"Chat and I are going to London to-morrow—to shop. Perhaps we may go on to Paris. I thought you might like to say good-by."

"That's very kind of you. I'm glad we're not to part in—well, as we parted this afternoon."

"If you regretted that, you might have done something to prevent it. Light your pipe again; you'll be able to think better—and I want you to think a little."

I obeyed her direction, she sitting for the moment silent. I came and stood opposite to her, leaning my elbow on the mantelpiece.

"When I first knew Mr. Powers, I was sixteen, and I'd been with the Smalls since I was eleven. You didn't get very discriminating, living with the Smalls. I met him at a subscription dance: I didn't know anything about his wife. He was clerk to an architect, or surveyor, or something of that sort. I met him a good many times afterwards—for walks. He was good-looking in his way, and he said he was in love with me. I fell in love with him and, when I couldn't get away to meet him, I wrote letters. Then I heard about the wife—and I wrote more letters. You know the sort—very miserable, and, I suppose, very silly—that I didn't know what to do, only the world was over for me—and so on. You can imagine the sort of letter. And I saw him—once or twice. He told me that he was in great trouble; he'd been racing and playing cards and couldn't pay; he'd be shown up, and lose his place—and what would become of his wife and child? I flared up and said that I was the last person who was likely to care about his wife and child. Then he suggested that I should get money from my father—he knew all about my father—by saying that I was in some trouble. I told him I couldn't possibly; I was never allowed to write and should only get an answer from a lawyer if I did—and certainly no money. He persisted —and I persisted. He threatened vaguely what he could do. I told him to do as he liked—that I'd done with him for good. I never wrote again—and I never saw him till to-day."

"When you asked him to dinner!"

She smiled, but took no more heed. "Well, I was in a scrape, wasn't I? I saw that clearly—rather a bad scrape. I didn't see what to do, though I did a

ON THE USE OF SCRAPES

lot of thinking. Being in a scrape does teach one to think, doesn't it? Then suddenly—when I was at my wits' end—it flashed across me that possibly it might all have happened for the best. My great object all through my girlhood was, somehow or other, to get into touch with my father. I believed that, if I could get a fair chance, I could win him over and persuade him to let me pay him a visit—even live with him perhaps. That was my great dream—and I was prepared to go through a lot for the hope of it. Well, it didn't come off. I don't know what Mr. Powers did—but it was not my father who came, it was Mr. Cartmell. I was taken away from the Smalls, but not allowed to come here. I was sent to the Simpsons. My father never wrote one word, good or bad, to me. Mr. Cartmell gave me a lecture. I didn't mind that. I was so furious with him for coming that I didn't care a straw what he said."

" His coming upset your brilliant idea? "

" Yes—that time. One can't always succeed. Still it's wonderful how often a scrape can be turned to account, if you think how to use it. You're in a corner: that sharpens your brains; you hit on something."

" Perhaps it does. You seem to speak from experience."

" Well, nobody means to get into them, of course, but you get drawn on. It's fun to see how far you can go—and what other people will do, and so on."

" Rather dangerous! "

" Well, perhaps that's part of the fun. By the by, I suppose I might get into a little scrape if I stayed here much longer. Chat would be very shocked—Loft, too, I expect!"

"It is getting on for eleven o'clock."

"Yes." She rose and drew her cloak round her. "Mr. Powers didn't come to dinner," she said. "On reflection, I wrote to him and told him that it was better not to renew our acquaintance, and that he must accept that as my final decision."

"That's something gained, anyhow," said I, with a sigh of relief.

"Something gained for you?" she asked quickly and suspiciously.

"I don't believe I was thinking of myself at the moment."

She looked at me closely. "No, I don't think you were—and there's no real reason why it should make any difference to you. Well, that depends on yourself! Mr. Powers is of no consequence one way or the other. The question is—are we two to try and get on together."

"I got on with your father," said I.

"You didn't tell my father what he was to do and not to do."

"Yes, sometimes—in social matters. It may surprise you to hear it, but your father was always ready to learn things that other people could tell him."

"Well, here are my concessions. Never mind what I said this afternoon—I was in a rage. I won't call you a servant again; I won't make you come to dinner when you don't want to; I won't demand that you meet my friends if you don't want to."

"That's very kind and handsome of you."

ON THE USE OF SCRAPES

"Wait a minute. Now for my side. Mr. Austin, if you're not a servant here, neither are you a master. Oh, I know, you disclaim any such idea, but still—think over this afternoon! You can't stay here as a master. I daresay you think I want a master. I don't think so. If I do, I suppose I can marry!"

"For my own part I venture to hope you will marry—soon and very happily."

"But my father? 'Suspect and fear marriage.' 'You need fear no man except the man to whom you have given yourself.'"

"Your father's experience was, you know, unhappily not fortunate."

Her face clouded to melancholy. "I don't believe mine would be," she murmured. Then she raised her voice again and smiled. "Neither servant nor master—but friend, Mr. Austin?" And she held out her hand to me.

"I accept most heartily, and I'll try to keep the bargain." I put out my hand to take hers, but, as if on a sudden thought, she drew hers back.

"Wait a moment still. What do you mean by a friend? One who likes me, has my happiness at heart?"

"Yes."

"Gives me the best advice he can, speaking his mind honestly, without fear and in friendship?"

"Yes."

A touch of mockery in her eyes warned me neither to take the questions too seriously nor to make my answers too grave. The mockery crept into her tone with the next interrogation.

"When I don't take his advice and get into a scrape, says, 'I told you so. I'm all right—you get out of your scrape in the best way you can?'"

"Call me no friend when I say that," I answered.

"Ah!" she whispered and gave me the hand which she before had withdrawn. "Now really!" she cried gayly, with a glance at the clock. "You go back to sleep—I have to get ready for a journey. No, don't come with me. I'll run up to the house by myself. Good night, my—friend!"

I opened the door for her, answering, "Good night." But she had one more word for me before she went, turning her face to me, merry with a smile and twinkling eyes—

"I suppose you haven't got a wife anywhere, have you, Mr. Austin?" She ran off, not waiting for an answer.

The appearance of Mr. Powers had not cost me my place: but it had defined my position—to Jenny's complete satisfaction! It had also elicited from her some interesting observations on the value of scrapes—the place they hold in life, and how a man—or woman—may turn them to account. I felt that I knew Jenny better for our quarrel and our talk.

CHAPTER IV

AN UNPOPULAR MAN

MISS DRIVER stayed away longer than her words had led me to expect. London and Paris—the names are in themselves explanation enough. The big world was entirely new to Jenny; though she could not yet take—shall I say storm?—her place in society, much instruction, and more amusement, lay open to her grasp even in the days of her obligatory mourning. On the other hand that same period could not but be very tedious to her if passed at Breysgate. In regard to her father's memory she felt a great curiosity and displayed a profound interest; for the man himself she could have had little affection and could entertain no real grief; in fact, though she professed and tried to forgive, she never shook herself quite clear of resentment, even though she, if anybody, ought to have come nearest to understanding his stern resolve. That nobody should ever again come so near to him, or become so much to him, as to be able sorely to wound him—that was how I read his determination. Jenny ought to have been able to arrive at some appreciation of that. I think she did—but she protested in her heart that his daughter should have been the one exception. No good lay in going back to the merits of that question. In the result they had been—strangers: her mourning, then, was a matter of propriety, not the true demand of her feelings. Viewed in this light, London and Paris, surveyed from the decent obscurity of a tourist, offered a happy compromise—and bridged a yawning gulf— between duty and the endurable.

Meanwhile the Great Seal was in Commission; Cartmell, Loft, and I administered the Kingdom— Cartmell Foreign Affairs, Loft the Interior, I the Royal Cabinet. Cartmell's sphere was the largest by far—all the business both of the estate and of the various commercial interests; Loft's territory was merely the house, but his sense of importance magnified the weight of his functions; to me fell such of Miss Driver's work as she did not choose to transact herself. In fact I was kept pretty busy and was in constant communication with her. In reply to my letters I received a few notes—very brief ones—and many telegrams—very decisive ones. As I expected, it was not long before she took the reins into her own hands. In matters of business she always knew her mind—even if she did not always tell it; indecision was reserved for another department. But neither in notes, nor in telegrams did she disclose anything of her doings, except that she was well and enjoying herself.

So time rolled on; we came to the month of June —and to the Flower Show. The great annual festivity of the Catsford Horticultural and Arboricultural Association had always, of recent years, been held in

AN UNPOPULAR MAN 51

the grounds of Breysgate Priory, and at the Mayor's request (Councillor Bindlecombe was also President of the Association) I had obtained Miss Driver's consent to the continuance of this good custom. In Jenny's absence the Show was to be opened by Lady Sarah Lacey. I have mentioned that no open rupture had taken place between Fillingford and Breysgate—there was only a very chilly feeling. Lady Sarah came, with her brother Lord Fillingford and his son. Sir John and Lady Aspenick from Overington Grange, the Dormers from Hingston, Bertram Ware—our M.P.—from Oxley Lodge, and many others—in fact all one side of the county—graced the occasion, mingled affably with the elect of Catsford, and made themselves distantly agreeable to the non-elect. (This statement does not, for obvious reasons, apply in all its exactitude to the M.P. If the bulk of the male guests were not elect, they were electors.) Everybody was hospitably entertained, but there was a Special Table, where, in years gone by, Mr. Driver himself had welcomed the most distinguished guests. His death and his daughter's absence—I fear I must add, Cartmell's also (he would have taken place of me, I think)—elevated me to this august position. In fact I had to play host, and so came for the first time into social relations with our august neighbors. I was not without alarm.

Lady Sarah questioned me about Jenny with polite but hostile curiosity. Her inquiries contrived to suggest that, with such a father and such a childhood, it would be wonderful if Miss Driver had really turned out as well as Lady Sarah hoped. I was not surprised, and set the attitude down to a natural touch of jealousy: between the two ladies titular precedence and solid power would very likely not coincide. Lord Fillingford talked to the Mayor—who sat between him and me—with a defensively dignified reserve. He was slightly built, and walked rather stiffly; he wore small whiskers, and inclined to baldness. Indisputably a gentleman, he seemed to be afflicted with an unreasonable idea that other people would not remember what he was; a good man, no doubt, and probably a sensible one, but with no gift for popularity. His handsome son easily eclipsed him there. At this time young Lacey was bordering on eighteen; he out-topped his father in stature as in grace. He was a singularly attractive boy with a hearty gayety, a flow of talk, and an engaging conviction that everybody wanted to listen. Childless old Mrs. Dormer was delighted to listen, to feast her eyes on his comeliness, and to pet him to any extent he desired.

As a whole the company was a little stiff, and the joints of conversation rather in want of oiling, until they struck on that most fruitful and sympathetic subject—a common dislike. The victim was our neighbor and tenant at Hatcham Ford, Leonard Octon. I knew him, for he had been something of a friend of old Mr. Driver's, and had been accorded free leave to walk as he pleased in the park; I had understood —and could well understand—that he was not generally liked, but never before had I realized the sum of his enormities. He had, it seemed, offended everybody. Charitable young Lacey did indeed qualify the

AN UNPOPULAR MAN

assertion that he was a "bounder" by the admission that he was afraid of nobody and could shoot. All the other voices spoke utter condemnation. He had got at odds with town, county, and church. His opinions were considered detestable, his manners aggressive. On various occasions of controversy he had pointed out to the Rector of Catsford that the pulpit was not of necessity a well of truth, to the Mayor that a gilt chain round his neck had no effect on the stuff inside a man's head, to Sir John Aspenick that one might understand horses and fail to understand anything else, to a large political meeting that of all laws mob-law was the worst, to Lord Fillingford that the rule of intelligence (to which Octon wished to revert) was no more the rule of country gentlemen than of their gardeners—perhaps not so much—and so on. These outrages were not narrated by the victims of them: they were recalled by sympathetic questions and reminders, each man tickling the other's wound. It could not be denied that they made up a sad catalogue of social crimes.

"The fellow may think what he likes, but he needn't tread on all our toes," Sir John complained.

"A vulgar man!" observed Lady Sarah with an acid finality.

Here, somewhat to my surprise, Fillingford opposed. He was a dry man, but a just one, and not even against an enemy should more than truth be said.

"No, I don't think he's that. His incivility is aggressive, even rough sometimes, but I shouldn't call it vulgar. I don't know what you think, Mr. Mayor, but it seems to me that vulgarity can hardly exist without either affectation in the man himself or cringing to others. Now Octon isn't affected and he never cringes."

Bindlecombe was a sensible man, and himself—if Fillingford's definition stood—not vulgar.

"You know better than I do, Lord Fillingford," he said. "But I should call him a gentleman spoiled—and perhaps that's a bit different."

"Meant for a gentleman, perhaps?" suggested Lady Aspenick, a pretty thin woman of five-and-thirty, who looked studious and wore double glasses, yet was a mighty horsewoman and whip withal.

I liked her suggestion. "Really, I believe that's about it," I made bold to remark. "He is meant for a gentleman, but he's rather perverse about it."

Lady Sarah looked at me with just an involuntary touch of surprise. I do not think that, in the bottom of her heart, she expected me to speak—unless, of course, spoken to.

"I intensely dislike both his manners and his opinions—and what I hear of his character," she observed.

"I mean," Lady Aspenick pursued, "that he's been to so many queer places, and must have seen such queer things——"

"And done 'em, if you ask my opinion," interposed her husband.

"That he may have got—what? Rusty? Well, something like that. I mean—forgotten how to treat people. He seems to put everybody down as an enemy at first sight! Well, I'm irritable myself!"

Bertram Ware joined in for the first time. "At the

clubs they say he's really a slave-driver in Central Africa, and comes over here when the scent gets too hot after him."

"Really," said Lady Sarah, "it sounds exceedingly likely. But if he teaches his slaves to copy his manners, they'll get some good floggings."

"That's what the fellow wants himself," growled unappeasable Sir John.

"You take it on, Johnny," counseled young Lacey. "He's only a foot taller and four stone heavier than you are. You take it on! It'd be a very sporting event."

This extract—it is no more—from our conversation will show that it was going on swimmingly. In the pursuit of a common prey we were developing a sense of comradeship which leveled barriers and put us at our ease with one another. No doubt our nascent cordiality would have sprung to fuller life—but it suffered a sudden check.

"Well, how have you all got on without me?" said a voice behind my chair.

I turned round with a start. The man himself stood there, his great height and breadth overshadowing me. His face was bronzed under his thick black hair; his mouth wore a wicked smile as his keen eyes ranged round the embarrassed table. He had heard the last part of Lacey's joking challenge to Aspenick.

"What's Sir John Aspenick got to take on? What's the event?"

The general embarrassment grew no less—but then it had never existed in young Lacey. He raised his fearless fresh blue eyes to the big man.

"To give you a thrashing," he said.

"Ah," said Octon, "I'm too old. I'm not like you." Lacey flushed suddenly. "And perhaps I'm a bit too big—and you're hardly that yet, are you?"

Perhaps he was too big! I noticed again his wonderful hands. They were large beyond reasonable limits of size, but full of muscle—no fat. They were restless too—always moving as if they wanted to be at work; if the work were to strangle a bull, I could imagine their being well pleased. He might need a thrashing—but, sturdy as the sons of Catsford were, there was none in the park that day who could have given him one.

Young Lacey was very red. I was a little uneasy as to what he would say or do; Fillingford saved the situation. He stood up and offered his hand to Octon, saying, "We're always glad to welcome a neighbor safely back. I hope your trip was prosperous?"

It was the right thing wrongly said—at least, inadequately said. It was civil, not cordial. They made a contrast, these men. Fillingford was too negative, Octon too positive. One defended where none attacked, the other attacked where no offense had been given. Unnecessary reserve against uncalled-for aggression! Fillingford was not popular—Octon was hated. Octon did not mind the hatred—did Fillingford feel the lack of liking? His reserve baffled me: I could not tell. With all Octon's faults, friendship with him seemed easier—and more attractive. The path might be rough—but the gate was not locked.

"Sure, Mr. Austin, it's time for the prizes?" said Lady Sarah.

AN UNPOPULAR MAN

It was not time, but I hastily said that it was, and with some relief escorted her to the platform. The rest followed, after, I suppose, a formal greeting to the unwelcome Prodigal; he himself did not come with us.

When Lady Sarah had distributed the prizes, I made a little speech on my chief's behalf—a speech of welcome to county and to town. Fillingford replied first, his speech was like himself—proper, cold, composed. Then Bindlecombe got up, mopping his forehead—the Mayor was apt to get hot—but making no mean appearance with his British solidity of figure, his shrewd face, and his sturdy respect for the office he exercised by the will of his fellow-citizens.

"My lords, ladies, and gentlemen—as Mayor of Catsford I have just one word to say on behalf of the borough. We thank the generous lady who has welcomed us here to-day. We look forward to welcoming her when she's ready for us. All Catsford men are proud of Nicholas Driver. He did a great deal for us—maybe we did something for him. He wasn't a man of words, but he was proud of the borough as the borough was proud of him. From what I hear, I think we shall be proud of Miss Driver, too —and I hope she'll be proud of the borough as her father was before her. We wish her long life and prosperity."

Bravo, Bindlecombe! But Lady Sarah looked astonishingly sour. There was something almost feudal in the relationship which the Mayor's words suggested. Jenny as Overlord of Catsford would not be to Lady Sarah's liking.

I got rid of them; I beg pardon—they civilly dismissed me. Only young Lacey had for me a word of more than formality. He did me the honor to ask my opinion—as from one gentleman to another.

"I say, do you think Octon had a right to say that?"

"The retort was justifiable—strictly."

"He need hardly——"

"No, he needn't."

"Well, good-by, Mr. Austin. I say—I'd like to come and see you. Are you ever at home in the evenings?"

"Always just now. I should be delighted to see you."

"Evenings at the Manor aren't very lively," he remarked ingenuously. "And I've left school for good, you know."

The last words seemed to refer—distantly—to Leonard Octon. Without returning to that disturbing subject I repeated my invitation and then, comparatively free from my responsibilities, repaired alone to the terrace.

Octon was still there—extended on three chairs, smoking and drinking a whisky and soda. I asked him about his travels—he was just back from the recesses of Africa (if there are, truly, any recesses left)—but gained small satisfaction. His predominant intellectual interest was—insects! He would hunt a beetle from latitude to latitude, and by no means despised the pursuit of a flea. My interest in the study of religion assorted ill with this: when I questioned on my subject, he replied on his. All other incidents of his journeys he passed over, both in talk and in writing (he had written two books eminent in their own line), with a brevity thoroughly Cæsarean. "Having taken the city and killed the citizens"—Cæsar invaded another tribe!—That was the style. Only Octon's tribes were insects, Cæsar's patriots. It was, however, rumored—as Bertram Ware had hinted in a jocose form—that Octon's summaries were, sometimes and in their degree, as eloquent as Cæsar's own.

"Hang my journeys!" he said, as I put one more of my futile questions. "I got six bugs—one indisputably new. But I didn't hurry up here—I only got home this morning—to talk about that. I hurried up here, Austin——"

"To annoy your neighbors—knowing they were assembled here?"

"That was a side-show," he assured me. "Though it was entertaining enough. And, after all, young Lacey began on me! No—I came to bring you news of your liege lady. I've been in Paris, too, Austin."

"And you met her?"

"I met her often—with her cat."

"Miss Chatters?"

"Precisely. And sometimes without her cat. How do you like the change from old Driver?"

"I hold no such position, either in county or borough, as need tempt you—to say nothing of entitling you—to ask impertinent questions, Octon."

He chuckled out a deep rumbling laugh of amusement. "Good!" he said. "Well-turned—almost witty! Austin, I've my own pursuits—but I'm inclined to wish I had your position."

"You're very flattering—but my position is that of an employé—at a salary which would hardly command your services."

"You can be eyes and ears and hands to her. If I had your position, I'd "—one of his great hands rose suddenly into the air—" crunch up this neighborhood. With her resources she could get all the power." His hand fell again, and he removed his body from two of the three chairs, shifting himself with easy indolent strength. " Then you'd have it all in your own control."

"She'd have it in her own control, you must mean," said I.

"Come, you're a man!" he mocked me. But he was looking at me closely, too—and rather inquisitively, I thought.

"Since you've met her often, I thought you might understand better than that." To answer him in his own coin, I infused into my tone a contempt which I hoped would annoy him.

He was not annoyed; he was amused. In the insolence of his strength he mocked at me—at Jenny through me—at me through Jenny. Yet, pervading it all, there was revealed an interest—a curiosity—about her that agreed ill with his assumed contemptuousness.

"She's given you her idea of herself—and you've absorbed it. She thinks she's another Nick Driver—and you're sure of it! It's all flim-flam, Austin."

"Have it your own way," said I meekly. "It's no affair of mine what you choose to think."

"Well, that's a more liberal sentiment than one generally hears in this neighborhood."

He rose and stretched himself, clenching his big fists in the air over his head. "At any rate she's told me I may take my walks about here as usual. I'll drop in and have a pipe with you some day."

Another guest proposed himself! I hoped that the company might always prove harmonious.

"As for Chat," he went on, "I don't want to boast of my conquests—but she's mine."

"My congratulations are untouched by envy."

"You may live to change your mind about that. Anyhow I hold her in my hand."

The truth about him was that, as he loved his strength, so, and no less, he loved the display of it. A common, doubtless not the highest, characteristic of the strong! Display is apt to pass into boast. He was not at all loath to hint to me—to force me to guess—that his encounters in Paris had set him thinking. (If they had set him feeling, he said nothing about that.) Hence—as I reasoned it—he went on, with a trifle more than his usual impudence, "Your goose will be cooked when she marries, though!"

After all, his impudence was good-humored. I retorted in kind. "Perhaps the husband won't let you walk in the park either!"

"If Fillingford were half a man—Lord, what a chance!"

"You gossip as badly as the women themselves. Why not say young Lacey at once?"

"The boy? I'd lay him over my knee—at the first word of it."

"He'd stab you under the fifth rib as you did it."

The big man laughed. "Then my one would be worse than his sound dozen! And what you say isn't at all impossible. He's a fine boy, that! After all, though, he's inherited his courage. The father's no coward, either."

We had become engrossed in our interchange of shots—hostile, friendly, or random. One speaks sometimes just for the repartee, especially when no more than feeling after the interpretation of a man.

Moreover Loft's approach was always noiseless. On Octon's last words, he was by my side.

"I beg pardon, sir, but Miss Driver has telephoned from London to say that she'll be down to-morrow and glad to see you at lunch. And I was to say, sir, would you be so kind as to send word to Mr. Octon that she would be very pleased if he would come, too, if his engagements permitted."

"Oh—yes—very good, Loft. This is Mr. Octon."

"Yes, sir," said Loft. The tone was noncommittal. He knew Octon—but declared no opinion.

I was taken aback, for I had received no word of her coming; I had been led not to expect her for four or five weeks. Octon's eye caught mine.

"Changed her mind and come back sooner? Well, I did just the same myself."

By themselves the words were nothing. In connection with our little duel—backed by the man's broad smile and the forceful assertion of his personality—they amounted to a yet plainer boast—"I've come—and I thought she would." That is too plain for speech—even for Octon's ill-restrained tongue—but not too plain for his bearing. But then I doubted whether his bearing were toward facts or merely toward me—were proof of force or effort after effect.

"Clearly Miss Chatters can't keep away from you!" I said.

"Clearly we're going to have a more amusing time than we'd been hoping," he answered and, with a casual and abrupt "Good-by," turned on his heel, taking out another great cigar as he went.

Perhaps we were—if amusing should prove to be the right word about it. So ran my instinct—with no express reason to be given for it. Why should not Jenny come home? Why should Octon's coming have anything to do with it? In truth I was affected, I was half dominated for the moment, by his confidence and his force. I had taken the impression he wanted to give—just as he accused me of taking the impression that Jenny sought to give. So I told myself consolingly. But I could not help remembering that in those countries which he frequented, where he got his insects and very probably his ideas, men were said as often to win or lose—to live or die—by the impression they imparted to friends, foes, and rivals as by the actual deeds they did. I could not judge how far that was true—but that or something like it was surely what they called prestige? If a man created prestige, you did not even try to oppose him. Nay, you hastened to range yourself on his side—and your real little power went to swell his asserted big power—his power big in assertion but in fact, as against the present foe, still unproved. Had the prestige been brought to bear on Chat—so that she was wholly his? Was it being brandished before my eyes, to gain me also—for what I was worth?

After all, it was flattering of him to think that I mattered. I mattered so very little. If he were minded to impress, if he were ready to fight, his display and his battle must be against another foe—or—if the evidence of that talk at the Flower Show went for anything—against several. If an attack on Breysgate Priory were really in his mind, he would find no ally —outside its walls.

CHAPTER V

RAPIER AND CLUB

ANY account of Jenny Driver's doings is in danger of seeming to progress by jumps and jerks, and thereby of contradicting the truth about its subject. Cartmell, her principal man of business, scoffed at the idea that Jenny was impulsive at all; after six months' experience of her he said that he had never met a cooler, saner, more cautious judgment. That this was true of her in business matters I have no reason to doubt, but (I have noted this distinction already) if the remark is to be extended to her personal affairs it needs qualification —yet without admitting of contradiction. There she was undoubtedly impetuous and impulsive on occasion; a certain course would appeal to her fancy, and she made for it headlong, regardless, or seeming regardless, of its risks. But even here, though the impulses prevailed on her suddenly in the end, they were long in coming to a head, long in achieving mastery, and preceded by protracted periods either of inaction or of action so wary and tentative as not to commit her in any serious degree. She would advance toward the object, then retreat from it, then stand still and look at it, then walk round and regard it from another point of view. Next she was apt to turn her back on it and become, for a time, engrossingly interested in something else; it seemed essential to her ease of mind that there should be an alternative possible and a line of retreat open. All this circumspection and deliberation—or, if you like, this dawdling and shilly-shallying (for opinions of Jenny have differed very widely on this and on other matters)—had to happen before the rapid and imperious impulse came to set a limit to them; even then it is doubtful whether the impulse left her quite unmindful of the line of retreat.

These characteristics of hers were exhibited in her treatment of the question of the Institute. Although this was a public matter, it was (or she made it) closely connected with certain private affairs which inevitably had a profound interest for all of us who surrounded her. My own belief is that a lift of Lady Sarah Lacey's brows started the Institute. When she called—this necessary courtesy was punctually forthcoming from the Manor to the Priory—she heard from Jenny about the proposed Driver Memorial Hall, how it was to look, where it was to be, and so forth. She put a question as to funds; Jenny owned to the ten thousand pounds. All Lady Sarah said was, " Do you feel called upon to do as much as that? " But she also lifted her brows—conveying thereby (as Jenny confidently declared) that Miss Driver was taking an exaggerated view of her father's importance and of her own, and was assuming a position toward the borough of Catsford which properly belonged to her betters (perhaps Lady Sarah was recollecting the Mayor's feudal speech!) At any rate from that day forward Jenny began to hint at bigger things. The Memorial Hall by itself no longer sufficed. She made a great friend of Mr. Bindlecombe, and he often came up to Breysgate. Where his beloved borough was concerned, Bindlecombe was openly and avowedly unscrupulous; he meant to get all he could out of Miss Driver, and made no concealment about it. Jenny delighted in this attitude; it gave her endless opportunities of encouraging and discouraging, of setting up and putting down, the hopes of Bindlecombe. Between them they elaborated the idea—Jenny was great at elaborating it, but careful to insist that it was no more than an idea—of extending the Memorial Hall into a great Institute, which was to include a memorial hall but to comprise much besides. It was to be a Driver Literary, Scientific, and Technical Institute on the handsomest scale. Bindlecombes' patriotic and sanguine mind hardly hesitated to see in it the nucleus of a future University for the City of Catsford. (Catsford was in the future to be promoted to be a "city," though I did not see how Jenny could have anything to do with that!) The notion of this great Driver Institute pleased Jenny immensely. How high it would lift Lady Sarah's eyebrows! It made Cartmell apprehensive about the expense—and she liked to tease him by suggested extravagance. Finally, it would, she declared, provide me with a splendid post—as librarian, or principal, or something—which would give me a worthier scope for my abilities and yet (Jenny looked at me almost tenderly) let me stay in my dear little home—near Breysgate—" and near me, Mr. Austin."

She played with the idea—as she played with us. Some gossip about it began to trickle through Catsford. There was much interest, and Jenny became quite a heroine. Meanwhile plans for the poor old Memorial Hall were suspended.

According to Bindlecombe the only possible site for the visible realization of this splendid idea—the only site which the congested condition of the center of the borough allowed, and also the only one worthy of the great Institute—was the garden and grounds of Hatcham Ford. The beautiful old house itself was to be preserved as the center of an imposing group of handsome buildings; the old gardens need not be materially spoiled—so Bindlecombe unplausibly maintained. The flavor of antiquity and aristocracy thus imparted to the Institute would, Bindlecombe declared, give it a charm and a dignity beyond those possessed by any other Institute the world over. I was there when he first made this suggestion to Jenny. She looked at him in silence, smiled, and glanced quickly at me. The look, though quick, was audacious—under the circumstances.

"But what will Mr. Octon say to that?"

Bindlecombe deferentially hinted that he understood that Mr. Octon's lease of Hatcham Ford expired, or could be broken, in two or three years. He understood—perhaps he was wrong—that Mr. Driver usually reserved a power to break leases at the end of seven years? Mr. Cartmell would, of course, know all about that.

"Oh, if that's so," said Jenny, "of course it would be quite simple. Wouldn't it, Mr. Austin?"

"As simple as drawing a badger," I replied—and Bindlecombe looked surprised to hear such a sporting simile pass my lips. It was by no means a bad one, though, and Jenny rewarded it with a merry little nod.

At this point, then, her public project touched her private relations—and her relations with Octon had been close ever since her return from Paris. He had been a constant visitor at Breysgate, and my belief was that within a very few weeks of her arrival he had made a direct attack—had confronted her with a downright proposal—demand is a word which suits his method better—for her hand. I did not think that she had refused, I was sure that she had not accepted. She was fond of referring, in his presence, to the recent date of her father's death, to her own immersion in business, to the "strangeness" of her new life and the necessity of "finding her feet" before doing much. These references—rather pathetic and almost apologetic—Octon would receive with a frown of impatience—sometimes even of incredulity; but he did not make them an occasion of quarrel. He continued to come constantly to the Priory—certainly three or four times a week. There is no doubt that he was, in his way, very much in love with Jenny. It was an overbearing sort of way—but it had two great merits: it was resolute and it was disinterested. He was quite clear that he wanted her; it was quite clear that he did not care about her money, though he might envy her power. And if he tried to dominate her, he had to submit to constant proofs of her domination also. She could, and did, make him furiously angry; he was often undisguisedly impatient of her coynesses and her hesitations: but he could not leave her nor the hopes he had of her. And she, on her side, could not—at least did not—send him away. For that matter she never liked sending anybody away—not even Powers; it seemed to make her kingdom less by one—a change in quite the wrong direction. Octon would have been a great loss, for he had, without doubt, a strong, and an increasingly strong, attraction for her. She liked at least to play at being subjugated by his masculine force; she did, in fact, to a great extent approve and admire his semi-barbaric way (for her often mitigated by a humor which he kept for the people he liked) of speaking of and dealing with women. Down in her heart she thought that attitude rather the right thing in a man, and liked to think of it as a power before which she might yield. At the theater she was always delighted when the rebellious maiden or the charming spitfire of a wife, at last, in the third act, hailed the hero as her "master." So far she was primitive amidst all her subtlety. But to Jenny's mind it was by no means the third act yet; even the plot of the play was not laid out so far ahead as that. If this masterful, quick, assertive way of wooing were proper to man, woman had her weapons; she had her natural weapons, she had the weapons a civilized state of society gave her, and she had those which casual chance might add to her arsenal. Under the last of these three categories fell the project of the Driver Institute, to be established at Mr. Octon's present residence, Hatcham Ford.

It was a great chance for Jenny. Institutes as such, and all similar works, Octon hated—why educate people who ought to be driven? The insolence not of rank but of intellect spoke in him with a strong voice. Bindlecombe he hated, and it was mainly Bindlecombe's idea. Catsford he hated, because it was gradually but surely spreading to the gates of his beautiful old house. Deeper than this, he hated being under anybody's power; it was bitter to him that, when his mind was to stay, anybody—whether Jenny or another —should be able to tell him to go. Finally, his special position toward Jenny made the mere raising of the question of his future residence a rare chance for her—a chance of teasing and vexing, of coaxing and soothing, or of artful pretense that there was no underlying question at all.

She told him about the project—it was nothing more, she was careful to remark—after dinner one evening, in her most artless manner.

"It's a perfect idea—only I hope you wouldn't mind turning out?"

He had listened sullenly, pulling hard at his cigar. Chat was watching him with alarmed eyes; he had cast his spell on Chat, that was certain; there his boast did not go beyond truth.

"Being turned out, you mean, I imagine! I'd never willingly turn out to make room for any such nonsense. Of all the humbugs——"

"It's my duty to do something for the town," she urged—very grave.

"Let them do their work by day and drink their beer by night. Fancy those fellows in my house!"

"I'm sorry you feel like that. I thought you'd be interested—and—and I'd try to find you a house somewhere else. There must be some other houses, Mr. Austin?"

"One or two round about, I fancy," said I.

"Nice little ones—to suit a single man?" she asked, her bright eyes now seeking, now eluding, a meeting with his.

"I suppose I can choose the size of my house for myself," Octon growled. "I don't want Austin's advice about it."

"Oh, it wasn't poor Mr. Austin who—who spoke about the size of the house." A sudden thought seemed to strike her. "You might stay on and be something in the Institute!"

"I'd burn the house over my head sooner."

"Burn my pretty house! Oh, Mr. Octon! I should be so hurt—and you'd be sent to prison! What a lot of police it would need to take you there!"

The last sentence mollified him—and it was clever of her to know that it would. He had his primitive side, too. He was primitive enough to love a compliment to his muscles.

"I'd be out of the country before they came—with you under my arm," he said, with a laugh.

"That would be very forgiving—but hardly proper, would it, Chat? Unless we were— Oh, but what nonsense! Why don't you like my poor Institute?"

He relapsed into ill-humor, and it developed into downright rudeness.

"It's nothing to me how people make fools of themselves," he said.

Jenny did not always resent his rudeness. But she never compromised her right to resent it. She exercised the right now, rising with instantaneous dignity. "It's time for us to go, Chat. Mr. Austin, will you kindly look after Mr. Octon's comfort for the rest of the evening?" She swept out, Chat pattering after her in a hen-like flutter. Octon drank off his glass of wine with a muttered oath. Excellent as the port was, it seemed to do him no good. He leaned over to me—perfectly sober, be it understood (I never saw him affected by liquor), but desperately savage. "I won't stand that," he said. "If she sticks to that, I'll never come back to this house when I've walked out of it to-night."

I was learning how to deal with his tempests. "I shall hope to have the pleasure of encountering you elsewhere," I observed politely. "Meanwhile I have my orders. Pray help yourself to port."

He did that, but at the same moment hurled at me the order—"Take her that message."

"There's pen and ink behind you, Octon."

Temper is a terrible master—and needs looking after even as a servant. He jumped up, wrote something—what I could only guess—and rang the bell violently. I could imagine Jenny's smile—I did not ring like that.

"Take that to your mistress," he commanded. "It's the address she wanted." But he had carefully closed the envelope, and probably Loft had his private opinion.

We sat in silence till the answer came. "Miss Driver says she is much obliged, sir, for the address," said Loft as, with a wave of his hand, he introduced a footman with coffee, " and she needn't trouble you any more in the matter—as you have another engagement to-night."

Under Loft's eyes he had pulled himself together; he received the message with an appearance of indifference which quite supported the idea that it related to some trifle and that he really had to go away early; I had not given him credit for such a power of suddenly regaining self-control. He nodded, and said lightly to me, " Well, since Miss Driver is so kind, I'll be off in another ten minutes." The presence of servants must, in the long run, create a great deal of good manners.

When Loft was out of the room Octon dropped his disguise. He brought his big hand down on the table with a slap, saying, " There's an end of it! "

" Why shouldn't she build an Institute? If you take a lease for only seven years, how are you aggrieved by getting notice to quit at the end of the term? "

" Don't argue round the fringe of things. Don't be a humbug," he admonished me, scornfully enough, yet for once, as I fancied, with a touch of gentleness and liking. " You've damned sharp eyes, and I've something else to do than take the trouble to blind them."

" No extraordinary acuteness of vision is necessary," I ventured to remark.

He rose from his chair with a heavy sigh, leaving his coffee and brandy untouched. I felt inclined to tell him that in all likelihood he was taking the matter too seriously: he was assuming finality—a difficult thing to assume when Jenny was in the case. He came to me and laid his hand on my shoulder. "They manage 'em better in Africa," he said with a sardonic grin. "Of course I'd no business to say that to her—but hadn't she been trying to draw me all the time? She does it—then she makes a shindy!"

"I'll see you a bit on your way," I said. He accepted my offer by slipping his hand under my arm. I opened the door for us to pass out. There stood Chat on the threshold. Octon regarded her with an ill-subdued impatience. Chat was fluttering still.

"Oh, Mr. Octon, she's—she's so angry! Might I —oh, might I take a message to her room? She's gone upstairs and forbidden me to follow."

"Thank you, but there's no message to take."

"If you would just say something——!"

"There's no message to take." Again his tone was not rough—it was moody, almost absent: but, as he left Chat behind in her useless agitation, he leaned on my arm very heavily. Though I counted his whole great body as for me less than her little finger, yet a subtle male freemasonry stirred in me. He had behaved very badly—for a man should bear a pretty woman's pin-pricks—yet he was hard hit; all against him as I was, I knew that he was hard hit. Moreover, he had summed up Jenny's procedure pretty accurately.

We put on our coats—it was now September—undid the big door, and went out, down the steps, into a clear frosty night. We had walked many yards along the drive before he spoke. At last he said, very quietly—

"You're a good chap, Austin, and I'm sorry I've made a row to-night. Yes, I'm sorry for that. But whether I'm sorry I've been kicked out or not—well, that's a difficult question. My temper—well, sometimes I'm a bit afraid of it."

"Oh, that's nothing. You've both got tempers. You'll make it up."

He spoke with a calm deliberation unusual with him. "I don't think I'd better," he said. "I don't quite trust myself: I might do something—queer."

In my opinion that possibility about him attracted Jenny; but it needed no artificial fostering, and I held my peace.

There were electric lights at intervals down the drive: at this moment I could see his face plainly. I thoroughly agreed with what he said and understood his judgment of himself. But it was hard to see him look like that about it. Suddenly—as I still looked—his expression changed. A look of apprehension came over him—but he smiled also, and gripped my arm tightly. A figure walked out of the darkness into the light of the lamp.

I recalled how I had found her sitting by my hearth one night—in time to make me recall my resignation. Was she here to make Octon unsay his determination?

She came up to us smiling—with no air of surprise, real or affected, and with no explanation of her own presence.

"Both of you! What luck! I didn't think you'd come away from the house yet."

"I've come away from the house, Miss Driver," said Octon—rather grimly.

"In fact you've—'walked out of the house'—?" asked Jenny, smiling. The dullest ears could not miss the fact that she was quoting.

"Yes," answered Octon briefly, leaving the next move with her. She had no hesitation over it.

"Let not the sun go down upon your wrath!" she cried gayly. "The sun is down, but the moon will be up soon, and if you won't quarrel any more I'll keep you company for a little bit of the way." She turned to me, "Do you mind waiting at the house a quarter of an hour? I've had a letter from Mr. Cartmell that I want to consult you about."

Octon had not replied to her invitation and did not now. As I said, "All right—I'll smoke a pipe outside and wait for you," she beckoned lightly and merrily to him. After an almost imperceptible pause he moved slowly after her. Gradually their figures receded from the area of lamplight and grew dim in the darkness. The moon peeped over the hill but gave no light yet by which they could be seen.

I had never believed in the permanence of that quarrel. Though it was a strong instance, yet it was hardly more than a typical instance of their quarrels —of the constant clashing of his way against hers— of the play between her rapier and his club. If their intimacy went on, they might have worse quarrels than that. For me the significance of the evening lay not in another proof that Jenny, while saving her pride and scoring her formal victory, would still not let him go—and perhaps would go far to keep him;

that was an old story, or, at least, a bit of discernment of her now months old; rather it lay in Octon's account of his own disposition toward her proceedings —in his puzzle whether he were glad or sorry to be "kicked out"—in that fear of himself and of his self-restraint which made him relieved to go, even while his face was wrung with the pain of going. In view of that, I felt that I also should have been relieved if he had really gone—gone not to return—not to submit himself again to the variety of Jenny's ways—to the quick flashing alternation of her weapons, natural, conventional, casual, or whatsoever they might be. He was right about himself—he was not the man for that treatment. He could not appreciate the artistic excellence of it; he felt, even if he deserved, its cruelty. Moreover, it might prove dangerous. What if he beat down the natural weapons—and ignored the rest? One thing at least was clear; he would not again tell me—or even pretend to me —that her power was "all flim-flam."

She came back in half an hour, at a leisurely pace, looking much pleased with herself.

I was smoking on the steps by the hall door.

"That's all right," she assured me with a cheerful smile. "We're quite friends, and he's not going to be such a bear any more—if he can help it, which, Mr. Austin, I doubt."

"How did you manage it?" I asked—not that there was much real need of inquiry.

"Of course I told him that the Institute was nothing but an idea, and that, even if it were built, its being at Hatcham Ford was the merest idea, and that, even if it had to be at Hatcham Ford—well, I pointed out that two years are two years—(You needn't take the trouble to nod about that—it was quite a sensible remark)—that two years are two years and that very likely he wouldn't want the house at all by then."

"I see."

"So, of course, he apologized for his rudeness and promised not to be so foolish again, and we said good night quite friends. What have you been thinking about?"

"I don't think I could possibly tell you."

I was just opening the door for her. She paused on the threshold, lifting her brows a little and smiling as she whispered, "Something uncomplimentary?"

"That depends what you want to be complimented on," I answered.

"Oh, as long as it's on anything!" she cried. "You'll admit my compliments to-night have been terribly left-handed?"

"I don't know that mine hasn't a touch of that. Well—I think it's very brave to play games in the crater of an active volcano—exceedingly brave it is!"

"Brave? But not very——?"

"Let's leave it where it is. What about Cartmell's letter?"

"That'll do to-morrow." (Of course it would—it had been only an instrument of dismissal.) "I'm tired to-night." Her face grew grave: she experienced another mood—or touched another note. "My friend, you must believe that I always listen to what you say. I mayn't see things just as you seem to, sometimes, but what you say always makes me think. By the bye, are you very busy, or could you ride to-morrow?"

"Of course!" I cried eagerly. "Seven-thirty, as usual?"

"A quarter to eight sharp. Good night." She gave me a contented friendly smile, with just a hint of triumph about it, and went upstairs.

It shows what a good thing life is that I, too, in spite of my questionings and apprehension, repaired home forgetful of them for the time and full of exultation. I loved riding; and Jenny on horseback was a companion for a god.

On reflection it might have occurred to me that it was easier for her to invite me to ride than to listen too exactly to my counsels—quite as easy and really as well calculated to keep me content. Happily the youth in me found in her more than the subject of fears or the source of questionings. She could also delight.

CHAPTER VI

TAKING TO OPEN SEA

ON her morning rides Jenny wore a habit of russet brown and a broad-brimmed hat to match; her beautiful mare was a golden chestnut; the motive and the crown of all the scheme showed in her brilliant hazel eyes. On this fine morning—there was a touch of autumn frost, slowly yielding before the growing strength of the sun, but the ground was springy under us—Jenny bore a holiday air; no cares and no schemes beset her. To my poor ability I shared and seconded her mood, though my black coat and drab breeches were a sad failure in the matter of outward expression. She made straight for the north gate of the Priory park; we passed through it, crossed the road, and entered, by a farm-gate, on to Fillingford territory. "I almost always come here," she told me. "There's such a splendid gallop. Now and then I meet Lord Lacey, and we have a race."

Not being an habitual party to these excursions—it was my usual lot to lie in wait for the early post and reduce the letters to order for our after-breakfast session—I had seen and heard nothing of her encounters with young Lacey. I conceived that the two houses were still on the terms of distant civility to which Lady Sarah's passive resistance had endeavored to confine them. A formal call from each lady on the other—a no less formal visit to Jenny from Lord Fillingford (who left his son's card also)—there it had seemed to stop, the Mayor of Catsford and the Memorial Hall perhaps in some degree contributing to that result. Fine mornings a-horseback and youthful blood had, however, sapped Lady Sarah's defenses. I was glad—and I envied Lacey. He had much to be thankful for. True, they talked of sad financial troubles at Fillingford Manor, but you may hear many a fine gentleman rail at the pinch of poverty, as he pours, in no ungenerous measure, his own champagne down his throat at half-a-crown a glass. Perhaps at Fillingford that luxury did not rule every day; but at any rate Lacey had a good horse to ride—to say nothing of pleasant company.

Well, all he had he deserved, if only because he looked what he was so splendidly. If Providence, or nature, or society makes a scheme of things, it is surely a merit in us poor units to fit into it? Let others attack or defend the country gentleman. Anyhow, if you are one, look it! And for such an one as does look it I have a heartfelt admiration, from the crown of his head to the sole of his foot—with a special affection for his legs in perfect boots and breeches. Young Lacey was such a consummate type; I did not wonder that Jenny's ever liberal appreciation smiled beams of approval as he appeared over the crest of a rising hillock and rode on to meet us. Excellent, too, were the lad's manners; he appeared really glad to see me—which in the nature of the case he hardly can have been in his heart.

"I'm going to win this morning!" he cried to Jenny. "I feel like winning to-day!"

"Why to-day? You don't win very often."

"That's true," he said to me. "Miss Driver's won two to my one, regular. At sixpence a race I owe her three shillings already."

I had a feeling that Jenny glanced at me, but I did not look at Jenny. I did not even do the sum, though it was easy arithmetic.

"But to-day—well, in the first place I've got my commission—and in the second Aunt Sarah's gone to London for a week."

"I congratulate you on the commission."

"And you're loftily indifferent about Aunt Sarah?" he asked, laughing. "I say, though, come along! Are you a starter, Mr. Austin?"

I declined the invitation, but I managed to keep them well in sight—and my deliberate opinion is that Jenny pulled. She could have won, I swear it, if she had liked; as it was, she was beaten by a length. The lad was ingenuously triumphant. "Science is beginning to tell," he declared. "You won't hold your lead long!"

"Sometimes it's considered polite to let a lady win," Jenny suggested.

"Oh, come! If she challenges she must take her chance in fair fight."

"Then what chance have we poor women?" asked deceptive Jenny—who could have won the race.

"You beat us in some things, I admit. Brains, very

often, and, of course, charm and all that sort of thing." He paused a moment, blushed a little, and added, "And—er—of course—out of sight in moral qualities."

I liked his "moral qualities." It hinted that reverence was alive in him. I am not sure it did not indicate that the reverence due to woman in the abstract was supremely due to the woman by his side.

"Out of sight in moral qualities?" she repeated thoughtfully. "Yes, I suppose even a woman may hope that that's true. Don't you think so, Mr. Austin?"

"It has always been conceded in civilized communities," I agreed.

"What I hate about that fellow Octon— Oh, I beg pardon—isn't he a friend of yours?"

"I know him pretty well. He's rather interesting."

"I hate the fellow's tone about—about that sort of thing. Cheap, I call it. But I don't suppose he does it to you; you wouldn't stand it."

"I'm very patient with my friends," said Jenny.

"Friends! You and that—! Oh, well, let's have another gallop."

The gallop brought us in full view of Fillingford Manor; it lay over against us in the valley, broad expanses of meadow and of lawn leading up to a formal garden, beyond which rose the long low redbrick façade half covered with ivy, and a multitude of twisting chimneys.

"Jolly old place, isn't it?" cried Lacey. "I say, wouldn't you like to see over it? I don't expect Aunt Sarah showed you much!"

"I should like to see over it very much, if your father would ask me."

"Oh, he will—he'll be delighted. I say, come this week—while we're by ourselves?"

"Yes, if he invites me."

"He'll invite you. He likes you very much—only he's not exactly expansive, you know, the governor!"

"Never mind, you are. Now Mr. Austin and I must go back to breakfast and to work."

"By Jove, I must be getting back, too, or I shall keep the governor waiting, and he doesn't like that."

"If you do, tell him it's my fault."

The boy looked at her, then at me, again blushed a little, and laughed. The slightest flush appeared on Jenny's smiling face. I took the opportunity to light a cigarette. The morning races had not been talked about at Fillingford!

"Well no—you mustn't put it on the woman, must you?" said Jenny, as she waved a laughing farewell.

On our way home she was silent and thoughtful, speaking only now and then and answering one or two remarks of mine rather absently. One observation threw some light on her thoughts.

"It's very awkward that Mr. Octon should make himself so unpopular. I want to be friends with everybody, but—" She broke off. I did no more than give a nod of assent. But I knew—and thought she must —how Octon stood. He was considered to have made himself impossible. He was not asked to Fillingford; Aspenick had bluntly declared that he would not meet him on account of a rude speech of Octon's, leveled at Lady Aspenick; Bertram Ware and he were at daggers drawn over some semipolitical semiprivate squabble in which Octon's language had been of more than its usual violence. The town loved him no better than the county. Jenny wanted to be popular everywhere—popular, influential, acclaimed. She was weighted by this unpopular friendship—which yet had such attraction for her. The cares of state had fastened on her again as we jogged homeward.

Well, they were the joy of her life—it would have needed a dull man not soon to see that. The real joy, I mean—not what at that moment—nay, nor perhaps at any moment—she would herself have named as her delight. Her joy in the sense in which we creatures—and the wisest among us long ago—come nearest to being able to understand and define the innermost engine or instinct whose working is most truly ourselves—the temptation to live and life itself which pair nature has so cunningly coupled together. Effective activity—the reaching out to make of external things and people (especially, perhaps, things and people that obstinately resist) part of our own domain—their currency coinage of ours, with the stamp of our mint, bearing our superscription—causing the writ of our issuing to run where it did not run before—is not this, however ill-expressed (and bigger men than I have failed, and will fail, fully to express it), something like what the human spirit attempts? Or is there, too, a true gospel of drawing in—of renouncing? In the essential, mind you!—It is easy in trifles, in indulgences and luxuries. But to surrender the exercise and expansion of self?

If that be right, if that be true—at any rate it was not Jenny Driver. She was a srong, natural-born swimmer, cast now for the first time into open sea—after the duck ponds of her Smalls and her Simpsons. It was not the smooth waters which tested, tried, or in innermost truth delighted her most.

All this in a very tiny corner? Of course. Will you find me anywhere that is not a corner, please? Alexander worked in one, and Cæsar. "What does it matter then what I do?" "No more," I must answer, being no philosopher and therefore unprepared with a theory, "than it matters whether or not you are squashed under yonder train. But if you think—on your own account—that the one matters, why, for all we can say, perhaps the other does."

That duck pond of the Simpsons'! By apparent chance—it may be, in fact, by some unusual receptivity in my own bearing—that very day Chat talked to me about it. I had grown friendlier toward Chat, having perceived that the cunning in her—(it was there, and refuted Cartmell's charge of mere foolishness)—ran to no more than a decent selfishness, informed by years of study of Jenny, deflected by a spinsterish admiration of Octon's claim to unquestioned male dominion. Her reason said—"We are very well as we are. I am comfortable. I am 'putting by.' Jenny's marriage might make things worse." The spinster added, "But this must end some day. Let it end—when it must—in an irresistible (perhaps to Chat's imagination a rather lurid) conquest." Paradoxically her instinct (for if anything be an instinct, selfishness is) squared with what I had deciphered of Jenny's strategy—in immediate action at least. Chat would not have Octon shown the door; neither would she set him at the head of the table—just yet. Being comfortable, she abhorred all chance of convulsions—as Jenny, being powerful, resented all threat of dominion. But if the convulsion must come—as it must some day—Chat wanted it dramatic—matter for gossip and for flutters! To her taste Octon fulfilled that æsthetic requirement.

Naturally Chat saw Jenny at the Simpsons' from her own point of view—through herself—and by that avenue approached the topic.

" Of course things are very much changed for the better in most ways, Mr. Austin—if they'll only last. The comforts!—And, of course, the salary! Well, it's not the thing to talk about that. Still I daresay you yourself sometimes think—? Yes, of course, one must consider it. But there were features of the rectory life which I confess I miss. We had always a very cheerful tea, and supper, too, was sociable. In fact one never wanted for a chat. Here I'm thrown very much on my own resources. Jenny is out or busy, and Mrs. Bennet—the housekeeper, you know—is reserved and, of course, not at her ease with me. And then there was the authority!" (Was Chat also among the Cæsars?) " Poor Chat had a great deal of authority at the rectory, Mr. Austin—yes—she had! Mrs. Simpson an invalid—the rector busy or not caring to meddle—the girls were left entirely to me. My word was law." She shook her head regretfully over the change in her position.

"We all like that, Miss Chatters, when we can get it!"

"Jenny, of course, was different—and that made it difficult sometimes. Besides being the eldest, she was very well paid for and, although not pampered and, I must say, considering all things as I now know them, very ill-supplied with pocket money, there were orders that she should ride every day. Two horses and the hostler from the Bull every day—except Sundays! It couldn't but make a difference, especially with a girl of Jenny's disposition—not altogether an easy one, Mr. Austin. It had to be give-and-take between us. If she obeyed me, there were many little things I could do—having, as I say, the authority. If she would do her lessons well—and her example had great influence on the others—I didn't trouble to see what books she had in her bedroom (with the other girls I did), nor even ask questions if she stayed out a little late for supper. Of course we had to be very much on our guard; it didn't do to make the Simpson girls jealous."

"You had a little secret understanding between yourselves?"

"Never, Mr. Austin! I wouldn't have done such a thing with any of my pupils. It would be subversive of discipline."

"Of course it would; I beg your pardon." (Here a little " homage to virtue " on both our parts!)

"She knew how far she could go; she knew when I must say 'Stop!' She never put me to it—though I must say she went very near the line sometimes. She came to us very raw, too, with really no idea of what was ladylike. What those Smalls can have been like! You see what she is now. I don't think I did so badly."

I saw what she was now—or some of it. And I seemed to see it all growing up in that country rectory—the raw girl from the Smalls (those deplorable Smalls!) at Cheltenham, learning her youthful lessons in diplomacy—how far one can go, where one must stop, how keen a bargain can be struck with Authority. Chat had been Authority then. There was another now. Yet where the difference in principle?

" I can't have managed so very badly, because they were all broken-hearted to lose me—I often think how they can be getting on!—and here I am with Jenny! Well, poor Chat would have had to go soon, anyhow. They were all growing up. That time comes. It must be so in my profession, Mr. Austin. Indispensable to-day, to-morrow you're not wanted! "

" That sounds sad. You must be glad, in the end, that you didn't stay? "

" It'll be the same here some day. For all you or I know, it might be to-morrow. The only thing is to suit as long as we can, and to put by a little."

I vowed—within my breast—that henceforth Chat's little foibles — or defenses? — her time-serving, her cowardice, her flutters, her judgment of Jenny's concerns from a point of view not primarily Jenny's, her encroachments on the port and other stolen (probably transient!) luxuries—all these should meet with gentle and sympathetic appraisement. She was only trying to " suit "—and meanwhile to put by a little. But I was not sure what she had done, or helped to do, to

Jenny, nor that her ex-pupil's best course would not lie in presenting her with her *congé* and a substantial annuity.

An invitation came from Fillingford in which Chat and I were courteously included. Jenny, however, found work for poor Chat at home (alas, for the days of Authority!) and made me drive her over in the dog-cart. As we drove in at the gates, she asked suddenly, " How am I to behave? "

" Don't look at anything as if you wanted to buy it," was the best impromptu advice I could hit on.

" I might do it tactfully! Don't you remember what my father said?—' You may succeed in your way better than I in mine.' "

" I remember. And you think he referred to tact? "

Jenny took so long to answer that there was no time to answer at all; we were at the door, and young Lacey was waiting.

The house was beautiful and stately; I think that Jenny was surprised to find that it was also in decent repair. There was nothing ragged, nothing poverty-stricken; a grave and moderate handsomeness marked all the equipment. The fall in fortune was rather to be inferred from what was absent than rudely shown in the present condition of affairs. Thus the dining-room was called the Vandyke Room—but there were no Vandykes; a charming little boudoir was called the Madonna Parlor—but the Madonna had taken flight, probably a long flight across the Atlantic. In giving us the names Lord Fillingford made no reference to their being no longer applicable —he seemed to use them in mechanical habit, forgetful of their significance—and Jenny, mindful perhaps of the spirit of my warning, refrained from questions. But for what was to be seen she had a generous and genuine enthusiasm; the sedate beauty and serenely grand air of the old place went to her heart.

But one picture did hang in the Madonna Parlor—a half-length of a beautiful high-bred girl with large dark eyes and a figure slight almost to emaciation. Lacey and I, who were behind, entered the room just as the other two came to a stand before it. I saw Jenny's face turn toward Fillingford in inquiry.

"My wife," he said. "She died thirteen years ago—when Amyas was only five." His voice was dry, but he looked steadily at the picture with a noticeable intentness of gaze.

"This was mother's own room, Miss Driver," Lacey interposed.

"Yes. How—how it must have suited her!" said Jenny in a low voice.

Fillingford turned his head sharply round and looked at her; with a slight smile he nodded his head. "She was very fond of this room. She had it furnished in blue—instead of yellow." Then he moved quickly to the door. "There's nothing else you'd care to see here, I think."

After lunch Lacey carried Jenny off to the garden—his father seemed to think that he had done enough as host and to acquiesce readily in the devolution of his duties—and I sat awhile with Fillingford, smoking cigarettes—well, he only smoked one. It seemed to me that the man was like his house; just as the state of its fortune was not rudely declared in anything unbecoming or shabby, but had to be gathered from the gaps where beauties once had figured, so the essence of him, and the road to understanding him, lay in his reserves, his silences, his defensiveness. What he refrained from doing, being, or saying, was the most significant thing about him. His manners were irreproachable, his courtesy cast in a finer mold than that of an ordinary gentleman, yet he did not achieve real cordiality and remained at a very long arm's length from intimacy. His highest degree of approval seemed to consist in an absence of disapprobation; yet, feeling that this negative reward of merit was hard to win, the recipient took the unsubstantial guerdon with some gratification. My own hope was to escape from his presence without having caused him to think that I had done anything offensive; if he had nothing against me, I should be content. I wondered whether he were satisfied to have the like measure meted out to him. His son had said he was " not expansive " : that was like denying silkiness to a porcupine. Yet there was that about him which commanded respect—at least a respect appropriately negative; you felt certain that he would do nothing sordid and touch nothing unclean; he would always be true to the code of his class and generation.

We heard laughter from Jenny and Lacey echoing down the long passages as they returned from the garden; from the noise their feet made they seemed to be racing again. The sounds interrupted a rather perfunctory conversation about Nicholas Driver and the growth of Catsford. Rather to my surprise—I must confess—his face lit up with a smile—a smile of pensive sweetness.

"That sounds cheerful," he said. "More like old days!" Then he looked at me apprehensively, as though afraid that he had proffered an uninvited confidence. He went on almost apologetically. "It's very quiet here. My health doesn't fit me for public life, or even for much work in the county. We do our duty, I hope, but we tend rather to fall out of the swim. It wasn't so in my wife's time. Well, Amyas will bring all that back again some day, I hope."

"I'm glad to hear that he's got his commission," said I.

"Yes, he must go and do some work, while I hold the fort for him at home. Landed property needs a great deal of attention nowadays, Mr. Austin." Again he smiled, but now wearily, as though his stewardship were a heavy burden.

The laughing pair burst into the room. Amyas was flushed, Jenny seemed out of breath; they had a great joke to tell.

"We've found a picture of Miss Driver in the West Gallery," cried Amyas. "Really it must be her—it's exactly like!"

"Fancy my picture being in your house all this time, Lord Fillingford—and you never told me!"

Fillingford was looking intently at Jenny now. He raised his brows a little and smiled, as the result of his survey.

"Yes—I'm afraid I know which picture Amyas means, though I don't often go to the West Gallery. The one on the right of the north door, Amyas?"

TAKING TO OPEN SEA

"Yes—in a wonderful gown all over pearls, you know."

"Who is she—besides me?" asked Jenny. "Because I believe she has a look of me really."

"She's an ancestress—a collateral ancestress at least—of ours. She was one of Queen Elizabeth's ladies. But we're not proud of her—and you mustn't be proud of the likeness—if there is one, Miss Driver."

"But I am proud of it. I think she's very pretty—and some day I'll have a gown made just like that."

"Why aren't we proud of her, father?" asked young Lacey.

"She got into sad disgrace—and very nearly into the Tower, I believe. Elizabeth made her kinsman Lord Lacey—one of my predecessors—take her away from Court and bring her down to the country. Here she was kept—in fact more or less imprisoned. But it didn't last many years. Smallpox carried her off, poor thing—it was very bad in these parts about 1590—and, unluckily for her, before the queen died.

"What was her name?"

"Mistress Eleanor Lacey."

"And what had she done?" pursued Jenny, full of interest.

"Ah, well, what was the truth about it—who can tell now? It was never important enough to get put on record. But the family tradition is that the Queen was jealous of her place in Leicester's affections." He smiled at Jenny. "I wish Amyas had found you a more acceptable prototype!"

"Oh, I don't know," said Jenny thoughtfully. "I

like her looks. Do you believe that what they said was true?"

"I'm sorry to say that, again according to the family tradition, it was."

Our dog-cart had been ready for some minutes. Jenny said good-by, and both father and son escorted her to the door.

"I hope we shall see you at dinner as soon as my sister comes back," said Fillingford, as he helped her to mount into the cart. "We must have a little festivity for Amyas before he joins."

Jenny was all thanks and cordiality, and drove off smiling and waving her hand gayly.

"Isn't that really rather interesting about Eleanor Lacey? Mind you go and see the picture next time you're there! It's really very like."

I promised to see the picture, and asked her how she had got on with Fillingford.

"Oh, I like him well enough, but—" She paused and smiled reflectively. "Down at the Simpsons' there was a certain young man—boy he really was—whom we called Rabbit. That was only because of the shape of his mouth, and has nothing to do with the story! I used sometimes to walk hcme with Rabbit—from evening church, or lawn-tennis parties, and so on, you know." (Were these the occasions on which she was rather late for supper—without incurring Chat's rebuke?) "We girls used to laugh at him because he always began by taking great pains to show you that he didn't mean to flirt—well, at all events, didn't mean to begin the flirtation. If you wanted to flirt, you must begin yourself—that was Rabbit's attitude, and he made it perfectly plain in his behavior.

"Rabbit can't have been a very amusing youth to walk home with in the gloaming?" I ventured to suggest.

"He wasn't, but then there wasn't much choice down at the Simpsons', you know. Besides, it could be made rather funny with Rabbit. You see, he wouldn't begin because he had such a terror of being snubbed." She laughed in an amused reminiscence. "I think I shall call Lord Fillingford Rabbit," she ended.

"It'll be very disrespectful."

"Oh, you can't make all the nicknames for yourself!" She paused and added, apparently with a good deal of satisfaction—"Rabbit—and Volcano—yes!"

CHAPTER VII

THE FLICK OF A WHIP

JENNY spent a large part of the winter in Italy, Chat being with her, Cartmell and I left in charge at home. But early in the New Year she came back and then, her mourning being over, she launched out. Without forgetting her father's injunction against spending all her income, she organized the household on a more extensive scale; new carriages and more horses, a couple of motors, and a little electric launch for the lake were among the additions she made. The out-of-doors staff grew till Cartmell had to ask for an estate-steward to take the routine off his shoulders, while Mrs. Bennet and Loft blazed with pride at the swelling numbers of their subordinates in the house itself. Jenny's taste for splendor came out. She even loved a touch of the gorgeous; old Mr. Driver's dark blue liveries assumed a decidedly brighter tint, and I heard her express regret that postilions and four horses were in these days thought ostentatious except for very great national or local potentates. " If I were a peeress, I would have them," she declared rather wistfully. If that were the condition and the only one, after all we might perhaps live to see the four horses and the postilions at Breysgate before we were many months older. By now, there was matter for much speculation about her future; the closer you were to her, the more doubtful any speculation seemed.

This was the time of her greatest glory—when she was fresh to her state and delighting in it, when all the neighborhood seemed to be at her feet, town and county vying in doing her honor—and in accepting her hospitality.

Entertainment followed entertainment; now it was the poor, now it was the rich, whom she fed and fêted. The crown of her popularity came perhaps when she declared that she would have no London house and wanted no London season. Catsford and the county were good enough for her. The *Catsford Herald and Times* printed an article on this subject which was almost lyrical in its anticipation of a return of the good old days when the aristocracy found their own town enough. It was headed " Catsford a Metropolis—Why not? " And it was Jenny who was to imbue the borough with this enviable metropolitan character! This was *Redeunt Saturnia regna* with a vengeance!

To all outward appearance she was behaving admirably—and her acquaintance with Fillingford had reached to as near intimacy as it was ever likely to get while it rested on a basis of mere neighborly friendship. Lady Sarah had been convinced or vanquished—it was impossible to say which. At any rate she had withdrawn her opposition to intercourse between the two houses and appeared to contemplate with resignation, if not with enthusiasm, a prospect of which people had now begun to talk—not always under their breath. Fillingford Manor and Breysgate were now united closely enough for folk to ask whether they were to be united more closely still. For my own part I must admit that, if Lord Fillingford were wooing, he showed few of the usual signs; but perhaps Jenny was! I remembered the story of Rabbit—without forgetting the subject of the other nickname!

Old Cartmell was a great advocate of the Fillingford alliance. House laid to house and field to field were anathema to the Prophet; for a family lawyer they have a wonderful attraction. An estate well-rounded off, spacious, secure from encroachment and, with proper capital outlay, returning three per cent.—he admires it as the rest of us a Velasquez—well, some of us—or others, a thoroughbred. Careful man as he was, he declined to be dismayed at Jenny's growing expenditure. "The income's growing, too," he said. "It grows and must grow with the borough. Old Nick Driver had a very long head! She can't help becoming richer, whatever she does—in reason." He winked at me, adding, "After all, it isn't as if she had to buy Fillingford, is it?" I did not feel quite sure that it was not—and at a high price; but to say that would have been to travel into another sphere of discussion.

"Well, I'm very glad her affairs are so flourishing. But I wish the new liveries weren't so nearly sky-blue. I hope she won't want to put you and me in them!"

Cartmell paid no heed to the liveries. He took a puff at his cigar and said, "Now—if only she'll keep

THE FLICK OF A WHIP

straight!" That would have seemed an odd thing to say—to anyone not near her.

Yet trouble came—most awkwardly and at a most awkward moment. Octon himself was the cause of it, and I—unluckily for myself—the only independent witness of the central incident.

He had—like Jenny—been away most of the winter, but I had no reason to suppose that they had met or even been in communication; in fact, I believe that he was in London most of the time, finishing his new book and superintending the elaborate illustrations with which it was adorned. He did, however, reappear at Hatcham Ford close on the heels of Jenny's return to Breysgate, and the two resumed their old—and somewhat curious—relations. If ever it were true of two people that they could live neither with nor without one another, it seemed true of that couple. He was always seeking her, and she ever ready and eager to welcome him; yet at every other meeting at least they had a tiff—Jenny being, I must say, seldom the aggressor, at least in the presence of third persons: perhaps her offenses, such as they were, were given in private. But there was one difference which I perceived quickly, but which Octon seemed slower to notice: I hoped that he might never notice it at all, or, if he did, accept it peaceably. Jenny preferred, if it were possible, to receive him when the household party alone was present; when the era of entertaining set in, he was bidden on the off-nights. No doubt this practice admitted of being put—and perhaps was put by Jenny—in a flattering way. But it was impossible to be safe with him—

there was no telling how his temper would take him. So long as he believed that Jenny herself best liked to see him intimately, all would go well; but if once he struck on the truth—that she was yielding deference to the wishes of his enemies, her neighbors—there might very probably be an explosion. "Volcano" would get active if he thought that "Rabbit" and company—Jenny had concealed neither nickname from him—were being consulted. Or he might get just a wayward whim; if his temper were out, he would make trouble for its own sake—or to see with how much he could make her put up; each was always trying the limits of his or her power over the other.

The actual occasion of his outburst was, as usual, trivial, and perhaps—far as that was from being invariably the case—afforded him some shadow of excuse. Neither did Chat help matters. He had sent up from Hatcham Ford a bunch of splendid yellow roses, and, when he came to dinner the same evening, he naturally expected to see them on the table. "Where are my roses?" he asked abruptly, when we were half-way through dinner.

"I love them—they're beautiful—but they didn't suit my frock to-night," said Jenny, smiling. She would have managed the matter all right if she had been let alone, but Chat must needs put her oar in.

"They'll look splendid on the table to-morrow night," she remarked—as though she were saying something soothing and tactful.

"Oh, you've got a dinner-party to-morrow?" he asked—still calm, but growing dangerous.

"Nobody you'd care about," Jenny assured him; she had given Chat a look which immediately produced symptoms of flutters.

"Who's coming?"

"Oh, only Lord Fillingford and Lady Sarah, the Wares, the Rector, the Aspenicks, and one or two more."

"H'm. My roses are good enough for that lot, but I'm not, eh?"

Jenny's hand was forced; Chat had undermined her position. Not even for the sake of policy did she love to do an unhandsome thing—still less to be found out in doing one. To use the roses and slight the donor would not be handsome. She knew Aspenick's objection to meeting Octon, but probably she thought that she could keep Aspenick in order.

"I had no idea you'd care about it. I thought you liked coming quietly better. I like it so much better when I can have you to myself."

No use now! His prickles were out; he would not be cajoled.

"So I may as a rule—but it's rather marked when you never ask me to meet anyone."

"I shall be delighted to see you at dinner to-morrow," said Jenny. "Will you come?"

"Yes, I will come—I hope I know how to behave myself, don't I?"

"Oh, yes, you know well enough," she answered, delicately emphasizing the difference between knowledge and practice. "All right, I shall expect you."

"I know the meaning of it. That little Aspenick

minx and her fool of a husband are trying to get me boycotted—that's it."

Jenny, as her wont was, tried to smooth him down, but with little success. He went off early, still very sulky, and growling about the Aspenicks. For what it is worth, there was no doubt that they were now busy leaders in the cabal against him, and he knew it.

"It won't be very pleasant, but we must carry it off with brave faces," said Jenny, referring to the next day's dinner. She looked vexed, though, at this crossing of her arrangements.

Probably the dinner would have passed off tolerably, if not comfortably—for Aspenick was a gentleman, and even Octon might feel that he ought to be on his good behavior—when his temper recovered. But unluckily his temper had not recovered by eleven o'clock the following morning, and it was then that the lamentable thing happened.

I had finished my after-breakfast work with Jenny and had left the house, to go down the hill to the Old Priory. The road through the park crosses the path I had to follow, at about seventy yards from the house. Approaching this road, I saw Lady Aspenick's tandem coming along on my right. She was, as I have said before, an accomplished whip, and tandem-driving was a favorite pastime of hers. To-day she appeared to be trying a new leader; at any rate the animal was very skittish, now rearing, now getting out of line, now sidling along—doing anything, in fact, but his plain duty. She was driving slowly and carefully, while the two grooms were half-standing, half-kneeling behind, looking over her

THE FLICK OF A WHIP

shoulders and evidently ready to jump down and run to the leader's head at any moment. I stood watching their progress; it was pretty to see her drive. Then I became aware of Octon's massive figure coming from the opposite direction; he was walking full in the middle of the road, which at this point is not very broad—just wide enough for two carriages to pass one another between the banks, which rise sharply on either side to the height of nearly three feet.

As Lady Aspenick drew nearer to Octon, one of the grooms whistled. Octon gave way—a little. Apparently the groom—whether Lady Aspenick spoke to him or not I could not see—thought that there was not yet room enough, for he whistled again, waving his hand impatiently. Octon edged a little more to the side of the road and then stood still, apparently waiting for them to pass. He was by no means at the side of the road—neither was he now in the middle; perhaps he was a third of the way across; and, so far as I could judge, there was room for them to pass—and a sufficient margin, at any rate for a steady team. Now the groom shouted—a loud " Hi! " or some such word—in a peremptory way. I heard Octon's reply plainly. " There's plenty of room, I tell you." Lady Aspenick had her whip in her hand—ready, no doubt, to give her restless leader a flick to make him mind his manners as they went by. While this happened, I had begun to walk on again slowly, meaning to speak to Octon when the lady had passed. I was about fifteen yards away—and the tandem was just approaching where Octon stood.

Just as she came up to him, Lady Aspenick loosed the long lash of her whip; it flew out and I looked to see a jump from the leader, who was dancing and capering in a very restive way. But unless she took great care—or Octon moved a bit——

The next instant, while the idea was till incomplete in my mind, the end of the lash caught him full on the face. He jumped back with a shout of rage. The leader gave a wild plunge toward the other side of the road; the cart swayed and rocked. The grooms leaped down and ran as hard as they could to the leader's head. Octon sprang forward, caught hold of the whip, wrenched it from Lady Aspenick's hand, almost pulling her out of her seat, broke it in the middle across his knee, and flung the fragments down on the road. I ran up hastily.

"You did that on purpose," he said, his voice shaking with rage. There was a red streak across his face from the cheek bone to the chin.

She was pale, but she looked at him calmly through her eyeglasses.

"Nonsense," she answered, "but if I had, it would have been only your deserts. Why didn't you give me room?"

"There was plenty of room if you knew how to drive; and, if you wanted more, you could have asked for it civilly."

"You must have seen I had a young horse." She turned to me. "Give me my whip, please, Mr. Austin. You saw what happened? I'll ask my husband to come and see you about it." Then she ordered her men to take out the refractory leader, and lead him home;

she would drive back with the wheeler. She took no more notice of Octon, nor he of her (unless to watch her grooms' proceedings with a sullen stare), but as she started off, holding the broken butt of the whip in her hand, she called to me, " Tell Miss Driver we're looking forward to dinner to-night."

The grooms had looked dangerously at Octon, and were now saying something to one another; but it needed at least one to hold the horse, and Octon would be far more than a match for either of them singly. His angry eyes seemed only to hope that they would give him some excuse for violence.

" Follow your mistress," I said to them. " It's no affair of yours."

I think that they were glad to get my sanction for their retreat. Off they went, and I was left alone with Octon.

" If it had been a man, I wouldn't have left a whole bone in his body. She struck me deliberately—on purpose."

" It wasn't a man. Why didn't you give her more room? "

" There was plenty of room? " he persisted. " The whole road isn't hers, is it? " With that he turned on his heel and sauntered off toward the south gate, in the direction of his own house.

There was the incident—and I had the grave misfortune of being the only independent witness of it. There was the incident—and there was the dinner-party in the evening, to which both the Aspenicks and Leonard Octon were bidden. Clearly the matter could not stand where it was; it was, alas! no less clear that I should have to give my evidence. Of course the meeting at dinner must not take place; whatever else might or might not follow from the affair, that much was certain. I went back to the house and asked to see Jenny.

I told her the story plainly and fully—all that I had seen and all that had been said; she did not interrupt me once.

"There it is," I ended. "His case is that he gave her plenty of room and that she purposely lashed him over the face. Hers is that he gave her too little room, deliberately annoying her, that her leader was restive and she had to use her whip, and that, if she hit him, it was his own fault for standing where he did."

"His snatching away the whip and breaking it—isn't that bad?" she asked. "Or if he thought she meant to hit him?"

"Then it's still bad, I suppose, since she's a woman; but it's perhaps understandable—above all in him."

"Well, what's your own opinion about it?"

"That's just what I don't want to give," I objected.

"But you must. I have to come to some decision about this."

"Well, then—I think he did leave her room—enough and a little more than enough; but I also think that he meant to annoy her. I'm sure he didn't mean to put her in danger of an upset, but I do think that, with such a horse as she was driving, an upset might have been the result, and he ought to have thought of that—only he doesn't know much about horses. On the other hand I don't think she deliberately made up her mind to hit him—but I do think she meant to go as near to it as she could without actually doing it; I think she meant to make him jump. That's about my idea of the truth of the matter."

"Yes, I daresay," she said thoughtfully. "When Sir John comes to you, bring him straight up here. They mustn't meet to-night, of course, but I should like to see Sir John first—if he comes this morning or soon after lunch."

"It's all very tiresome," said I lugubriously.

She suddenly put her hands in mine—in one of her moments of impulse. "Oh, yes, yes, dear friend!" she murmured with an acute note of distress in her voice. Tiresome as the affair was, it hardly seemed to call for that; but I had not yet realized her position in its full difficulty; I did not know what every new proof of Octon's "impossibility" meant to her.

Sir John arrived, hot-haste, before lunch. Happily Fillingford was with him. I say happily, for I gathered that the angry husband's first intention had been to go straight to Hatcham Ford and undertake the horse-whipping of Leonard Octon—which enterprise must have ended in broken bones for Sir John, and probably the police court for both combatants. Fillingford happened to be with him when Lady Aspenick arrived at home and told her story; with difficulty he dissuaded Aspenick from violent measures; above all, nothing must get into the papers; all the same, it was a case for decisive private action. According to my orders I took Sir John up to Jenny, and Fillingford came with us.

There—before her—we had the whole story over again. Sir John told his wife's version, I put Octon's forward against it—if only for fair play's sake. Sir John naturally would have none of Octon's, nor would Fillingford. Then I repeated my own impression of the affair. Any points in it which made for Octon Sir John violently rejected; Fillingford's attitude was wiser, the position he took up less open to the charge of prejudice; he disliked Octon intensely, but he would not rest his case on the weak foundation of an angry temper.

"I'm quite content to accept Mr. Austin's view of the facts, which he has given us so clearly and so impartially. Where does his view lead? Why to this— Not only was Mr. Octon inexcusably violent at the end, but he was the original aggressor. He did not, Mr. Austin is convinced, mean to cause danger to Lady Aspenick, but he did mean to cause her vexation—in fact to offer her an affront. In my opinion anything on her part that followed is imputable to his own fault, and he had no title to resent it. I base my decision not on Lady Aspenick's account, but on Mr. Austin's independent testimony; and I say that Mr. Octon behaved as no gentleman and as no good neighbor should."

Jenny had listened to all the stories in silence, and in silence also she heard Fillingford's summing-up. Now she looked at him and asked briefly, "What follows?"

"It follows that he must be cut," interposed Aspenick in dogged anger.

"We have a right to protect ourselves—above all the ladies of our families—from the chance of such

THE FLICK OF A WHIP

occurrences. They mustn't be exposed to them if we can help it; they certainly need not and must not be exposed to the unpleasantness of meeting the man who causes them. We have a right to act on that line—and I, for one, feel bound to act on it, Miss Driver."

"Not a man in the place will do anything else," declared Aspenick.

But I was wondering what Jenny would do. Almost without disguise they were presenting to her an ultimatum. They were saying, "If you want him, you can't have us. We can't come where he comes. Is he to go on coming to Breysgate? Is he to go on using your park?" She did not like dictation—nor did she like sending her friends away. To send them away on dictation—would she do that? Or would she fall into one of her rages, bid them all go hang, and throw in her lot with boycotted Octon? She turned to me.

"Do you agree with what these gentlemen say?" she asked.

In the end I liked Octon or, at any rate, found him very interesting, and I was therefore ready, for myself, to put up with his tempers and his tantrums. People who did not like him nor find him interesting could not be asked to do that. And he stood condemned on my own evidence.

"They are quite within their rights," I had to answer.

She was not in a rage; she was anxious and distressed. Nor was the anxiety all hers. Aspenick indeed had at the moment no thought but of anger on his wife's account, but Fillingford must have had other things in his mind. To put it at the lowest, he valued his acquaintance with the mistress of Breysgate Priory; there were good grounds for guessing that he valued it very much. If he had learned anything at all about her, he must have known that he was risking it now. But he showed no hesitation; he awaited her answer with a grave deference which declared the importance he attached to it but gave no reason to hope that his own course of action could be affected, whatever the answer might be.

Neither did she give the impression of hesitating—it was not exactly that. Whether in her heart she hesitated I cannot tell; if she did, she would not let them see it. Her demeanor betrayed nothing more than a pained reluctance to condemn utterly, to recognize that one who had been received as a friend and as a gentleman had by his own fault forfeited his claim to those titles. Her delay in giving her decision—for the real question now was whether she would join in Octon's ostracism—did not impugn their judgment nor seem to weigh their merits against the culprit's. It did not declare a doubt of their being right; it said only with what pain she would recognize that they were right.

"Yes—it's the only thing," she said at last.

"I was sure you would agree with us—painful as such a course is," Fillingford said.

"It's only cutting a cad," Aspenick grumbled, half under his breath. Jenny did not or would not hear him.

The bargain was struck, and fully understood without more words. Jenny's friends must not be exposed to meeting Octon at Breysgate or in Breysgate park.

THE FLICK OF A WHIP

They would be strangers to Octon; if Jenny would be their friend, she must be a stranger to him. Dropping Octon was the condition of holding her place in their society. She understood the condition and accepted it. There was no more to be said.

They took leave and she did not ask them to stay to lunch. Her farewell to Aspenick was cold, though she made a civil reference to seeing him again at dinner—nothing was said about Octon in that connection! But toward Fillingford she showed a marked, if subdued, graciousness. Clearly she meant to convey to him that, distressed as she was by the incident and its necessary consequences, she attached no blame to him for the part he had taken—nay, was grateful to him for his counsel and guidance.

"I never had any doubt of your coming to a right decision," he told her, holding her hand for a moment longer than he need. She looked into his eyes, but said nothing; she gave the air of being heartily content to surrender her judgment to his.

I saw them off and came back to her. She was still standing in the same place, looking very thoughtful and frowning slightly; it was by no means the trustful expression with which her eyes had dwelt on Fillingford's.

"Directly after lunch I must go down to Hatcham Ford and see Mr. Octon. I want you to come with me."

"I? Not Miss Chatters?"

"You—not Chat. Don't be stupid," she said.

CHAPTER VIII

A SECRET TREATY

JENNY'S first remark as we drove down together to Hatcham Ford seemed to have very little to do with the matter in hand. Still less to do with it, as one would think, had the fact that, just before starting, she had—I learned it afterwards—given Chat a piece of handsome old lace.

"I like your name," she remarked. "'Austin Austin'—quite a good idea of your parents'! One's only got to drop the 'Mr.' to be friendly at once. No learning a strange Algernon, or Edward, or things of that kind!"

"Do drop it," said I.

"I have, Austin," said Jenny. She edged ever so little nearer to me, yet looked steadily out of the window on the other side of the brougham. "I'm frightened," she added in a low voice.

"Upon my honor," said I, "I don't wonder at it."

Such was the beginning of a remarkable kindness, a gentleness, almost an appealing attitude, which Jenny displayed during several weeks that followed. I must not flatter myself—Chat shared the rays of kindly sunshine. If I were promoted to the Christian name, Chat got the lace.

"What will you call me?" she asked. "'Miss Driver' sounds—Say 'Jenny'!"

"Before the county? Impossible!"

"Well, then, when we're alone?"

"Shall it be Lady Jenny? For ourselves?"

She sighed acquiescence. "You're a great comfort to me," she added. "You'll come in, won't you, if you hear me scream?"

"Come in?"

"I've got to see him alone, you know." She raised her hands for an instant, as though in lamentation; Oh, why is he like that?"

There was no treating this lightly—for one who felt for her what I did. I was no such fool as not to see that her sudden access of graciousness had a purpose—I had to be conciliated and stroked the right way for some reason; so doubtless had Chat. But again I was, so I humbly trust, no such churl as to resent the purpose—though I did not know precisely what it was. I was her 'man,' as the old word was—her vassal. If my liking or my honor refused that situation, well and good—I could end it. While it lasted, I was hers. Within me the thing went deeper still than that.

She was frightened. Therefore she was very gracious, seeking allies however humble. I declare that I have always limited my expectation of attachments entirely disinterested. Are there any? Who cherishes a friend from whom there is neither profit nor pleasure to be had? Or, at any rate, from whom neither has been had? The past obligation is often acknowledged—and acquitted—with a five-pound note.

The westering sun caught her face through the window as we entered the outskirts of Catsford; her eyes looked like a couple of new sovereigns.

"Yes, I'm frightened."

"Not you! You've courage enough for a dozen."

"Ah, I like you to say that! But I must make terms with him, you know." She caught and pressed my hand. "But I don't believe I'm quite a coward."

All this could mean but one thing—Octon had a great hold on her; yet against him was a powerful incentive. Between the two—between his power, which was great, and the power against him whose greatness she had acknowledged to Fillingford that morning, she must patch up conditions of peace—a secret treaty. I had no idea what the terms could or would be. If Octon had the naming of them, they would not be easy.

Hatcham Ford just held its freedom against the encroaching town. No more than fifty yards from its gates was the last villa—a red-brick house of eccentric architecture but comfortable dimensions; its side windows looked toward the gate of the Ford, and on the left its garden ran up to the road on to which the shrubberies encircling the old house faced. A tall oak fence surrounded the garden—on the gate was written, in large gilt letters, "Ivydene." That house, like so many in Catsford, was on Jenny's land. I wished that Cartmell would keep a tighter hand on his builders.

Nearly swallowed by the flood of modern erections as it was, the old house still preserved its sequestered charm. The garden was hidden from the road by a close screen in front; at the back it ran gently down to the murmuring river. Within were low ceilings crossed by old beams, and oak paneling everywhere. Octon's tenancy and personality were marked by clusters of barbaric spears and knives, hung against the oak, burnished to a high polish, flashing against their time-blackened background.

Visitors were not expected. Octon's man—a small wizened fellow of full middle age—seemed rather startled by the sight of Jenny; he hastily pushed, rather than ushered, us into the dining room, a room on the left of the doorway. In a moment or two Octon came to us. He stood in the doorway, his big frame looking immense under the low lintel which his head all but touched.

"You're not the visitors I expected," he said with a laugh. "I've stayed in, waiting for Aspenick."

"Sir John won't come," said Jenny. "But I must speak to you—alone." She turned to me. "You're sure you don't mind, Austin?"

"Of course you must see him alone. Where shall I go?"

"Stay here," he said. "We'll go next door—in the study."

He held the door for her, and she went out. I heard them enter a room next to the one in which I was; the door was shut after them. Then for a long while I heard nothing more, except the murmur of the little river, which seemed loud to my unaccustomed ears, though probably people living in the house would soon cease to notice it.

Presently I heard their voices; his was so loud that,

for fear of hearing the words, I had deliberately to abstract my mind by looking at this, that, and the other thing in the room—more spears and knives on the walls, books about his subject on the shelves, a couple of fine old silver tankards gleaming on the mantelpiece. The voices died down again just as I had exhausted the interest of the tankards, and taken in my hand a miniature which stood on the top of the marble clock.

His voice fell to inaudibility; the welcome silence left me alone with the little picture. It represented a child perhaps fourteen years old—a small, delicate face, dark in complexion, touched on the cheeks with a red flush, with large dark eyes, framed in plentiful black hair which curled about the forehead. Whoever the young girl was, she was beautiful; her eyes seemed to gaze at me from some remote kingdom of childish purity; her lips laughed that I should feel awe at her eyes. How in the world came she on Octon's mantelpiece?

Picked up somewhere for half a sovereign—as a pretty thing! That was the suggestion of common sense, in rebellion against a certain sense of overstrained nerves under which I was conscious of suffering. Yet, after all, Octon, like other men, must have kith and kin. The style of the picture was too modern for it to be his mother's. There were such things as sisters; but this did not look like Octon's stock. An old picture of a bygone sweetheart—that held the field as the likeliest explanation; well, except the one profanely offered by common sense. Octon was, to and for me, so much a part of Jenny's life and surroundings that it was genuinely difficult to realize him as a man with other belongings or associations; yet I could not but recognize that in all probability he had many—perhaps some apart from those which he might chance to have inherited.

Suddenly, through the wall, I heard a wail—surely I heard a little sob? The picture was instantly forgotten. I stood intensely awake, alert, watchful. If that sound came again, I determined that I would break in on their conference. For minutes I waited, but the sound came no more. I flung myself into a chair by the fire and began to smoke. I fell into a meditation. No further sound came to break it; the murmur of the river already grew familiar.

I heard a door open; the next moment they were in the room with me.

" What a time we've kept you! Have you been very bored? " asked Jenny.

Her words and her tone were light, but her face was as I had never seen it. It was drawn with the fatigue of deep feeling: she had been struggling; if I did not err, her eyes bore signs of crying—I had never known her cry. At that moment I think I knew to the full that Octon was, for good or evil, a great thing in her life. How could it be for good? She herself, she alone, must bear the burden of answering that question.

But he, standing behind her, wore an unmistakable air of victory. So confident was it, and so assured the whole aspect of his dominant figure, that I prepared myself to hear that the verdict of the morning was reversed and that the neighborhood—and all that meant—were to go hang. Yet his first words contradicted both my forecast and his own appearance. He spoke in a chafing tone.

"Behold in me, Austin, the Banished Duke! Never again may I tread the halls of Breysgate—at any rate, not for the present! I have offended a proud baronet—a belted earl demands my expulsion. And my liege lady banishes me!"

"Don't be so silly," said Jenny—but gently, ever so gently, and with a smile.

"Serves you right, in my opinion," said I.

"I suppose so," he answered, "and I bear no malice. I'm glad Aspenick didn't force me to wring his neck. But I shall be very lonely—nobody comes here—well, not many are invited! Will you drop in on the exile and smoke a pipe now and then after dinner?"

"Oh, yes, I'll look you up." My tone was impatient, I know: his burlesque was neither intelligible nor grateful to me.

"After dinner, if that suits you. I'm going to take advantage of my solitude to work in the daytime. The door will be barred till nine o'clock."

I nodded—and looked at my watch.

"Yes," said Jenny, "we must be going. Everything's settled, Austin, and—and Mr. Octon has been very kind."

"I'm glad to hear that anyhow," I said grumpily. If he had been kind, why had I heard that wail?

In fact I was thoroughly puzzled—and therefore both vexed and uneasy. He accepted his banishment—and yet was friendly. That result seemed a great victory for Jenny—yet she did not look victorious. It was Octon who wore the air of exultation and self-satisfaction; yet he had been thrown to the wolves, abandoned to the pack of Fillingfords and Aspenicks. Well, that could not be the whole truth of it, though what more there might be I could not guess.

He came with us down the gravel path which led from the hall door to the road, where the brougham was waiting. Jenny pointed across the road—where Ivydene stood with its strip of garden.

"That's the house I meant, you know," she said, evidently referring to something that had passed in their private conversation.

He stood smiling at her, with his hands in his pockets. He really was, for him, ridiculously amiable, though his amiability, like everything else about him, was rough, almost boisterous.

"If you must go on with your beastly Institute," he said, "and msut have a beastly house for a beastly office, to make your beastly plans and do your other beastly work in, why, I daresay that beastly house will do as well as any other beastly house for your beastly purpose. Only do choose beastly clerks, or whatever they're going to be, who haven't got any beastly children to play beastly games and make a beastly noise in the garden."

Quite the first I had heard of this idea! Quite the first time, too, that Leonard Octon had been so agreeable—he meant to be agreeable, though the humor was like a schoolboy's—about the Institute!

"I think I'll speak to Mr. Bindlecombe about it," said Jenny, as she gave him her hand. Her farewell was more than gracious; it was grateful, it was even appealing. Nor for all my anger and vexation could I deny the real feeling in his eyes as he looked at her; he was admiring; he was affectionate; nay more, he seemed to be giving her his thanks.

She was very silent all the way home, answering only by a " yes " or a " no " the few remarks I ventured to make. On her own account she made only one—as the result of a long reverie. " It'll all blow over some day," she said.

If it was her only observation, at least it was a characteristic one. Jenny had a great belief in things " blowing over "—a belief that inspired and explained much of her diplomacy. What seemed sometimes in retrospect to have been far-sighted scheming or elaborate cunning had been in reality no more than waiting for a thing to " blow over "—holding the balance, maintaining an artificial equilibrium by a number of clever manipulations, until things should right themselves and gain, or regain, a proper and natural basis. The best opinion I could form of her present proceedings was that they rested on some such idea. For the moment she banned Octon under the pressure of her other neighbors; but in time the memory of his offenses would grow dimmer—and in time also her own position and power would be more firmly established. Then he could come back. She might have persuaded him into good humor by such a plea as that. If it were so, I thought that she had misled him and perhaps deceived herself. People have long memories for social offenses. And—one could not help asking the question—what of Fillingford?

A SECRET TREATY

Where was he to fit in, what part was he to play? Was a millennium to come when he was to lie down on Jenny's hearthrug side by side with Octon?

There was a lady too many at dinner—a man short! Jenny could have avoided this blot on her arrangements by eliminating Chat—and poor Chat was quite accustomed to being eliminated. But she chose not to adopt this course. I rather think that she liked to feel herself a bit of a martyr in the matter, but possibly she was also minded to make a little demonstration of her submission, to let them guess that Octon had been coming and that she had acted on their orders with merciless promptitude. In other respects the party was one of her most successful. Great as was the strain which she had been through in the afternoon, she herself was gay and sparkling. And how they petted her! Lady Aspenick might naturally have looked to be the heroine of the occasion—nor had she any reason to complain of a lack of interest in her story (I had to complain of a great deal too much interest in mine)—but it was for Jenny that the highest honors were reserved; the most joy was over the one sinner that repented.

Fillingford, of course, took her in to dinner. It was not in the man to pay what are called "marked attentions" before the eyes of others, but his manner to her was characterized by a pronounced friendliness and deference; he seemed to be trying to atone for the coercion which he had been compelled to exert earlier in the day. He did not fall into the mistake of treating her acquiescence as a trifle or the case as merely that of "cutting a cad," to use Aspenick's curtly contemptuous phrase. He raised her action to the rank of an obligation conferred on her neighbors and especially on himself. He was man of the world enough to convey this impression without departing too far from the habitual reserve of his demeanor.

Lady Aspenick looked at the pair through her eye-glasses; we had at last exhausted the incident of the morning—though we had not settled the precise degree of accidentality which attached to the collision between her whip and Octon's face; under a veiled cross-examination she had become rather vague about it—that may weigh a little in Octon's favor.

"It's a long while since I've seen Lord Fillingford so lively," she remarked. "He seems to get on so well with Miss Driver. As a rule, you know, we women despair of him."

"Has he such a bad character among you as that?"

"He seemed to have given himself up to being old long before he need. He's only forty-three, I think." She laughed. "There, in my heart I believe I'm matchmaking, like a true woman!"

"Yes, I believe you are. Well, these speculations are always interesting."

"We're beginning to make them in the neighborhood, I can tell you, Mr. Austin."

"And—knowing the neighborhood—I can believe you, Lady Aspenick."

"You've no special information?" she asked, laughing. "It would make me so important!"

"Oh, you're important enough already—after this morning. And I know nothing—absolutely nothing."

"You mean to say Miss Driver doesn't tell you——?"

"Actually she does not—and I'm not sure I should know if she did."

"Of course I'm only chaffing. But it would be rather—ideal."

"H'm. Forty-three may not be senile, but would you call it ideal? For a romance?"

"Who's talking of romances? I'm on the question of marriage, Mr. Austin."

"But if one can afford a romance? What's the use of being rich?"

"No, no, it's the poor people who can go in for romance. They've nothing to lose! Divide nothing a year between two—or, presently, four—and still it's no less."

"But the rich have nothing to gain—except romance."

"Oh, yes, sometimes. At the time of the Coronation I had quite a quarrel with Jack because he wasn't a peer. He said I ought to have thought of it before, but I said that that would have been quite disloyal." She lowered her voice to a discreet whisper. "I do hope she's not distressed about this morning?"

"A little, I'm afraid. Octon had his interesting side for her."

"I'm so sorry! I must be very nice to her after dinner."

Lady Aspenick was very "nice" to Jenny after dinner, and so were all of them. She seemed to take new rank that evening—to undergo a kind of informal but very real adoption into the inner circle of families which made the local society. She was no longer a stranger entertaining them; she had become one of themselves. This could not all be reward for ostracizing Octon. Lady Aspenick's conversation, in itself not remarkable for depth or originality, was a surface sign of another current of opinion bearing strongly on Jenny's position. But no doubt acquiescence in the ostracism was a condition precedent both to the adoption and to that remoter prospect which inspired it.

Jenny's eyes were very clear. After they had all gone, I returned to the drawing-room to bid her good night. Chat had already scuttled off to bed—dinner parties kept her up later than was to her liking. Jenny was leaning her elbow on the mantelpiece.

"Well," she said, "I've been good—and I've had my sugar-plums."

"Yes, and they've got plenty more for you if you go on being good."

"Oh, yes." Her voice sounded tired, and her face looked strained.

"Even some very big ones!"

Up to now she had shown no sign of resenting the pressure put upon her; she had been sorrowful, but had displayed no anger. She did not even now challenge the justice of Fillingford's decision; but she broke out into a rage against the control claimed over herself.

"They force me to things," she said in a low voice, but in a tone full of feeling. "They tell me I must do this or do that, or else I can't be one of them, I can't rank with them, I can't, I suppose, marry Lord Fillingford! Well, I yield where I must, but sometimes I get my own way all the same. Let them look out for that! Yes, I get my own way in the end, Austin."

"No doubt—not that I know what is your way in this particular matter."

Her little outbreak of anger passed as quickly as it had come. She shrugged her shoulders with a woeful smile.

"My own way! So one talks. What is one's way? The way one would choose? No—it's generally the way one has to tread. It's in that sense that I shall get my own way."

"You'll try for it in the other sense, though, I fancy."

"Yes, perhaps I shall—and I shan't try less because Lord Fillingford and the Aspenicks either scold or pet me."

"Well, but it's hardly reasonable to expect to have things both ways, is it?"

She came to me, laughing, and took hold of my hands: "But if I choose to have them both ways, sir?" she asked.

"Then, of course," said I, "the case is different."

"I will have them both ways," said Jenny.

"You can't."

"See if I don't!" she cried in merry defiance. "Only, mind you, not a word of it—to the county!" She pressed my hands and let them go. "Oh, I'm so tired!"

"Stop thinking—do stop thinking—and go to sleep."

She nodded at me kindly and reassuringly as Loft came in to put out the lights. I left her standing there in her rich frock, with her jewels gleaming, yet with her eyes again weary and mournful. She had had a bad day of it, for all her triumph in the evening. Trying to have it both ways was hard work.

CHAPTER IX

THE INSTITUTE CLERK

MR. BINDLECOMBE was jubilant. Jenny's vacillations were over—the Institute was really on the way. A Provisional Committee had been formed; it was composed of Bindlecombe (in the Chair, in virtue of his office of Mayor, which he still held), Fillingford, Cartmell, Alison the Rector of the old parish church, and Jenny. I was what I believe they term in business circles "alternate" with—or to?—Jenny; when she could not attend, I was to act and, if need be, vote in her place. As a fact, I generally went even when she did. Since the Institute was to serve for women as well as for men, a subsidiary and advisory Ladies' Committee was formed—and Lady Sarah Lacey was induced to accept the chairmanship of it. Jenny was justifiably proud of this triumph; but the Ladies' Committee had nothing to do with finance, and finance was, of course, the question of paramount interest, in the early stages at least. The original ten thousand pounds which I had allocated to the Memorial Hall looked a mere trifle now. The talk was of eighty thousand—with a hundred thousand for a top limit. Over these figures Cartmell looked important, but not outraged—evidently the Driver estate was shaping well. But it was, as Jenny remarked, impossible to be precise on the subject of figures, until we had more definite ideas about what we wanted to do. Plans were, she declared, the first necessity—provisional plans, at all events—and she was for having them drawn up at once. Bindlecombe was in no way reluctant, but opined that plans depended largely on site; must not the question of site be taken in hand simultaneously? Jenny replied that Mr. Bindlecombe had so convinced her of the unique suitability of Hatcham Ford that she was in negotiation with Mr. Octon. Cartmell looked a trifle surprised—I do not think that he had heard of these negotiations. Jenny added that in two years' time she would be free to act of her own will; but in the first place two years was long to wait, and in the second she was anxious to deal with Mr. Octon in a friendly spirit. There was a feeling that this was carrying neighborliness too far, but Fillingford, content with what Jenny had already done in regard to Octon, came to her help, pronouncing that the diplomatic way was expedient: No excuse for any opposition should be given; you could never tell who might or might not, for his own purposes, get up a party. If Mr. Octon proved unapproachable—he chose the word with care and gave it with a neutral impassiveness—it would be time enough to talk of rights.

"We can begin on something at once," Jenny declared. "I'm going to ask Mr. Cartmell to make arrangements to put a house at our disposal for offices. We should hold our meetings there, and I should propose to employ a clerk to keep our records and, as time goes on, to help with the plans and so on." She turned to Bindlecombe. " You know that house next to Hatcham Ford—a new red house? It's got very good windows and an open outlook. Wouldn't that do for us? I forget the name—something rather absurd."

" Ivydene," said Cartmell. He had every detail of her property at his finger ends.

" Yes, that's it," said Jenny, with a nod of recollection.

Everybody approved of Ivydene for the suggested purpose, and the Committee broke up with the usual expressions of gratitude to and admiration of Miss Driver. " She does things so handsomely—and with such head, too! " said Bindlecombe.

I walked away with Alison, the Rector, for whom I had a great liking. He was a fine fellow, physically and mentally—a tall, strong-built man of forty, with a keen blue eye. He had " done wonders," as they say, in Catsford and was on the sure road to promotion—if he would take it. He was sincere, pious, and humble; but his humility was personal. It did not extend to his office or to the claims of the Church he represented.

He asked me if I would lay before Jenny the merits of a fund he was raising to build yet another new district church, to meet the ever growing needs of Catsford. I replied that I had no doubt she would be glad to give a donation.

" So far, so good," said Alison—but his tone did not sound contented.

"She's sure to give something substantial—she's like her father in that."

"In the way of money I had nothing to complain of from Mr. Driver. Anything else I suppose you'll tell me I couldn't expect, as he was a Unitarian."

"I remember he used to say he'd been brought up a Unitarian."

"That's what we seem to be coming to! When it's a question of a man's religion, you remember what he used to say he was brought up as!" Alison's tone became sarcastic. "Well, then, his daughter's a Church-woman, isn't she—by the same excellent evidence?"

"She lived five years in a clergyman's family," I answered discreetly—feeling that it was safer to stick to indisputable facts. "She attends church fairly often, doesn't she?"

"Yes, fairly often." He repeated my words with a contemptuous grimace. "People who attend church fairly often, Austin, are the people whom, if the good old days could come back, I should like to burn."

"Of course you would. You all would, if you dared say so."

"Just two or three to start with. I should like it done very conspicuously—in the market place."

"The worst of it is that you're really quite sincere in all this."

He pressed my arm. "I don't want to burn you. You've thought, though you've thought wrong. And you've been through tribulation. It's the people who in their hearts just don't——"

"Care a damn?" I profanely suggested.

THE INSTITUTE CLERK

"Yes," he agreed with a laugh and a grip on my wrist which distinctly hurt.

"But I don't think Miss Driver's quite one of those. At any rate she's intellectually interested—talks about things, and so on."

He nodded. "Yes, I daresay. Well, she's a remarkable girl. Look here—she's worth having, and I'm going to try to get hold of her."

"You never will, though you try for ever—not in your sense. She never surrenders."

"Not even to God?"

"Speaking through you?"

"Through my office—yes."

"Aye, there's the rub! Besides—well, I can't discuss her from a moral point of view; any information I may have seems somehow to have been acquired confidentially."

"That's quite right, Austin."

"I'll only put before you a general suggestion. Doesn't our disposition determine our attitude to these things much oftener than our attitude is shaped by our opinions? Hence individual modifications—variations from the general trend, whatever that may be. What a man—or woman—is in worldly relations, isn't he apt to be in regard to religious affairs? If a man thinks for himself in worldly affairs——"

"I'm not against thought," he broke in. "That's the eternal misunderstanding!"

"But so often against the results of it?" I suggested. "And one reason among others for that is because the result of individual thought is often a decision to suspend generally accepted views in one's own case—which you fellows don't like. I don't mind going so far as to say that I think Miss Driver would be capable of suspending a generally accepted view in her own case—but she wouldn't do it without thought or indifferently. She would do it as a well-considered exercise of power. Some people like power—I don't know whether a priest can understand that?"

We had come to the "Church House" where he dwelt in barracks with his curates. His eyes twinkled. "I know what you mean—and you can chaff as much as you like—but I shall have a go at Miss Driver."

After a conversation a man of candid mind will often—and, if the discussion has partaken in any degree of an argumentative character, I would say generally—be left reflecting whether what he has said was even as true as he meant to make it. As I had hinted, I talked to Alison about Jenny with reserves, but even within their limits I doubted whether I had given him the impression I had meant to convey. Perhaps he understood, though he could never acknowledge as legitimate, my view that she would feel entitled to treat herself as a special case. He might even act on this view—always without acknowledging it; surely Churches have been known to do that? He might approach her on that footing—with the hope of changing it. I had meant to point out an impossibility; I fancied I had indicated a task and communicated a stimulus. Had I cast aside the reserves, I should have told him plainly that in my judgment the emotional basis for his appeal was lacking in her. Emotions existed, but not in that direction; that was

THE INSTITUTE CLERK

more what I had wanted to say, but, not feeling at liberty to adduce evidence, I had lost myself in generalities. My poor modicum of truth stopped at the dictum that to Jenny Jenny would seem an exceptional person; I had at least come near to putting it in the hazardous and unorthodox form that everybody might have a right, on sufficient occasion, so to treat himself. And he himself judge of the sufficiency of the occasion? That amounts to anarchy—as Alison, of course, perceived, and, had we pursued the argument, I must have found myself in a very tight place.

I was shaking my head over my own controversial incompetence—with, perhaps, a furtive saving plea that it was very hard to tell all one's thoughts to an ecclesiastic—when I was suddenly brought back to more tangible matters; perhaps also to my modicum of truth—that Jenny would seem to Jenny an exceptional person. In short, on turning the next corner, I all but ran into Mr. Nelson Powers.

He looked as greasily insinuating as ever. He also appeared to be more prosperous than when I had last seen him. He looked, so to say, established—as if he had a right to be where he was, not so much as if he were " trying it on "—with eyes open for kicks or the police. He was strolling about the streets of Catsford quite with the air of belonging to it.

He did not recognize me, or would not. He was almost by me when I stopped him.

" Mr. Powers? Surely it is? What brings you to Catsford? "

" Mr. Austin? Yes! Well, now, how do you do, sir?

I'm glad to meet you again. I was unlucky in missing that dinner—well, never mind! But you've heard? Miss Driver has mentioned my appointment?"

"I've heard nothing of any appointment."

"Ah, perhaps I'm premature in mentioning it. I'll say good afternoon, Mr. Austin."

I seemed to have nothing to say to him. I was rather bewildered; I thought that we had really seen the end of Powers.

He stretched out his hand, and took hold of mine, depriving me of all initiative in the matter.

"Miss Driver will speak in her own time, sir. I—I should only like to say, sir, that I—I recognize the change in Miss Driver's position. One learns wisdom, Mr. Austin. Good afternoon, sir." He pressed my hand—he was wearing gloves and I was not sorry for it—and was round the corner while I was still gaping.

I walked up to the Priory, immersed in a rather scandalized, rather amused, would-be psychological line of reflection. "She can't help it!" I said to myself. "She can't let anyone go! Not even Powers! At the first chance (I did not yet guess what the chance was) she calls him to heel again. Even the meanest hound must keep with the pack. It's very curious, but that's it!"

In fact that was only part of it—and not the most significant for present purposes.

Jenny had gone from the Committee to call on Mrs. Jepps, a person of much consideration in Catsford, wife of its first Mayor (now deceased), owner of an important business house in the drapery line, *vir* (save that she was a woman) *pietate gravis,* and eminently meet to be enrolled among the active adherents of the Institute.

"And I've got her!" said Jenny complacently, as she gave me my tea.

"Mr. Alison wants to get you—I've been talking to him."

"Oh, well, I like Mr. Alison."

"He wants to get you. Don't misunderstand. He doesn't want you to get him, you know."

"Friendship is surely mutual?" suggested Jenny, with a lurking smile.

I mentioned the matter of the subscription: Jenny was satisfactorily liberal.

"Not that you'll be quit of him with that," I warned her.

"I'm not afraid. Going? Will you come back to dinner?"

I stood for a moment looking at her. We might just as well have it out now.

"You remember your promise? I'm not to be called upon to meet Mr. Powers? I happened to meet him in the town this afternoon."

Jenny began to laugh—without the smallest sign of embarrassment. "I was going to break it to you over your glass of port. That's why I asked you to dinner. Now don't look grave and silly. Can't you really see any difference between me as I am and the girl who came here a year ago? Well, then, you're stupider than poor Powers himself! He sees it clearly enough and accepts the position—he won't expect to come to dinner. Besides he's very sorry for what happened. Besides why shouldn't I give a chance to an old acquaintance rather than to a stranger? Besides—how I'm piling up 'besides' just to keep you quiet!—Mrs. Powers has come, too, and all the children—three now instead of one! So really it must be all right."

"But what are you going to do with him?"

"Why, he's a first-class draughtsman—trained in a very good architect's office. Mr. Bindlecombe has seen specimens of his work and says it's excellent. I should think that Mr. Bindlecombe knew!" (Meaning thereby, as the lawers say, that I did not!)

"Well?"

"Can't you really guess? He's to be the Institute clerk. He'll draw plans and so on for us—and she'll keep the house, and have it all ready for our Committees."

"He's to live at Ivydene?"

"Have you any objection?"

Up to now Jenny's tone had been evenly compounded of merriment—over my absurdities—and plausibility for her own admirable management. Now a slightly different note crept in. "Have you any objection?" was not said in a very conciliatory manner.

"I might have anticipated," she went on—"in fact I do anticipate—these stupid objections from Mr. Cartmell—and I'm prepared to meet them. But from you I looked for more perception. The man is a clever man; he's out of employment. Why shouldn't I employ him? Is it to be fatal to him that he was once unwise—worse than unwise? Against that, put that he's an old friend, and that even I have my human feelings. I was a fool, but I was fond of him once."

"It's for you to judge," I said.

"Can't you see—can't you understand?" she exclaimed. "Powers is nothing—it's all over, gone, done with!" She clasped her hands excitedly. "Oh, when I've so much on my shoulders, why do you worry me with trifles?"

"If you've so much on your shoulders, why add even trifles?"

"I add nothing," she said. "On the contrary I—" She broke off suddenly, and added quickly, "It's done—I'm pledged to him. Oh, don't bother me about Powers!" She calmed down again. She returned to plausibility. She went on with a smile, "You've found me out in one way, of course. I do want my own man there. I want my own way in everything, so I want a man who'll back me up—a man who'll always be on my side, who won't suddenly go over to Lord Fillingford, or the Rector—or even Lady Sarah! Poor Powers will have to agree with me always—he'll have to be a blind adherent. He can't afford to differ."

"That's frank, at all events," I commented.

Jenny's face lit up. "Yes, it is," she said, with much better temper. "Quite frank—the whole truth about Jenny Driver! He'll be what I want—and do you seriously mean to say that you think there's any danger? Nobody here knows anything about him, except you and Mr. Cartmell. Are you traitors? Will Powers speak—and lose his livelihood? It's absurd to talk of danger from Powers."

I had come to agree with her that it was. So far as I could judge, there was no longer any appreciable danger from the man—neither from his presence in

Catsford nor from Jenny's meetings with him. He could not afford to threaten; she had grown far out of any peril of being cajoled. But if not dangerous, neither was the arrangement attractive to one's taste. It was difficult to suppose that Jenny herself liked it, unless indeed my highly philosophical speculations covered the whole ground. Did they? Must she really recall Powers? Couldn't she help it? Was a present and immediate domination over even such as Powers essential to her content?

I could not believe it and accused my own speculations, if not of entire error (they had an element of truth), yet of inadequacy. In fact a doubt had begun to creep into my mind. Never in my life had I heard so many sound reasons for doing a thing that was obviously quite uncalled for—unless there was one other reason still—a reason not plausible, nor producible, but compelling. Yet what? For I was convinced that the man had no hold, that she was not in the least afraid of Powers.

"I hate your standing opposite me and thinking about me," remarked Jenny suddenly. "I'm sure it's not comfortable, and I don't think it's polite. Besides, after all, it's possible that you might find out something!"

"Surely that 'Besides' is superfluous, anyhow?"

"I don't know—I don't quite trust you. But shall I tell you your mistake? You're too ready to think that I have a reason for everything I do. You're wrong. Where reason comes in with me is about the things I don't do. If you reason about things, most of them look either dull or dangerous. So you let them alone. But if you don't reason, you chance it—either the dullness or the danger, as the case may be."

"A juggle with words! You reason all the same."

"Not always. Sometimes you're—driven."

On her face was a look almost as if she were being driven. I fancied that I might have said too much about deliberate exercises of power in my conversation with the Rector.

"I suppose you'd explain that, if you wished to," I remarked after a pause. "You appear to be as free from being driven as most people. You're pretty independent!"

"I should explain it if I wished—perhaps even if I could. But do you always find it easy to explain yourself—even to yourself, to say nothing of other people?"

"It seems to me that you've only got yourself to please."

"And it also seems to you that that would be very easy?"

"Now you're in one of your fencing moods—there's no plain English to be got out of you."

"Fencing is useful to parry thrusts, Austin."

"Heavens, have I been making thrusts at you? You mean about that miserable Powers?"

She sat there looking at me, with the mystery smile on her lips; but her brow was knit. "Yes, about Powers," she said—after a pause, but without hesitation. The manner of her answer said plainly "Call it about Powers—it is about something else." So I think she meant me to read it. She told me that there was some trouble lest, suspecting but not knowing, I should make wild thrusts and wound her blindly.

"No one but you would put up with such an impertinent retainer," I said.

"You always stop when I want you to. And I rather like—sometimes—to try over my feelings and ideas in talk. One gets a kind of outside look at them in that way." She broke into a little laugh. "And I must keep you in a good temper, because I've a favor to ask. Are we going to be terribly busy in the immediate future?"

"I should think so—with your Institute!"

"No time for riding?" she suggested insinuatingly.

"Oh, well, one must consider one's health."

"I don't want to give up my morning ride; but I want you to come with me—well, as often as you can. Make it the regular thing to come, barring most pressing business."

"I see what I get out of this, Lady Jenny. Now what do you?"

"I knew you'd ask that. Of course I'm never disinterested!"

"I won't ask. I'll take the gift Heaven sends!"

"I daren't leave it like that. You're too conscientious; you'd stay at home and work. I'm afraid I must give you the reason."

Her thoughts had passed away, it seemed, from the difficulty which had made her now irritable, now melancholy, while we talked about reasoning and being "driven." She was gay and chaffed me with enjoyment. If there were any perplexity in the case here,

THE INSTITUTE CLERK

evidently it struck her as a comedy, complicated by no threat of a tragic catastrophe. Her lips twitched with merriment.

"Yes, you must have it—and really plain English this time—no fencing—the downright blunt truth!"

"I wait for it."

"Lord Lacey comes home on leave to-morrow."

The explanation here was certainly plain. In fact it was both plain and pregnant. While it confessed to a flirtation in the past, it also admitted a project for the future.

"I must ride as often as possible," I said gravely. "Does he stay long?"

"I should think that might depend," answered Jenny. She laughed again as she added, "Not even you can ask 'On what?'"

CHAPTER X

A FRIENDLY GLASS

I HOPE that my company on the morning rides was agreeable to Jenny, but I cannot be persuaded that it was necessary; she showed such perfect ability to handle a situation which, if not precisely difficult, might easily have become so under less skillful management. There had, of course, never been any serious lovemaking between her and Lacey; whatever he may have been inclined to feel, or to tell himself that he felt, she had always kept him to his position as "a boy." Yet young women in the twenties do not always scorn the attentions of boys, and Jenny had certainly not despised Lacey's. In fact, they had flirted, and flirted pretty hard—and, as has been seen, Jenny was at no trouble to deny it. But now the thing had to stop—or rather the flirtation had to be transformed, the friendship established on a new basis. Into this task Jenny put some of her best work. Her finest weapon was a frank cordiality—such as could not but delight a friend, but was really hopeless for a lover. To every advance it opposed a shield of shining friendliness, of a hearty, almost masculine, comradeship. It left no room for the attacks and defenses, the challenges and evasions, the pursuit, the flight, and the collusive capture. It was all such immensely plain sailing, all so pre-eminently above-board, in its unmitigated cunning. But it was charming also, and Lacey, though naturally a little puzzled at first, soon felt the charm. He was wax in those clever hands; she seemed to be able not only to make him do what she wanted, but even to make him feel toward her as she wished—to impart to his emotions the color which she desired them to take. Positively I think he began to forget the flirtation in the friendship, or to charge his memory with twisting or misinterpreting the facts. All the time, though, he would have been ready to resume the old footing at the smallest encouragement, the lightest touch of coquetry or allurement. But Jenny's masterpiece of honest friendship was without any such flaw; if she was great at flirtation, she was no less a mistress of the art of baffling it. With such ability and such self-confidence what need had she of my presence? She was wiser than I was when I put that question to myself. I thought only of what would happen; she remembered what people might say—that the neighbors had tongues, and that Fillingford had ears to his head like other folks. While the buckler of cordiality fronted Lacey, I was her shield against a flank attack.

Had she really made up her mind then? It looked like it. If she rode in my company with Lacey in the morning, she received his father without my company in the afternoon. There could be no doubt what he came for; middle-aged men of many occupations do not pay calls two or three afternoons a week without a purpose. What passed at these interviews remained, of course, a secret; I confess to a suspicion that Jenny found them dull. Fillingford's wariness of exposing himself to rebuff or ridicule, his habitual secretiveness as to his emotions, cannot have made him either an ardent or an entertaining suitor. In truth I do not believe that he seriously pretended to be in love. He liked her very much; he thought that she would fill well the place he had to offer, and that she, in her turn, would like to fill it, and might find him agreeable enough to accept with it. That would content him. With that I thought she, too, would be content—considering the other advantages thrown in. She would not have cared for his love, but she could endure his company. That carried with it only a limited liability—and good dividends in the form of rank, position, and influence. In dealing with the Drivers one had a tendency to fall into commercial metaphors; caught from old Nicholas, the trick extended itself to Jenny.

But if he were resolved and she ready, why did the thing hang fire? It did—and surely by Jenny's will? She was reasoning; the affair could not look dangerous; then it looked dull? But it would look no less dull the longer she looked at it. Her feelings were not engaged; unless caught up by strong emotions, she shunned the irrevocable, liked open alternatives, hated to close the line of retreat; he who still parleys is still free, he who still bargains is still master. That attitude of her mind—reënforced by her father's warning—was aways strong with her and had always to be remembered. Was it enough to account for her

A FRIENDLY GLASS

continuing to keep Fillingford at bay? The answer might well be yes—for these natural predispositions will knock the bottom out of much speciously logical reasoning about people. But there was another factor in the case—a thing which could not be overlooked. Why was Leonard Octon keeping quiet? Or if quiet perforce, why did he seem placid, content, and, contrary to all expectation of him, amiably trustful?

One evening I availed myself of his invitation—Jenny did not always bid me to dinner, and sometimes I was lonely even as he was—and walked down to Hatcham Ford. Passing Ivydene, I was interested to observe lights in the window, though it was nine o'clock at night. Presumably friend Nelson Powers did not merely use the place as his office (Cartmell's protest had, of course, not produced the smallest effect on Jenny—my own having failed, I should have been annoyed if it had), but was established there with his family. Certainly Jenny did not always procrastinate—she seemed to delay least when the transaction was most doubtful! But I had come to accept Powers's position as one of her freaks and, save for a rather sour amusement, thought at the moment little more about him.

That night—it seems strange to say it, but it expresses my inmost feelings—I made friends with Leonard Octon; before I had been merely interested, amused, and exasperated in turn. He chose to remove from me the ban which he laid on and maintained over most of his fellow-creatures—from no merit of my own, as I believe, but because I stood near to Jenny; or, if I can claim any part in the matter, because of a certain openness of mind which, as he was good enough to declare, existed in me. This was to say no more than that, to a certain and limited extent, I agreed with some of his prejudices—his own openness of mind consisting mainly in a hatred of the views and opinions of most other people. I was a very pale copy of him. Things toward which my meditations and my temper bred in me a degree of indifference he frankly and cordially hated. Respectability may be chosen as the word to sum them up; if I questioned its merits, he hated and damned it utterly. This was one of the things which interested and amused—and, when it issued in rudeness to Lady Aspenick, also exasperated. It was not for this that I made friends with him.

"When I saw that woman owning that road—coming along in her twopenny glory, with her flunkeys to whistle me out of the way—she looked at me herself, too, mind you, and without a gleam of recognition—I got angry. Not even the public road, mind you! She was a guest as I was."

"But you weren't driving a tandem with a restive leader."

"And oughtn't she to apologize for driving restive horses? Must I dodge for my life—or for hers—without even a civil word or look—just an order from a flunkey?"

"For some reason or another," I observed, "people who are angry always call grooms and footmen flunkeys."

He burst into a guffaw of laughter. "Lord, yes, asses all of us, to be sure! And what, after all, does a flick in the face come to, Mr. Philosopher? Nothing at all! It hardly even hurts. But a man calls it a deadly insult—when he's angry; between man and man there must be blood for it when they're angry."

"There's the police court," I suggested mildly.

"As you say, for sheep there's the police court. I came as near behaving right as one can with a woman when I broke her whip."

"You really think that?"

"Yes, Austin, I really do—and that shows, as you were going to say, that I'm utterly hopeless. I don't fit the standards." He was sitting hunched up over the fire, monopolizing its heat, his great shoulders nearly up to his ears. He condemned himself with much better humor than he judged other people. "I don't fit them, I don't agree with them, I hate them. Left to myself, I'd get out of this."

"Who's stopping you?" I asked, pulling at my pipe and trying to edge nearer the fire.

He took no notice of my question—which was indeed no more than an indifferently civil way of suggesting that he was at liberty to please himself. He took no notice of my futile edging either.

"Now if I had Jenny Driver's gifts for the game," he went on, "I daresay I should like it. Oh, you were quite right there! She's equal to ruling the county, and ruling it well. Since she can do it, I don't blame her for trying. Perhaps I'd try myself in the same case. But, mind you, in her heart she thinks no more of them than I do. They can give her what she wants, they can't give me what I want—that's all the difference. So it's worth her while to fool them—and it's not worth mine. Not that I could do it half as well as she does!"

His admiration of Jenny was unmistakably affectionate as well as amused. There is a way a man draws at his pipe—long pulls with smiles in between. It tells a tale when a woman's name has just passed his lips.

"Then all she's got — the big place and the money—the influence and so on—wouldn't attract you?"

He turned slowly to me. "It might, if I thought that I could make terms with the people. But I can't do that. So I should hate it. Why did you ask me that question, Austin?"

"Why not? We were discussing your character, and any sidelights—" I ended with a shrug.

"You humbug, you infernal humbug!" he said. Then he fell into silence, staring again at the fire.

"Not at all. My interest is quite speculative. What else should it be? Is she likely to die and leave you her property?" I spoke in sincerity, having in my mind Jenny's purpose with regard to Fillingford, for a settled purpose it had by now, to my thinking, become.

My sincerity went home to him, and carried with it an uncontrollable surprise. He turned his head toward me again with a rapid jerk. His eyes searched my face, now rather suspiciously. Then he smiled. "Yes, that's true. I suppose I ought to beg your pardon!" he said.

He had recovered himself in time and had told me

A FRIENDLY GLASS

no secret. But he had been surprised to find that I considered any relation of his to Jenny's place and property as a mere speculation—no more than the illustration to an argument. Then he must consider it as more than that himself. But then how could he—he, the ostracized? Yet there was the secret treaty, whose terms availed to keep him quiet—quiet and at Hatcham Ford. There were a lover's obstinate hopes. And—the thought flashed into my mind—had he any knowledge of Fillingford's frequent calls or of the dexterous management of Lacey? It was probable that he knew as little of them as Fillingford knew of the mysterious treaty.

Suddenly he started a new topic; between it and the previous one there seemed no connection—unless Jenny were the link.

"I say, that's a rum fish—my new neighbor Nelson Powers!"

"You've made acquaintance? You haven't been long about it!"

"He smokes his pipe, leaning over his garden fence; I smoke mine, leaning over my gate. Hence the acquaintance."

"Of course; you're always so affable, so accessible to strangers."

He dropped his scarcely serious pretense of having made Powers's acquaintance casually. "Miss Driver told me something about him. We've been in communication about this house and the Institute, you know."

"Did she tell you anything interesting about him?"

"Only that he'd been a humble friend in days gone by. You're looking rather sour, Austin. Don't you like Mr. Nelson Powers?"

"He's not one of my particular fancies," I admitted.

"Miss Driver says he's devoted to her."

"He's in debt to her, anyhow, I expect—and perhaps that'll do as well."

"Perhaps." He was speaking now in a ruminative way—as though he were comparing in his mind Jenny's account of Powers, my opinion of Powers, and his own impression of the man. He seemed to me to give more thought to Powers than I should have expected from him; a rude and contemptuous dismissal would have been Powers's more probable fate at his hands.

"Are you going to clear out for the Institute?" I asked.

"I shall be out of this house in less than a year, anyhow. That's settled."

"Oh, then your negotiations have been very satisfactory! You had a right to stay here two years."

"The present state of affairs can't drag on for two years," he said, looking at me steadily. His ostensible reference might be to his uncomfortable relations toward his neighbors; I was sure that he meant more than that—and did not mind letting me see it. A restlessness betrayed itself in his movements; he seemed to be on the edge of an outbreak and to hold himself back with a struggle. His victory was very imperfect: he could not keep off the subject which perturbed him; he could only contrive to treat it with a show of lightness and contempt. The subject had been in my thoughts already.

"Seeing much of our friend Fillingford just now at the Priory?"

"He comes a certain amount. I don't see much of him."

"And that sets fools gossiping, I suppose?"

"Need you ask me, Octon? I fancy you've heard something for yourself."

He rubbed his big hands together, giving a laugh which sounded rather uneasy under its cloak of amusement.

"It won't be much trouble to her to make a fool of Fillingford—he's a conceited ass. She'll use him as long as she wants him, and then—!" He snapped his fingers scornfully.

Had he struck on that explanation for himself? Possibly—he had studied Jenny. Yet it sounded rather like an inspired version of her policy. The weak spot about it was that, by now, Jenny could have little need of Fillingford—except in one capacity. As her husband he could give her a good deal; he could offer her no obvious advantages in any other relation. I wondered that this did not occur to Octon—and then decided that it did. He knew that the argument was weak; he hoped that I would afford it the buttress of my confirmatory opinion.

"Well?" he growled impatiently, for I said nothing.

"I didn't understand that you asked me a question—and, if you had, I shouldn't have answered it.

It's no business of mine to consider how Miss Driver treats Fillingford or means to treat him."

At that his temper suddenly gave, his hold on himself was broken. "But it is of mine, by God!" he cried.

Our eyes met for a moment; then he turned his head away, and a long silence followed. At last he spoke in a low voice.

"I call other people fools—I'm a fool myself. I can't hold my tongue. I oughtn't to be at large. But it's pretty hard to bottle it all up sometimes." He laid his hand on my knee. "I shall be obliged if you'll forget that little remark of mine, Austin."

"I can't forget it. I can take no notice of it," I said.

"It's not merely that I gave myself away—which, after all, doesn't matter as you happen to be a loyal fellow—I know that" (he smiled for a moment), "having tried to pump you myself. But what I said was against a pledge I had given."

"I wish you hadn't said it—most heartily. I'll treat it as unsaid—so far as my allegiance allows."

"Yes, I see that. She must come first with you, of course."

"And with you, too, I hope?"

"In my sort of case a man fights for himself."

"I'll say one thing to you—since you have spoken. You'd much better go away—before that year is up."

He made an impatient gesture with his hands. "I can't!" Then he leaned forward and half-whispered, "You put your money on Fillingford?"

"I don't intend to tell you what I think—if you can't gather it from what I've said already."

Again his laugh came—again sounding more like bravado than real confidence. "You're wrong, I can tell you that," he said. "I shouldn't be here if I wasn't sure of that."

I had better have said no more, but temptation overcame me. "I don't think you are sure of it."

I expected him to be very angry, I looked for some bluster. None came. He shrugged his shoulders and wearily rubbed his brow with his hand. The case was very plain; he had been told, but he was not sure that he had been told the truth. Many people might have told him that Jenny meant to marry Fillingford. Only one on earth could have assured him that she did not. The assurance had been forthcoming—not in so many words, perhaps, yet plainly enough to be an assurance for all that. But was it an assurance of truth?

It grew late, and I took my leave. Octon put on his hat and walked to the gate with me. "Come and see me again," he said. "I'm always ready for you—after dinner. A talk does a man good—even if he talks like a fool."

"Yes, I'll come again—not that I've been very comforting."

"No, you haven't. But then, you see, I don't believe a word you say." He went back to that attitude —to that obstinate assertion. It was not for me to argue the question with him; even if my tongue were free, why should I? He would argue it quite enough —there at Hatcham Ford, by himself.

"Is that your estimable neighbor?" I asked. Through the darkness, by help of the street lamp, a man's figure was visible, standing at the gate of the new house which Jenny had taken for the Institute office.

"That's the fellow," said Octon, and he walked on with me. "Good evening, Mr. Powers," he said, as we came to the gate.

Powers bade him good evening, and also accorded to me a courteous greeting. In this hour of leisure he had assumed a pseudo-artistic garb, a soft shirt with trimmings along the front and a turndown collar cut very low, and a voluminous tie worn in an ultra-French fashion; his jacket appeared to be of velveteen, rather a light brown.

"You find me star-gazing, gentlemen," said he. "I take delight in it. The immensity of the heavens!"

"And the littleness of man! Quite so, Mr. Powers," said Octon, refilling his pipe.

"These thoughts will come—sometimes to encourage us, sometimes—er—with an opposite effect."

"Don't let them discourage you, Powers. That would be a pity. After all, the Institute will be pretty big."

To a refined ear Octon was not treating Powers precisely with respect—but Powers's ear was not refined. He was evidently quite comfortable and at his ease with Octon. I wondered that Octon cared to chaff him in this fashion, offering what was to Powers a good substitute for friendliness.

"Yes, sir. Miss Driver is giving us an adequate

A FRIENDLY GLASS

sphere for our ambitions. I have longed for one. Doubtless you have also, Mr. Austin?"

"I'm not very ambitious, Mr. Powers."

"Wise, sir, wise! But we can't help our dispositions. Mine is to soar! To soar upward by dint of hard work! Miss Driver will find I've not been idle when she next honors Ivydene with a visit. You don't know if she'll be here to-morrow?"

"Not I," I answered. "Miss Driver doesn't generally tell me what she's going to do to-morrow. The boot's on the other leg—she tells me what I'm going to do to-morrow."

"Ha-ha! Very good, sir, very good! And she's a lady one is proud to take orders from."

"Quite so. Good night." I think I must have spoken rather abruptly, for Powers's answering "Good night" sounded a little startled. I really could not bear any more of the fellow. But Octon—impatient, irascible, contemptuous Octon—seemed quite happy in his company. If he were not the rose, yet—? No, the proverb really could not be strained to embrace the moral perfume of Powers.

"Good night, Austin. I'll stop and smoke half a pipe here with Mr. Powers."

"You do me honor, Mr. Octon. But if you'd step inside—perhaps just a little drop of Scotch, sir? Don't say no. Drink success to the Institute! One friendly glass!"

What a picture! Octon drinking success to the Institute with Powers! But a short time ago I should have deemed it a happily ludicrous inspiration from Bedlam. To my amazement, though Octon hesitated for a perceptible space, he did not refuse. He glanced at me, laughed in a rather shamefaced way, and said, " Well, just a minute, and just one glass to the Institute—since you are so kind, Mr. Powers." With a nod to me he turned and followed Powers toward the house.

As I walked home, a picture of the position pieced itself together in my head. The process was involuntary—even against my will. I tried to remind myself all the time of Jenny's own warning—how she had accused me of too often imputing to her long-headed cunning, how her actions were, far oftener than I imagined, the outcome of the minute, not the result of calculation or subtle thought. Yet if in this case she had been subtle and cunning, she might have produced some such combination as now insisted on taking shape before my brain. For the sake of the neighborhood, and her position and prestige in its eyes, especially for the sake of Fillingford, she had abandoned Octon and had banished him. But she wanted to see him—and to see him without creating remark; in plain fact, to see him, if not secretly, yet as privately as she could. Next, she wished to make progress with the Institute, to establish an office with a clerk, an office where meetings could be held and plans made, and where she could come and see how matters were getting on—a clerk on whom she could depend to support her, always to be on her side—a clerk who, as she had said, could not afford to be against her. Hence came Ivydene—and Mr. Powers. Was it mere chance that Ivydene was just opposite Hatcham Ford? Was Mr. Powers's support—that subserviency on which Jenny had playfully laid stress —desired only against Lady Sarah and other possibly recalcitrant members of the Committee? If Powers could not afford to oppose her on the Committee's work, could he afford any the more to thwart her in her private concerns? Plainly not. There also he was bound to help.

So the picture formed itself; and the last bit to fit in, and thereby to give completeness, was what I had seen that night—the strange complaisance of Octon toward the intolerable Powers. Did Octon smoke his pipe in Powers's house and drink Powers's whisky for nothing? That "friendly glass"—what was its significance?

This was work for a spy or a detective. I thrust the idea away from me. But the idea would not depart. A man must use his senses—nay, they use themselves. The more I sought to banish the explanation, the more insolently it seemed to stare me in the face. "Pick a hole in me, if you can!" it challenged. The hole was hard to pick.

CHAPTER XI

THE SIGNAL AT "DANGER"

ALISON lost little time in making his promised attack on Jenny; he was not the man to let the grass grow under his feet. It might be improper to say that he chose the wrong moment—for no moment could be wrong from his point of view, and the one most wrong from a worldly aspect might well be to his mind the supremely right. Yet according to that purely worldly standpoint the time was unfortunate. Jenny had a great many other things to think of—very pressing things: as to many of us, so to her, her religious position perhaps seemed a matter which could wait. Moreover—by a whimsical chance—the Rector ran up against another difficulty: to Jenny it was a refuge, of which she availed herself with her usual dexterity. When one attack pressed her, I am convinced that she absolutely welcomed the advent of another from the opposite direction. Between the two she might slip out unhurt; at any rate, if one assailant called on her to surrender, she could bid him deal with the other first. The analogy is not exact—but there was a family likeness between her balancing of Fillingford against Octon and the way in which, assailed by Alison, she interposed, as a shield, the views urged on her by Mrs.

Jepps. Displayed in a less serious campaign—less serious, I mean, to Jenny's thinking—yet it was, in essence, the same strategy—and it was a strategy pretty to watch. Be it remarked that Jenny was busy keeping friends with everybody during these anxious weeks.

Mrs. Jepps—if I have said it before, it will bear repetition—was a power in Catsford, in the town itself. She might be said to lead the distinctively town society. Age, wealth, character, and a certain incisiveness of speech combined to strengthen her position. She was a small old lady, with plentiful white hair; she had been pretty—save for a nose too big; in her old age she bore a likeness to Cardinal Newman, but it would never have done to tell her so—she would as soon have been compared to the Prince of Darkness himself. For she was a most pronounced Evangelical, and her feud with Alison was open and inveterate. She disapproved profoundly of "the parish clergyman"; she called him by that title, whereas he called himself "the priest in charge"; for his "assistant priests" she would know no name but "curates." There had been an Education Question lately; the fight had waxed abnormally hot over the souls—almost over the bodies—of Catsford urchins, male and female, themselves somewhat impervious to the bearings of the controversy. Into deeper differences it is not necessary to go. The Rector thought her one of the best women he knew, but one of the most wrong-headed. Put man for woman—and she exactly reciprocated his opinion; and it is hard to deny, though sad to admit, that her zeal for Jenny's spiritual awakening was stirred to greater activity by the knowledge that Alison had put his hand to the alarm. To use a homely metaphor, they were each exceedingly anxious that the awakened sleeper should get out on what was, given their point of view, the right side of the bed.

To Jenny—need I say it?—this situation was rich in possibilities of staying in bed. In response to appeals she might put one foot out on one side, then the other foot out on the other; she would think a long while before she trusted her whole body to the floor either on the right or on the left. She did not appreciate in the least the fiery zeal which urged her to one side or the other: but she knew that it was there and allowed for its results. To her mind she had two friends—while she lay in bed; a descent on either side might cost her one of them. While she hesitated, she was precious to both. For the rest, I believe that she found a positive recreation in this ecclesiastical dispute; to play off Mrs. Jepps against Alison was child's play compared to the much more hazardous and difficult game on which she was embarked. Child's play—and byplay; yet not, perhaps, utterly irrelevant. It would have been easy to say " A plague on both your houses! " But even Mercutio did not say that till he was wounded to death, and Jenny was more of a politician than Mercutio. She asked both houses to dinner—and took pains that they should meet.

They met several times—with more pleasure to Mrs. Jepps than to the Rector. He fought for conscience' sake, and for what he held true. So did she

THE SIGNAL AT "DANGER"

—but the old lady liked the fighting for its own sake also. Jenny's attitude was "I want to understand." She pitted them against one another—Mrs. Jepps's "Letter of the Scriptures" against Alison's "Voice of the Living Church," his "Primitive Usage and Teaching of the Fathers" against her "Protestantism and Reformation Settlement." It is not necessary to deny to Jenny an honest intellectual interest in these and kindred questions, although her concern did not go very deep—but for her an avowed object always gained immensely in attraction from the possibility of some remoter and unavowed object attaching to it. If the avowed object of these prolonged discussions was the settlement of Jenny's religious convictions, the remoter and unavowed was to keep herself still in a position to reward whichever of the disputants she might choose finally to hail as victor. Policy and temperament both went to foster this instinct in her; the position might be useful, and was enjoyable; her security might be increased, her vanity was flattered. Jenny stayed in bed!

In secular politics her course was no less skillfully taken. She did indeed declare herself a Conservative —there was no doubt, even for Jenny's cautious mind, about the wisdom of that step—and gave Bertram Ware a very handsome contribution toward his Registration expenses; the expenses were heavy, Ware was not a rich man, and he was grateful. But at that time the question of Free Trade against Protection— or Free Imports against Fair Trade, if those terms be preferred—was just coming to the front, under the impetus given by a distinguished statesman. Fillingford, the natural leader of the party in the county division, was a convinced Free Trader. Ware had at least a strong inclination for Fair Trade. After talks with Fillingford and talks with Ware, Jenny gave her contribution, but accompanied it by an intimation that she hoped Mr. Ware would do nothing to break up the party. The hint was significant. Between the two sections which existed, or threatened to exist, in her party, Jenny—with her estate and her money—became an object of much interest. They united in giving her high rank in their Primrose League—but neither of them felt sure of her support.

To complete this slight sketch of the public position which Jenny was making for herself, add Catsford highly interested in and flattered by the prospect of its Institute, grateful to its powerful neighbor for her benefits, perhaps hopefully expectant of more favors from the same hand—proud, too, of old Nick Driver's handsome and clever daughter. Catsford was both selfishly and sentimentally devoted to Jenny, and of its devotion Mr. Bindlecombe was the enthusiastic and resonant herald.

Her private relations, though by no means free from difficulty, were at the moment hardly less flattering to her sense of self-importance, hardly less eloquent of her power. Fillingford was ready to offer her all he had—his name, his rank, his stately Manor; Octon lingered at Hatcham Ford, hoping against hope for her, unable to go because it was her will that he should stay: at her bidding young Lacey was transforming himself from a gay aspirant to her favor into the submissive servant of her wishes, her warm and obedient friend. To consider mere satellites like Cartmell and myself would be an anti-climax; yet to us, too, crumbs of kindness fell from the rich man's table and did their work of binding us closer to Jenny.

If she stayed as she was—the powerful, important Miss Driver—she was very well. If she married Fillingford, she hardly strengthened her position, but she decorated it highly, and widened the sphere of her influence. If she chose to take the risks and openly accepted Octon, she would indeed strain and impair the fabric she had built, but she could hardly so injure it that time and skill would not build it again as good as new. But she would make up her mind to none of the three. She liked independence and feared its loss by marriage. She liked splendor and rank, and therefore kept her hold on Fillingford's offer. Finally, she must like Octon himself, must probably in her heart cling more to him than she had admitted even to herself; there was no other reason for dallying with that decision. Across the play of her politics ran this strong, this curious, personal attraction; she could not let him go. For the moment she tried for all these things—the independence, the prestige of prospective splendor and rank, and—well, whatever she was getting out of the presence of Octon at Hatcham Ford, across the road from her offices at Ivydene.

It was a delicate equipoise—the least thing might upset it, and in its fall it might involve much that was of value to Jenny. There was at least one person who was not averse from anything which would set a check to Jenny's plans and shake her power.

Jenny and I had been to Fillingford Manor—where, by the way, I took the opportunity of inspecting Mistress Eleanor Lacey's picture, Fillingford acting as my guide and himself examining it with much apparent interest—and, as we drove home, she said to me suddenly:

"Why does Lady Sarah dislike me so much?"

"She has three excellent reasons. You eclipse her, you threaten her, and you dislike her."

"How does she know I dislike her?"

"How do you know she dislikes you, if you come to that? You women always seem to me to have special antennæ for finding out dislikes. I don't mean to say they're infallible."

"At any rate Lady Sarah and I seem to agree in this case," laughed Jenny. "She's right if she thinks I dislike her, and I'm certainly right in thinking she dislikes me. But how do I threaten her?"

"Come, come! Do you mean me to answer that? Nobody likes the idea of being turned out — any more than they welcome playing second fiddle."

"I'm always very civil to her—oh, not only at Fillingford! I've taken pains to pay her all the proper honors about the Institute. Very fussy she is there, too! She's always dropping in at Ivydene to ask something stupid. She quite worries poor Mr. Powers."

Jenny might resent Lady Sarah's excessive activity at Ivydene, but she gave no sign of being disquieted by it. To me, however, it seemed to be, under the circumstances, rather dangerous; but not being supposed to know, or to have guessed, the circumstances, I could say nothing.

Jenny's next remark perhaps explained her easiness of mind.

"We don't let her in if we don't want her. I must say that Mr. Powers is very good at keeping people out. Well, I must try to be more pleasant. I don't really dislike her so much; it's chiefly that family iciness which is so trying. It's a bore always to have to be setting to work to melt people, isn't it?"

I hold no brief against Lady Sarah, and do not regard her as the villain of the piece. She was a woman of a nature dry, yet despotic; she desired power and the popularity that gives power, but had not the temper or the arts to win them. Jenny's triumphs wounded her pride, Jenny's plans threatened her position in her own home at Fillingford Manor. Her dislike for Jenny was natural, and it is really impossible to blame very severely—perhaps, if family feeling is to count, one ought not to blame at all—her share in the events which were close at hand. It is, in fact, rather difficult to see what else she could have done. If she had a right to do it, it is perhaps setting up too high a standard to chide her for a supposed pleasure in the work.

When we got home, Cartmell was waiting for Jenny, his round face portentously lengthened by woe. He shook hands with sad gravity.

"What has happened?" she cried. "Not all my banks broken, Mr. Cartmell?"

"I'm very sorry to be troublesome, Miss Jenny, but I've come to make a formal complaint against

Powers. The fellow is doing you a lot of harm and bringing discredit on the Institute in its very beginnings. He neglects his work; that doesn't matter so much, there's not a great deal to do yet; he spends the best part of the mornings lounging about public-house bars, smoking and drinking and betting, and the best part of his evenings doing the same, and ogling and flirting with the factory girls into the bargain. He's a thorough bad lot."

Jenny's face had grown very serious. "I'm sorry. He's—he's an old friend of mine!"

"That was what you said before. On the strength of it you gave him this chance. Well, he's proved himself unworthy of it. You must get rid of him—for the sake of the Institute and for your own sake, too."

"Get rid of him?" She looked oddly at Cartmell. "Isn't that rather severe? Wouldn't a good scolding from you——?"

"From me? He practically tells me to mind my own business. If there are any complaints, the fellow says, they'd better be addressed to you!" He paused for a moment. "He gives the impression that you'd back him up through thick and thin, and, what's more, he means to give it."

"What does he say to give that impression?" she asked quickly.

"He doesn't say much. It's a nod here, and a wink there—and a lot of vaporing, so I'm told, about having known you when you were a girl."

"That's silly, but not very bad. Is that all?"

"No. When one of my clerks—Harrison, a very

steady man—gave him a friendly warning that he was going the right way about to lose his job, he said something very insolent."

"What?" She was sitting very still, very intent.

"He laughed and said he thought you knew better than that. Said in the way he said it, it—it came to claiming some sort of hold on you, Miss Jenny. That's a very dangerous idea to get about."

Cartmell was evidently thinking of the old story—of the episode of Cheltenham days. But had Powers been thinking of that? And was Jenny, with her bright eyes intent on Cartmell's face? She did not look alarmed—only rather expectant. She foresaw a fight with Powers, but had no doubt that she could beat him—if only the mischief had not gone too far."

"He seemed to refer to—Cheltenham?" she asked, smiling.

Cartmell was the embarrassed party to the conversation. "I—I'm afraid so, Miss Jenny," he stammered, and his red face grew even redder.

"Oh, I'll settle that all right," Jenny assured him.

"You'll give him the sack?" Cartmell asked bluntly.

She had many good reasons to produce against that, just as she had produced many for bringing him to Catsford. "I'll reduce him to order, anyhow," she promised.

That was what she wanted—to bring him to heel, not to lose him. But surely it was no longer for his own sake, nor even to satisfy that instinct of hers which forbade the alienation of the least of her human possessions? There was more than that in it. He was part of the scheme—he fitted into that explanation which my brain had insisted on conceiving as I walked home from Ivydene. Of this aspect of the case Cartmell was entirely innocent.

By one of her calculated bits of audacity—concealing much, she would seem to have nothing to conceal—she took me with her when she went down to Ivydene the next morning, to haul Powers over the coals. She would have me present at the interview between them. Well, it may also have been that she did not want too much plain speaking—or, rather, preferred to do what was to be done in that line herself.

She attacked him roundly; he stood before her not daring to resist openly, yet covertly insolent, hinting at what he dared not say plainly—certainly not before me, for he had not yet decided what game to play. He waited to see what he could still get out of Jenny. She rehearsed to him Cartmell's charges as to his conduct; its idleness, its unseemliness, the disrepute it brought on her and on the Institute. Somehow all this sounded a little bit unreal—or, if not unreal, shall I say preliminary? Powers confessed part, denied part, averred a prejudice in Cartmell—this last not without some reason. She rose to her gravest charge.

"And you seem to have the impertinence to hint that you can do what you like, and that I shall stand it all," she said.

"I never said that, Miss Driver. I may have said you had a kind heart and wouldn't be hard on an old friend." He had his cloth cap in his hands and kept twisting it about and fiddling with it as he talked. He smiled all the time, insinuatingly, yet rather uneasily, too."

"It's not your place to make any reference to me," she said haughtily. "I'll thank you to leave me out of your conversation with these curious friends of yours, Mr. Powers."

He looked at her, licking his lips. I was a mere spectator, though I do not think either of them had for a moment, up to now, forgotten my presence; indeed, both were, in a sense, playing their parts before me.

"I don't know that my friends are more curious than other people's, Miss Driver. People choose friends as it suits them, I suppose."

She caught the insinuation—he must have meant that she should. Her eyes blazed with a sudden anger. I knew the signs of that; when it came, prudence was apt to be thrown to the winds. She rose from her chair and walked up to where he stood.

"What do you mean by that?" she demanded.

He was afraid; he cowered before her fury: "Nothing," he grumbled sullenly.

"Then don't say things like that. I don't like them. I won't have them said. It almost sounded as if you meant a reference to me."

Of course he had meant one. She saw the danger and faced it. She relied on her personal domination. He was threatening, she would terrify. She went on in a cool, hard voice—very bitter, very dangerous.

"Once before in your life you threatened me," she said. "I was a child then, and had no friends. You got off safe—you even got a little money—a little very dirty money." (He did not like that; he flushed red and picked at his cap furiously.) "Now I'm a woman and I've got friends. You won't get any money, and you won't get off safe. Be sure of that. Who'll employ you if I won't? What character have you except what I choose to give? I think, if I were a man, I'd thrash you where you stand, Mr. Powers."

This remark may perhaps have been unladylike—that would have been Chat's word for it. For my part I thoroughly appreciated and enjoyed it. She was a fine sight in a royal rage like this.

"But though I'm not a man, I've friends who are. If you dare to use your tongue against me, look out!"

He could not stand against her nor face her. Indeed it would have been hard to fight her, unless by forgetting that she was a woman. He cringed before her, yet with an obstinately vicious look in his would-be humble eyes.

"I beg your pardon, Miss Driver—indeed I do. I —I've been wrong. Don't be hard on me. There's my poor wife and family! You shall have no further cause of complaint. As for threatening, why, how could I? What could I do against you, Miss Driver?"

Did his humility, hardly less disagreeable than his insolence, disarm her wrath? Did her mood change—or had the moment come for an artistic dissimulation? I must confess that I do not know; but suddenly she struck him playfully on the point of the chin with her glove and began to laugh. "Then, you dear silly old Powers, don't be such a fool," she said. " Don't quarrel with your bread and butter, and don't take so much whisky and water. Because whisky brings vapors, and then you think you're a great man, and get romancing about what you could do if you liked. I've stood a good deal from you, haven't I? I would stand a good deal for old times' sake. You know that; but is it kind to presume on it, to push me too far just because you know I like you?"

This speech I defend less than the unladylike one; I liked her better on the subject of the thrashing. But there is no denying that it was very well done. Was it wholly insincere? Perhaps not. In any event she meant to conquer Powers, and was not without reason, or precedent, in trying to see if blarney would aid threats.

He responded plausibly, summoning his mock gentlemanliness to cover his submission, and, I may add, his malice. He regretted his mistakes, he deplored misunderstanding, he avowed unlimited obligation and eternal gratitude. He even ventured on hinting at the memory of a sentimental attachment. " I can take from you what I would from no other lady." (At no moment, however agitated, would Powers forget to say " lady.") The remark was accompanied by an unmistakable leer.

Even that, which I bore with difficulty, Jenny accepted graciously. She gave him her hand, saying, " I know. Now let's forget all this and work pleasantly together." She glanced at me. " And Mr. Austin, too, will forget all about our little quarrel? "

"I'm always willing to be friends with Mr. Powers, if he'll let me," I said.

"And so are all my friends, I'm sure," said Jenny.

Going out, we had a strange encounter, which stands forth vivid in memory. Jenny's brougham was waiting perhaps some thirty yards up the road toward Catsford: the coachman had got down and was smoking; it took him a moment or two to mount. In that space of time, while we waited at the gate, Octon came out from Hatcham Ford and lounged across the road toward us. At the same instant a landau drove up rapidly from the other direction, going toward Catsford. In it sat Lady Sarah Lacey. She stared at Octon and cut him dead; she bowed coldly and slightly to Jenny; she inclined her head again in response to a low bow and a florid flourish of his cap from Powers. I lifted my hat, but received no response. Jenny returned the salute as carelessly as it was given, bestowed a recognition hardly more cordial on Octon, and stepped into the brougham which had now come up. As we drove off, Powers stood grinning soapily; Octon had turned on his heel again and slouched slowly back to his own house.

Jenny threw herself into the corner of the brougham, her body well away, but her eyes on my face. For many minutes she sat like this; I turned my eyes away from her; the silence was uncomfortable and ominous. At last she spoke.

"You've guessed something, Austin?"

I turned my head to her. "I couldn't help it."

She nodded, rather wearily, then smiled at me. "The signal's at 'Danger,'" she said.

CHAPTER XII

SAVING A WEEK

SEEN in retrospect, the history of the ensuing days stands out clearly; subsequent knowledge supplies any essential details of which I was then ignorant and turns into certainties what were, in some cases, only strong suspicions at the moment. If it be wondered—and it well may be—that any woman should choose to live through such a time, it is hardly less marvelous that she could stand the strain of it. Brain and feelings alike must have been sorely taxed. Jenny never faltered; she looked, indeed, tired and anxious, but she had many intervals of gayety, and, as the crisis approached, she was remarkably free from her not unusual little gusts of temper or of petulance. To all around her she showed graciousness and affection, desiring, as it seemed, to draw from us expressions of attachment and sympathy, making perhaps an instinctive attempt to bind us still closer to her, to secure us for friends if anything went wrong in the dangerous work on which she was engaged.

She had a threefold struggle—one with Fillingford, one with Octon, the last and greatest—really involving the other two—with herself. Fillingford was pressing for her answer now. It was not so much that any heat of emotion, any lover's haste, urged him on; he had begun to be fearful for his dignity, to be apprehensive of the whispers and smiles of gossip, if Jenny played with him much longer. She had made up her mind to accept him. Not only were there the decorative attractions and the wider sphere of influence; she felt that in a marriage with him lay safety. She was not afraid of him; it would be a partnership in which she could amply hold her own—and more than that. The danger pointed out in her father's warning—so congenial to her that it sank deep into her own mind and was never absent from it—would here be reduced to a minimum. There the attractions of the project stopped. She was not the least in love with him; I do not think that she even considered him an actively agreeable companion. An absence of dislike and a genuine esteem for his honorable qualities—that was all she could muster for him. No wonder, perhaps, that, though her head had decided, her heart still pleaded for delay.

With Octon the case was very different. There she was fascinated, there she was in thrall—so much in thrall that I am persuaded that she would deliberately have sacrificed the attractions of the Fillingford alliance, braved her neighbor's disapproval, imperiled the brilliant fabric of popularity and power which she had been at such pains to create—save for one thing. She was fascinated to love by the quality which, above all others, she dreaded in marriage. In that great respect wherein Fillingford was harmless, Octon was to her mind supremely to be feared. The very difficulty she now felt in sending him away was earnest of the dominion which he would exercise. Since he was a lover, no doubt he made the usual lover's vows—or some of them; very likely he told her that her will would be his law, or spoke more impassioned words to that effect. Such protestations from his lips carried no conviction. The man could not help being despotic. She was despotic, too. If he would not yield, she could not answer for it that she would, and perhaps aspired to no such abdication. Her foresight discerned, with fatal clearness, the clash of their opposing forces, accentuated by the permanent contrast of their tastes and dispositions. The master of Breysgate Priory might again break Lady Aspenick's whip or insult the Mayor of Catsford! Trifles from one point of view, but Jenny would not have such things done. They were fatal to popularity and to power; they broke up her life as she had planned it. There would arise an inevitable conflict. In victory for herself—even in that—she saw misery. But she could not believe in victory. She was afraid.

Then she must let him go. She had the conviction clear at last; her delicate equipoise—the ignorance of Fillingford against Octon's suspicious but hopeful doubt—her having it both ways, could not be maintained forever. Sentence was passed on Octon. I think that in his heart he must have known it. But her fascination pleaded with her for a long day—that the sentence should not be executed yet. To determine to do it was one thing; doing it was quite another. Day by day she must have debated " Shall it be to-morrow?" Day after day she delayed and dallied. Day after day she saw him; whether they met at Ivydene with Powers for sentinel, or whether she seized her chance to slip across from Ivydene to Hatcham Ford, I know not. However that may be —and it matters little—every afternoon she went down to Ivydene—to transact Institute business— between tea and dinner. Late for business? Yes—but Fillingford came earlier in the afternoons—and now it grew dark early. A carriage or a car took her— but she never kept it waiting. She always came home on foot in the gathering darkness.

After her one explicit confidence, "The signal's at Danger," she became unapproachable on the subject which filled alike her thoughts and mine. Hence a certain distance came between us in spite of her affectionate kindness. There were no more morning rides; she went only once or twice herself; I did not know whether she met Lacey. I was less often at lunch and dinner. We confined ourselves more to our official relations. We were both awkwardly conscious of a forbidden or suppressed subject—one that could not be approached to any good purpose unless confidence was to be open and thorough. To that length she would not—perhaps could not—go; she had to fight her battle alone. Only once she came near to referring to the position of affairs, then no more than indirectly.

"You looked rather fagged and worried," she said one day. "Why don't you take a little holiday, and come back when things are settled?"

"Would you rather I went away for a bit? I want you to tell me the truth."

"Oh, no," she answered with evident sincerity, almost with eagerness. "I like to have you here." She smiled. "Somebody to catch me if I fall!" Then, with a quickness that prevented any answer or comment of mine, she returned to our business.

So I stayed and watched—there was nothing else to do. If anybody objects that the spectacle which I watched was not a pleasant one, I will not argue with him. If anyone asserts that it was not a moral one, not tending to edification, I may perhaps have to concede the point. I can only plead that to me it was interesting—painful, perhaps, but interesting. I believed that she would win; we who were about her got into the way of expecting her to win. We looked for some mistakes, but we looked also for dexterous recoveries and ultimate victories won even in the face of odds. I will volunteer one more confession—I wanted her to win—to win the respite she craved without detection and without disaster. The sternness of morality is apt to weaken before the appeal of a gallant fight—valor of spirit, and dexterity, and resource in maneuver. We forget the merits of the cause in the pluck of the combatant. As I believed, as I hoped, that Jenny would win, I also hoped that she would not take too great, too long, a risk. The signal pointed straighter to "Danger" every day.

Chat—whom I have been in danger of forgetting, though I am sure I mean her no disrespect—had her work in the campaign. It was to create diversions, to act as buffer, to cover up Jenny's tracks when that was necessary, to give plausible reasons for Jenny's movements when such were needed; above all, delicately to imply to the neighborhood that the Fillingford matter was all right—only they must give Miss Driver time! Chat was a loyal, nay, rabid Octonite herself, but she was also a faithful hound. She obeyed orders—and obeyed them with a certain skill. On the subject of Jenny's shrinking timidity when faced with an offer of marriage, Chat was beautifully convincing—I heard her do the trick once for Mrs. Jepps's edification. The ladies were good enough not to make a stranger of me. Mrs. Jepps, I may observe in passing, took a healthy—and somewhat imperious—interest in one's marriage, and one's means, and so on, as well as in one's religious opinions.

"Always the same from a girl, Mrs. Jepps!" said Chat. "And after five years of her I ought to know. I assure you we couldn't get her to speak to a young man!"

"Very unusual with girls nowadays," observed Mrs. Jepps.

"Ah, our little village wasn't like Catsford! We were, I suppose you'd call it, behind the times there. I had been brought up on the old lines, and I inculcated them on my pupils. But, as I say, with Jenny there was no need. The difficulty was the other way. Why, I remember a very nice young fellow, named Maunders (was Maunders Rabbit, I wondered), who paid her such nice attentions—so respectful! (Maunders was Rabbit, depend upon it!) She used to be angry with him—positively angry, Mrs. Jepps." Chat nodded sagely. "Comparing small things and great, it's the same thing here." Thus did Chat transform into girlish coyness Jenny's masterful grip on liberty!

"It's possible to carry it too far. Then it looks like shilly-shallying," said Mrs. Jepps.

"She does carry it too far," Chat hastened to admit candidly. "Much too far. Why, between ourselves, I tell her so every day." (Oh, oh, Chat, as if you dared!) "I try to use some of my old authority." Chat smiled playfully over this.

"Well," said Mrs. Jepps, rising to go, "I suppose the poor man's got to put up with anything from sixty thousand a year!"

In that remark Mrs. Jepps, shrewdly unconvinced by Chat's convincing precedent, hit off the growing feeling of the neighborhood—the feeling of whose growth Fillingford had begun to be afraid. He believed that all communication with Octon had been broken off; he had never considered Octon as a rival. He saw no ostensible reason for Jenny's hesitation; he was either sure that she would say yes if forced to an answer, or he made up his mind at last to take the risk. He came over to Breysgate Priory with a formal offer and the demand for a formal answer.

Needless to say, he did not confide this fact to me, but I had information really as good as first-hand. On the day in question I was sitting reading in my own house after lunch when, with a perfunctory knock, young Lacey put his head in at the door.

"Got any tobacco and a drink, Mr. Austin? We've walked over. I've dropped the governor up the hill."

I welcomed him, provided him with what he wanted, and sat him down by the fire; it was late autumn now and chilly. He was looking amused in a reflective sort of way.

"I say, I suppose you're pretty well in the know up there, aren't you?" He nodded in the direction of the Priory. "Not much danger of the governor slipping up, is there? Oh, you know what I mean! There's no reason you and I shouldn't talk about it."

"Perhaps I do, Lord Lacey. Your father's at the Priory now?"

"I've just left him there. It's a bit odd to do bottleholder for one's governor on these occasions. It'd seem more natural the other way, wouldn't it?"

"Depends a bit on the relative ages, doesn't it?"

"Yes, of course, that's it. The governor's getting on, though." He looked across at me. "He's a gentleman, though. The way he told Aunt Sarah and me about it was good—quite good. He said his mind had been made up for some time, but he couldn't formally take such a step without discovering the feelings of the—well, he called us something pleasant—the people who'd lived with him and done so much for his happiness for so many years, ever since mother—'your dear mother,' he said—died. So he told us what he was going to do, and asked our good wishes. Rather straight of him, don't you think?"

"I should always expect the straight thing of him," I said.

"Yes—and that'll suit her at all events." (Did he unintentionally hint that some other things would not?) "She's straight as a die, isn't she? Look at the straight way she's treated me! As soon as she saw me—well, inclined to be—oh, you know!—she put it all straight directly; and we're the best of pals—I'd go through fire and water for her—and I wished the old governor luck with all my heart."

"I'm delighted to hear you feel like that about it—I really am. And I'm sure Miss Driver would be, too. I hope Lady Sarah is equally pleased?"

His blue eyes twinkled. "You needn't put that on for me, Austin," he remarked, with a pleasant lapse into greater intimacy. "I imagine Aunt Sarah's feelings are no secret! However, she said all the proper things and pecked the governor's cheek. Couldn't ask more, could you?" He laughed as he stretched his shapely gaitered legs before the fire. "After all, there'll be two pretty big houses—Fillingford and Breysgate! Room for all!"

"You'll be wanting one presently."

"I shall live with the old folks—I say, how'd Miss Driver like to hear that?—till I get married—which won't be for a long while, I hope. Then we'll set Aunt Sarah up at Hatcham Ford. Octon will be gone by then, I hope! I saw the fellow in the town the other day. I wonder he doesn't go. It can't be pleasant to stop in a place where you're cut!"

"Octon has his own resources, I daresay."

"Sorry for the resources!" Lacey remarked. "I say, how long ought we to give the governor?"

"Don't hurry matters."

"It can't take very long, can it? The governor means to settle it out of hand; he almost said as much."

"But then there's the lady. Perhaps she——"

"Between ourselves, I fancy he thinks he's waited long enough."

I had the same impression, but my mind had wandered back to another point.

"When did you see Octon?" I asked.

"I trotted Aunt Sarah down to that place—what's it called?—where the Institute offices are. Aunt Sarah's got very keen on the Institute; she must mean to queer it somehow, I think! Well, Octon was there, talking to the clerk. She cut him dead, of course—marched by the pair of them with her head up. Powers ran after her, and I addressed an observation to Octon. You remember that little spar we had?"

"At the Flower Show? Yes, I remember."

"I was a bit fresh then," he confessed candidly, "and perhaps he wasn't so far wrong to sit on me. But the beggar's got a rough way of doing it. Well, it didn't seem civil to say nothing, so I said, 'I haven't had that thrashing yet, and I'm getting a bit too big for it, like you, Mr. Octon.'"

"Was that your idea of something civil?" I felt constrained to ask.

"He didn't mind," Lacey assured me. "But he said a funny thing. He grinned at me quite kindly and said, 'You're just coming to the size for something much worse.' What do you think he meant by that, Austin?"

"I haven't the least idea."

"He's a bounder—at least he must be, or he'd never have done that to Susie Aspenick; but he's got his points, I think. I tell you what, I shouldn't so much mind serving under him. One don't mind being sat on by the C. O."

"What was happening between Lady Sarah and Powers all this time?" I asked.

"Lord bless you, I don't know!" he answered scornfully. "Institute, I suppose! I should be inclined to call the Institute rot if Miss Driver wasn't founding it. At any rate Aunt Sarah and Powers—rather like a beach photographer, isn't he?—seem as thick as thieves." He finished off his whisky and soda. "Well, women must do something, I suppose," he remarked. "Shall we go and beat up the governor?"

He was impatient. I yielded, although I did not think that "the governor" would be ready for us yet; I thought that, if Lord Fillingford was to gain his cause that afternoon, he was in for a long interview with Jenny. Evidently Lacey meant to wait. I was game to wait with him. In these days I was all suspicion—on the alert for danger. It made me uneasy to hear that Lady Sarah and Powers were "thick as thieves." Mentally I paused to acknowledge the exquisite accuracy of Lacey's "beach photographer." On the genus it would have been a libel; for the species it was exact. I saw him with his velveteens, his hair, his collar—against a background of paper-littered sands and "nigger minstrels"; the picture recalled childhood, but without the proper sentimental appeal.

I was right. We had to walk up and down the terrace in front of the house for a long while. Lacey talked all the time—his views, his regiment, sports, races, what not. From the top of my mind—the surface responsive to externals—I answered. Within I was following in imagination the struggle of my dear, wayward, unreasonable mistress—of her who wanted both ways, who would lead half a dozen lives, and unite under her sway kingdoms between which there could be neither union nor alliance.

It was almost five o'clock by the time Fillingford came out; the sun had begun to lose power; the peace of evening—and something of its chill—rested on the billowing curves of turf and the gently swaying treetops. As we saw him we came to a standstill, and so awaited his approach.

Under no circumstances, I imagine, could Lord Fillingford have looked radiant. Even any overt appearance of triumph his taste, no less than his nature, would have rejected; and his taste was infallible in negatives. Yet on his face, as he came to us, there was unmistakable satisfaction; he had done quite as well as he had expected—or even better. I was glad —with a sharp pang of sorrow for the limitations of human gladness. In my heart I should have been glad for Jenny to be allowed to break rules—to have it all ways—as she wanted—for as long as she wanted. There was the moral slope of which I have before made metaphorical mention!

He greeted me with a cordiality very marked for him, and laid a hand on his son's shoulder affectionately. "I've kept you a terribly long time, Amyas, and we mustn't bother Miss Driver any more. She's tired, I fear. We'll go home for a cup of tea."

Lacey was excited and anxious, but he knew his

father better than to put even the most veiled question to him in my presence.

"All right, sir. Austin's been looking after me first-rate."

I could not be mistaken; a touch of ownership over me—the hint of a right to approve of me—came into Fillingford's voice. I seemed to feel myself adopted as a retainer—or, at least, my past services to one of the family acknowledged.

"I'm sure Mr. Austin is always most kind."

The impression was subtle, but it confirmed, more than anything that had yet happened, my certainty of Jenny's answer. I had further confirmation the next moment. He stood on the edge of the terrace, his arm through his son's, and looked over the view.

"A fine position!" he said. "If it had been the fashion to build on the top of a hill three centuries ago, we should have put the house here, I suppose, instead of selling to the Dormers. It was part of our land originally, you know, Mr. Austin." He pulled himself up with a laugh. "A feudal lord's reminiscences! We do well enough if we can keep what we've got nowadays—without regretting what we used to have. Come along, Amyas, or your aunt will have given us up for tea!"

He had sought to correct the impression he had given—to withdraw the idea implicit in his words about Breysgate Priory; yet the withdrawal seemed formal, made in deference to an obligation rather than really effective or important. I was sure that, as he trod Breysgate park that evening, he trod the soil as, in his own mind, already part of the Fillingford domains. The most reserved of men cannot but tell something; only a god or a brute, as the philosopher has it, can be absolutely unrevealing. If Fillingford could have succeeded in attaining to that—and I have no doubt that he tried—his son would have spoiled the mystery. Familiarity taught him to read more clearly his father's visage. His face beamed with exultation; as he had "wished the governor luck with all his heart," now, without question, the moment I was out of hearing, he wished him joy.

I went in to Jenny, without stopping to think whether she had bidden me come or not. I could not keep away; it even seemed to be something like hypocrisy to keep away now on the pretext that I had not been expressly summoned. She had told me that she liked me to stay—as "somebody to catch her if she fell." That was, surely, at least a permission to be near her?

She was alone, save for Loft who was setting out the tea-tray in his usual deft, speedy, deliberate way. She sat in the middle of the sofa, looking straight in front of her. But she spoke to me directly I came in, while Loft and the footman were still in the room.

"You've just missed Lord Fillingford. Or did you see him as he went away?"

"Yes, I met him and had a little talk with him. Young Lacey's been gossiping with me most of the afternoon."

Loft must have wanted to hear, but you'd never have known it! He withdrew, imperturbable and serene. I think that Loft should be added to the god and the brute, to form a trinity of impeccable illegibility.

At a sign from Jenny I took my tea and drank it. She sat very quiet, exhausted as it seemed, yet still thinking hard. I did not speak.

"A long call, wasn't it?" she said at last, and a faint smile flickered on her lips.

"It was—and it seemed so, I daresay."

"How did he look?"

"Exceedingly well-content. And Lacey seemed most contented with his appearance."

She shrugged her shoulders and smiled again rather contemptuously. I set down my cup and came to her. "Well, good-night, Lady Jenny," I said.

She looked up at me and suddenly spoke out the truth—in a hard voice, bitter and resentful.

"With prayers and vows—yes, and tears," she said, "I've saved a week."

"Before you give your answer?"

"No. The answer is given. Before the engagement is announced."

"If you've given your answer, announce it to-night."

She did not resent my counsel. But she shook her head. "I've fought that battle with him already. I—I can't." She rose suddenly to her feet and stood before me. "I've done it. I've managed to do it. It's done—and I stand by it. But not to-day! I must have a week." She stretched out her hands to me in appeal; there was a curious mixture of mockery and of passion in her voice. She mocked me for certain—perhaps she mocked herself, too; yet she was strongly moved. " Dear old, kind, little-understanding Austin, you must give poor Jenny Driver her last week! "

The last week, which she must have, did all the mischief.

CHAPTER XIII

THE BOY WITH THE RED CAP

JENNY had failed with Powers; that seemed to be the state of the case—or, at least, her success was so precarious as to put her whole position in extreme peril. Neither storm nor sunshine, neither wrath nor cajolery, had won him securely. Behind each he could discern its true object —to gain time, to tide over. When Jenny had finished her equivocal proceedings, when she had settled down either to Fillingford or to Octon—Octon's success must still have seemed a possibility to the accomplice of their meetings—what would she do with her equally equivocal partner? Reward him? Yes, if she had trusted him. He knew very well that she trusted him no longer; her threats and her wheedling combined to prove it. Presumably Mr. Powers was acquainted with the parable of The Unjust Steward; he, too, was a child of this world—indeed his earthly parentage was witnessed to beyond the common by his moral features. What should he do when he was no longer steward, when Jenny was safely wedded to Fillingford, or had thrown off, of her own motive or on compulsion, all secrecy about Octon? Lady Sarah should receive—or at least introduce—him into a comfortable habitation and put money in his pocket to pay its rent. Jenny had overrated her domination; and she had forgotten that rogues are apt not to know when they are well off. Even when their own pockets are snugly lined, a pocket unpicked is a challenge and a temptation.

Lady Sarah's conduct is sufficiently accounted for by most praiseworthy motives—moral principle, family pride, loyalty to her brother. Let, then, no others be imputed. But if Jenny would not credit these to her, well, there were others of which she might have thought. She had chosen not to think of Lady Sarah at all—in connection with Powers at all events. The very omission might stand as a compliment to Lady Sarah, but Jenny was not the person who could afford to pay it; her own safety and honor still rested in those unclean hands.

The last days—the week of Jenny's hard-won respite—passed for us at Breysgate like the interval between the firing of a fuse and the explosion. How would it go? Clear away obstacles and open the adit to profitable working? Or blow all the mine to ruins, and engulf the engineer in the *débris*? Nerves were on trial and severely tried. Chat was in flutters beyond description. I do not suppose that I myself was a cheerful companion. Jenny was steel, but the steel was red-hot.

At last—the last day! Jenny's week of respite drew to its end. Be sure I had counted! But if I had not, Octon himself came, most welcomely, to announce it. With a mighty relief I heard him say, as he threw himself into my armchair at the Old Priory, "I've just dropped in to say good-by, Austin. I'm off tomorrow."

"Off? Where to?" I had sooner have asked "For how long?" His reply answered both questions.

"Right out of this hole—for good." He smiled. "So, for once, I chanced meeting Lady Aspenick again in the park." He took up the poker and began to dig and prod my coals: all through our talk he held the poker, now digging and prodding, now using it to emphasize his words with a point or a wave. "I'm done with here, Austin. I've played a game that I never thought I should play again—and I've come to feel as if I'd never played it before. I've played it with all the odds against me, and I've made a good fight."

"Yes, too good," I said.

"Aye, aye! But I've lost. So I'm off." He lay back in the big chair—the same one in which Lacey had stretched his graceful, lithe young body—and looked up at me where I stood on the rug. "There's not much more to say, is there? I thought I'd say that much to you because you're a good fellow."

"And you're not," I retorted angrily—(Remember our nerves!) "Have you no care for what you love?"

"Am I so much the worse man of the two?" he asked.

"What's that got to do with it? Well, thank God you're going to-morrow!"

"Everybody always thanks God when I go, and I generally thank Him myself—but not to-day, perhaps." His next prod at the coals in the grate was a vicious one. "I suppose that some day there'll be a general feeling that I must be wiped out—an instinctive revolt against my existence, Austin. This neighborhood has felt the thing already. Some day it will be felt where stronger measures than cutting are in fashion. Then I shall be killed. Perhaps I shall kill, too, but they'll get me in the end, depend upon it!" Suddenly he smiled in a tender reflective way. "That was what poor little Madge was always so afraid of. Well, I had a good deal to try my temper while she was with me." He looked up at me, smiling now in mockery. "Don't be shocked, my excellent Austin. I'm talking about my wife."

"Your wife!" I cried in utter surprise and consternation.

That was exactly the effect he intended to produce and enjoyed producing. Amidst all his distress he found leisure to indulge his taste for administering shocks.

"You've always thought of me as a bachelor, haven't you? I suppose everybody thinks so—except one person. Well, it's no affair of theirs, and they've never chosen to inquire. I didn't mean to tell you, but the reference to her slipped out."

"You've had a wife all this time?" I gasped, sinking into a chair opposite to him.

He laughed openly at me. "Poor old Austin! No, it's not Powers over again." (So he knew about Powers!) "The poor child's been dead these twelve years."

I shrugged my shoulders impatiently. "Does it really amuse you to play the fool just now?"

"It amused me to make you jump." He watched me with a malicious grin for half a minute, then fell to prodding the coals again. "We were boy and girl —and I had only two years with her, and during that time I had the pleasure of seeing her nearly starve. I had no money and got very little work; in the usual way of things, I came into my little bit of money— it's precious little—too late. She was very pretty and a good girl, but not a lady by birth—no, not a lady, Austin. Consequently my folk—my respectable well-to-do folk—left her pretty nearly to starve—and me to look on at it. That's among the reasons why I'm so fond of respectable well-to-do people, why I have a natural inclination to acquiesce in their claim to all the virtues."

"Does Miss Driver know this?"

"Yes." He paused a moment. "She knows this— and a little more—which may or may not turn out material some day."

These words started my alarm afresh. Did he mean still to be in touch with Jenny, still to keep up communication with her—a hold on her—even though he went? If that were so, there was no end in sight, and no peace. The next instant he relieved me from that fear by adding in a low pensive voice, "But not while I live; we know each other no more after to-day."

Our eyes met again. He nodded at me, confirming his last words. "You may rely on that," he seemed to say.

"Do you leave by an early train to-morrow?" I asked.

"Yes—first thing in the morning."

"By this time to-morrow I shall feel very kindly toward you, Octon, and the more kindly for what you've told me to-day."

"I believe you will, and I understand the deferred payment of your love." He smiled at me again. "You're true to your salt, and I suppose you're a bit in love yourself, though you don't seem to know anything about it. Well, take care of her—take care of this great woman."

"I don't want to talk about her to you. I don't see the good of it."

"You ought to want to, because I understand her. But since you don't——" He dropped the poker with a clatter and reared himself to his height. "I'd better go, for, as heaven's above us, I can talk and think of nothing else—till to-morrow."

"Where are you going to?"

"Into the dark"—he laughed gruffly—"Continent. Did my melodrama alarm you? Not that it's dark any longer—more's the pity! It's not very likely we shall meet again this side the Styx." He held out his hand to me with a genuinely friendly air.

"We're both young!" I said as I clasped his hand. In the end, still, I liked him, and his story had moved me to a new pity. It was all of a piece with his perversity that he should have hidden so long his strongest claim to sympathy.

"I could have been young," he answered. "And that stiff fool can't." He squeezed my hand to very pain before he dropped it. "A great woman and a good fellow—well, in this hole it's something to have met! As for the rest of them—the fate of Laodicea, I think!"

"You're so wrong, you know."

"Yes? As usual? In the end I shall certainly be stamped out!" He shook his head with a whimsically humorous gravity. "Part of the objection to me is simply because I'm so large."

That was actually true when I came to think of it. His size seemed an oppression—a perpetual threat—in itself a form of bullying. Small men could have said the things he did with only half the offense; the other half lay in his physical security.

"Try to counteract that by improving your manners," I said, smiling at him in a friendly amusement.

"Let the grizzly bear put on silk knee-breeches—wouldn't he look elegant? Good-by, Austin. Take care of her!"

"Since you say that again—you know I would—with my life."

"And I—to my death. And I seem to die to-day."

There was nothing to be said to that. We walked out into the open air together. I rejoiced that he was going, and yet was sad. Something of what Jenny felt was upon me then—the interest of him, the challenge to try and to discover, the greatness of the effort to influence, the audacity of the notion of ruling. The danger of him—and his bulk! A Dark Continent he seemed in himself! I could not but be sorry that my little ship was now to lose sight of the coasts of it. But there was a nobler craft—almost driven on to its rocks, still tossing in its breakers. For her a fair wind off land and an open sea!

As we stood before my door, I awaiting Octon's departure, he perhaps loath to look his last on a scene which must carry for him such significance, I saw Lacey coming toward me on horseback. He beckoned to me in token that he wanted me.

"Ah, an opportunity for another good-by!" said Octon grimly.

Lacey brought his horse to a stand by us, but did not dismount.

"I'm trespassing, I'm afraid, Lord Lacey! My being in this park is against the law, isn't it?"

Octon's opening was not very conciliatory, but Lacey's good-humor was proof against him. Moreover the lad looked preoccupied.

"I'm not out for a row to-day, Mr. Octon," he said. "I want just one word with you, Austin."

"Then I'll be off," said Octon. He nodded to me; he did not offer to shake hands again.

"I'll come and see you off to-morrow morning. The eleven-five, I suppose?" That was the fast train to London.

"Yes. All right, I shall be glad to see you. To Lord Lacey—and his friends—this is good-by."

"You're going away?" asked Lacey, joy and relief plain in his voice.

"Yes. You seem very glad."

"I am glad," said young Lacey, "but I mean no offense, Mr. Octon."

Their eyes met fair and square. I expected an angry outburst from Octon, but none came; his look was moody again, but it was not fierce. He looked restless and unhappy, but he spoke with dignity.

"I recognize that. I take no offense. Good-by, Lord Lacey." With a slight lift of his hat, courteously responded to by Lacey, he turned his back on us and walked away with his heavy slouching gait, his head sunk low on his shoulders. We watched him go for a moment or two in silence.

"Is he going for good?" Lacey asked me.

"Yes, to-morrow."

He seemed to consider something within himself. "Then I don't know that I really need trouble you. It's a delicate matter and—" He beat his leg with his crop, frowning thoughtfully. "I wonder, Austin, whether you're aware how matters stand between Miss Driver and my father?" His use of "my father" instead of "the governor" was a significant mark of his seriousness.

"Yes, she told me."

"My father told me. To-morrow is the day for the announcement. Austin, the last two or three days my father has been very worried and upset. Aunt Sarah's been at him about something. I'm sure it's about—about Miss Driver. I can tell it is by the way they both look when her name's mentioned. And I—I tried an experiment. At lunch to-day I began to talk about that fellow Powers. I tried it on by saying I thought he was a scoundrel and that I hoped Miss Driver would give him the sack. I never saw a man look up with such a start as my father did. Aunt Sarah was ready to be on to me, but he was too quick. 'Why do you say that?' he snapped out—eagerly, you know—as if he was uncommonly anxious to hear my reasons. Well, of course, I'd none to give, only my impressions of the chap. Aunt Sarah looked triumphant and read me a lecture on envy, malice, and all uncharitableness. My father sat staring at the tablecloth, but listening hard to every word. Why the devil should my father be so interested in Powers? Can you tell me that, Austin?"

"No, I can't tell you," I said, "but I'm much obliged to you for this—information."

"I thought there would be—well, just no harm in mentioning it to you," he said. "Of course it's probably all right really. And if everything is settled, and announced, and all that, to-morrow—and—" He broke off, not adding in words what there was no need to add—"Octon gone to-morrow!"

But to-day was not to-morrow. Lady Sarah was at work, and Fillingford much interested in Mr. Powers! Worried, upset, and very much interested in Powers!

Lacey gathered his reins and prepared to be off. "Sorry if I've meddled in what's not my business," he said. "But I'm ready to take the responsibility." That was permission to me to use his information, and to vouch his authority to Jenny. He nodded to me. "See you to-morrow, perhaps, and we'll drink the health of the engaged couple!" He smiled, but he looked puzzled and not very happy, rather as though he were hoping for the best, and staving off anticipation of some hitch or misfortune.

As soon as he was gone, I went up to the Priory.

My task was not an easy one, but I had an overwhelming feeling—a feeling which refused all counter-argument—that it was necessary. There was still this one evening—an opportunity for a last bit of recklessness, and Heaven alone knew how great a temptation.

Jenny received me in her little upstairs sitting-room, next to the room where she slept. She wore an indoors gown and, in answer to my formal inquiry, told me that she had a cold and was feeling rather " seedy "—not a common admission for her to make. Then I went to work, stumbling at my awkward story—so full of implied accusation against her, if it were not utterly unmeaning—under the steady thoughtful gaze of her eyes. She heard me to the end in silence.

" If that rascal is trying to make mischief, if he has trumped up some story—" I tried so to put it that she could feel entitled to be on her guard without making any admissions.

She made none, and offered no direct comment on the story. She took up an envelope from the writing-table by her.

" This is my formal leave to Lord Fillingford to announce our engagement. I was going to post it to-night. I'll send it now by a groom. Please ring the bell for me, Austin."

Loft appeared. She gave him the letter and ordered that a groom should take it to Fillingford Manor on horseback. Loft glanced at the clock.

" The men will just be at their tea, miss," he said. It was now about half-past four.

"It'll do in half an hour's time," she answered. "But let it get there this afternoon without fail."

As Loft went out, she turned to me. "There now, that's settled."

Was it? There was still to-night. I suspected to-night desperately. I suspected Jenny's love of having it both ways to the very last moment that she could. I suspected the strength of the lure toward Octon. Whether she divined my suspicions I cannot tell. She went on in her simplest, most plausible way.

"Now I'm going to lie down, and I'm not sure I shall get up again. A plate of soup and a novel in bed look rather attractive! And I must get a good beauty-sleep—against my lord's coming to-morrow!"

She held out her hand to me. As I took it I gave her a long look. The bright eyes were candid and unembarrassed. Yet I had grave doubts whether Jenny was speaking the whole truth—and nothing but it!

On the stairs I encountered Chat. She broke out on me volubly about Jenny's indisposition.

"You've seen our poor Jenny—the poor child? So ill, such a cold! And she actually wanted to go down to Catsford to see Mr. Bindlecombe and Mr. Powers on some Institute business! As if she was fit to go out—a raw cold evening, too, and getting dark so much earlier nowadays! At any rate I persuaded her out of that, and I do hope she'll be sensible and go to bed."

"So do I—very much, Miss Chatters," I replied.

"And she's just given me to understand that she means to do it."

"That's the safe thing," Chat averred with emphasis; and, without a doubt, she was perfectly right —from more points of view than one. In bed at Breysgate, with her soup, her novel, and a watchful maid in attendance, Jenny would be safe. I did not, however, need quite as much convincing of it as Chat seemed disposed to administer to me.

There was nothing more to do. I went back home, brewed myself a cup of tea, and sat down to write letters; writing letters compels an attention which would wander from a book. I had an accumulation to answer, some on my own account, the greater part on Jenny's affairs, and I worked away steadily till it was nearly seven o'clock. Then I was suddenly interrupted by a loud knock on my door. As I rose, the door opened, and Lacey was again before me. He was still in riding dress, but his boots were covered with dust; he was hot and out of breath. He had been walking—walking fast, or even running. He seemed excited, but tried to smile at me.

"Here I am again!" he said. "I don't know whether I am a fool, Austin—I hope I am—but there's something I want you to hear." He shut the door behind him, glanced at the clock, and went on quickly. "Do you know a sandy-haired boy who wears a red cap and rides a girl's bicycle?"

"Yes," I answered. "That's Powers's boy—Alban Powers."

"I thought I remembered the young beggar. That

boy brought a note up to Aunt Sarah while we were having tea—about a quarter past five, it must have been, I think. Aunt Sarah pounced on the note, read it, said there was no answer, and then handed the note over to my father. 'Who's it from?' he asked peevishly. 'You'll see if you read it,' she said. I asked if I was *de trop*, but my father signed to me to sit where I was. He read the note, and handed it back to Aunt Sarah. 'What are you going to do?' she asked. 'Nothing,' he said. She pursed up her lips and shrugged her shoulders—she made it pretty plain what she thought of that answer. 'Nothing!' she sort of whispered, throwing her eyes up to the ceiling. Then he broke out: 'I've forbidden the subject to be mentioned!'—but he looked very unhappy and uncomfortable. Nobody said anything for a bit; Aunt Sarah looked obstinate-silent and my father unhappy-silent. I tried to talk about something or other, but it was no good. Then the man came in with another note, saying a groom had brought it for his lordship. Well, he read that—and it seemed to please him a bit better."

" Well it might! " I remarked. " It was from Miss Driver and it said what he wanted."

" Wait a bit, Austin. He sat with this note—Miss Driver's—in his hand, turning it over and over. He didn't offer to show it to either of us, but he kept looking across at Aunt Sarah. I took up a paper, but I watched them from behind it. He was weighing something in his mind; she wouldn't look at him—playing sulky still over the business of the first note, the one that boy in the red cap had brought. At last he got up and went over to her. He spoke rather low, but I heard—well, he could have sent me away, or gone away with her himself, if he hadn't wanted me to hear. 'A note I've had from Miss Driver makes it very proper for me to call on her this evening,' he said. Aunt Sarah looked up, wide awake in a minute. 'You'll go this evening—to Breysgate?' she asked. 'Yes, at seven.' 'At seven,' she repeated after him with a nod. 'But perhaps she'll be out.' 'That's possible,' he answered. 'But I shall wait for her—she must come in before dinner.' Aunt Sarah looked hard at him. 'They'll probably know where she's gone if she is out. You could go and meet her,' she said to him. I can't give you the way they talked—it was all as if what they said meant something different, or something more, at any rate. When Aunt Sarah suggested that he might go and meet Miss Driver, he started a little, then thought it over. At last he said, 'I shall try to find her to-night.' 'You're sensible at last!' she said—and added something in a whisper. My father nodded, and walked out of the room, pocketing his letter. Aunt Sarah went to the fire and burned hers. I wish I could have got a look at it!"

"So do I," I said. "It's just on seven now."

I was thinking hard. The boy with the red cap—Powers's boy—the note—the subterranean quarrel over it—the strange half-spoken half-suppressed conversation that followed—these gave plenty of matter for thought when I added to them my sore doubts of the way in which Jenny in truth meant to spend the evening.

"Of course it may be all nothing. I'm afraid all the time of being infernally officious."

"Your father will pretty nearly be at Breysgate by now."

"And she's there, I suppose, isn't she?" His question was full of hesitation.

In an instant, on his question, my doubts and suspicions seemed to harden into certainties. I knew—it was nothing less than knowledge—that she was not there, and that the note brought by the boy with the red cap told truly where she was. Fillingford would go to Breysgate—he would be referred to Chat. Chat would tell him that Jenny was in bed. Would he believe it and go home peacefully—to face Lady Sarah's angry scorn and the doubts of his own perplexed mind? He might—then all would be well. But he might not believe it. He had said that he would try to find her to-night. He knew where to find her—if he trusted the information which the boy in the red cap had brought.

"He doesn't know you've come here, of course?"

"Not he! I got a start—and, by Jove, I ran! Are you going to do anything about it?"

I was quite clear what I had to do about it. Chat must be in the secret; she might manage to send Fillingford home—or she might keep him at Breysgate long enough to give me, in my turn, a chance. No good lay in my going to meet him—Chat could lie as well as I, and, if he would not believe her, he would not believe me either. Neither would I send Lacey to him; any appearance of Lacey's in the matter would show that we were afraid, that we knew

THE BOY WITH THE RED CAP

there was something to conceal. My course was to take the start Lacey's warning gave me, to go where Jenny was, trusting to reach her in time to get her away before Fillingford came on from Breysgate. It was time to put away pretenses, scruples, formalities. I must find her wherever she was; I must meet her face to face with my message of danger.

I put on my hat and coat hastily. Lacey stood looking at me.

"Where are you going?" he asked.

"Where that boy came from," I answered.

"Do you mind if I come, too? As far as the house, say?"

"Why do you want to come?"

He spoke with a certain calm authority. "I think I've a right to come. You must excuse me for saying that I think I know with whom we're dealing. We may very likely be in for a row, Austin. I don't want to be seen, if I can help it, but I do want to be somewhere handy in case my father—well, in case there is a row, you know."

Yes, we knew with whom we might have to deal. A row was not unlikely.

"Very well, come along," I said.

The clock struck seven as we started out into a dull, foggy, chill evening. Darkness had fallen and the lights of Catsford twinkled in the valley beneath us. As we began to walk, I heard carriage wheels on the road behind us. Fillingford was on his way to Breysgate. Lie well, Chat! Be clever! Keep him there—keep him there, till the danger is overpast!

CHAPTER XIV

THE EIGHT-FIFTEEN TRAIN

IF Jenny were bound to see Leonard Octon that evening, why had she not sent for him to her own house? In order that the servants might not know, and spread the gossip among their friends in other households? For fear that some of the neighbors, to whom she had sacrificed him, might pass by and see him going in or coming out, or even might call and encounter him there? A visit from the Aspenicks, from Lacey, from Alison, was not impossible. Who could say that Fillingford himself would not do as, in fact, he had done, and go to Breysgate on receipt of her letter? There were plausible reasons to be given for her action, but they were not, coolly regarded, of sufficient strength to outweigh the great fact that, whereas a meeting at Breysgate might have been reckoned a bit of defiance and unfriendliness to Fillingford and his allies, a meeting at Ivydene or, above all, at Hatcham Ford was open to a far more damaging interpretation; it was a terrible risk, an indiscretion fatal if discovered.

For the motives which determined her action, it is necessary, I believe, to look deeper, less to her reasoning, more to her character, and to the feeling under whose sway she was. Her obstinate courage refused to show the white feather to her distrust of Powers; that very distrust itself appealed to her love of a risk. She would do the thing because it was dangerous—because, if it came off well, the peril of it would have made it so much sweeter to her taste, would have given the flavor of mystery she loved, and been such a defiance of fate as was an attraction to her spirit. " Once more! " always appealed to Jenny; to try once more—once again beyond the point of safety. " Once more! " has appealed to—and has ruined—many lovers. Is not the scene, too, something? To lovers a meeting in the old place is doubly a meeting, and becomes a memory of double strength. The shrine has its sacredness as well as the deity; the spirit of the encounter is half lost in alien surroundings. " Once more—in the old place! " So she felt on the evening when she was to meet for the last time the man whom she dared not keep with her, but whose going wrung her heart. Farewell it was—it should be full farewell!

Lacey and I ran till we nearly reached the gates of the park; then we walked quickly, pausing now and again to listen for carriage wheels behind us. We heard none. Fillingford was lingering at Breysgate—Chat must be playing her game well! Jenny was in bed and perhaps would get up—or Jenny was out and would soon be back; by some story or other Chat was fighting to keep him where he was. The thought gave hope, and I pushed on. Lacey kept pace with me; he never spoke till we came opposite to Ivydene, and saw the shrubberies of Hatcham Ford on our right.

"That's as far as I go," said Lacey, "for the present. It's no business of mine unless my father comes —and wants me."

I left him standing in the road, just opposite the gate of Hatcham Ford, which was open. I went on to Ivydene and knocked. I waited, but nobody came. I knocked again impatiently. There was a clatter of hob-nailed shoes along the stone passage inside. The door was opened by the boy in the red cap.

"Ah, Alban, how are you? Is your father in?"

"No, sir—mother's out, too, sir. I'm taking care of the house." The boy looked pleased and proud— almost as if he knew, though of course he did not, the importance he had possessed in our eyes that day.

"Do you know where your father is?"

"I think he's at Hatcham Ford, sir. Mr. Octon came across a little while ago and asked for father, and when father came to the door he told him to get his hat and come back to the Ford with him. I expect he's there still."

"Thank you, Alban. I'll go and have a look."

I expected to find Powers on guard, acting scout, before the door or in the shrubbery, and quickly crossed the road to the Ford. As I went, I looked about for Lacey, but could see him nowhere. Either he had gone back along the road toward Breysgate, to watch for Fillingford's possible approach, or else he had thought he might attract attention if he loitered in the road, and had taken refuge from observation in the shrubberies. I passed quickly along the

Jenny was crouching on the floor beside Powers

THE EIGHT-FIFTEEN TRAIN

gravel walk, went up to the hall door, and rang the bell.

A moment or two passed. Then Octon himself opened the door. The light of the gas jet over the doorway was full on his face; he was very pale, and drops of perspiration stood on his brow. But when he saw me his face lit up with a sudden relief. "You! Thank God!" he said. "The very man we wanted! Come inside."

"Is she here?"

"Yes."

"She mustn't stay a minute. There's danger."

"I know there is," he said grimly. "We found that out from Powers. I've killed him, Austin, or all but. Come into the dining-room."

I followed him into the room where I had once waited while he and Jenny talked. As we passed through the hall, I noticed a portmanteau and a bag standing ready packed.

In the dining-room Jenny was crouching on the floor beside Powers; she was giving him something to drink out of a wineglass. The man lay there inert. I went up and looked at him, bending down close. There were marks of fingers on his neck; he had been half strangled.

Jenny had taken no notice when I came in. Now she looked up. "It's all right, he's coming to," she said. "I thought he was gone, though. We made him confess what he'd done, you know. Then he grew insolent, and Leonard—" She turned to Octon with a smile. She seemed to say, "Well, you can guess what Leonard would do under those circumstances!"

"You must come away from here," I said in a low urgent voice. " Fillingford may be here at any moment. He went to Breysgate first—but he'll come on here. He knows—and he means to find you."

"If he knows, what does it matter whether he finds me or not? And what are we to do with Powers?"

"Leave him to me. I'll get him back to his own house." I had it in my mind that I could call Lacey to help me to carry him.

While I spoke, she was giving the man another drink. He gurgled in his throat and moved uneasily. She looked up again: "He's doing all right, but— hadn't Leonard better go?"

"Nonsense," said Octon. "I'm here to see it through."

"No, no," I said hastily. "She's right, you go. This may be a police matter, if he takes it that way— or if Fillingford comes and finds him. If you're here, you may be arrested. Then everything's got to come out! For her sake you ought to go."

"You must go, Leonard," said Jenny. She propped Powers's head on a footstool and rose to her feet.

"It would be the best thing," said Octon. "It's only to-night instead of to-morrow morning."

His decision was taken. He lingered only one minute. He held out both his hands to her, and she put hers in them. I looked away; by chance my eyes fell on the mantelpiece. It struck me differently somehow; in an instant it occurred to me that the picture of the beautiful young girl was not there.

"There's a fast train to London at 8.15. You can

catch that," I said. " And you'd better go abroad to-morrow. I can let you know what happens."

" Wire as soon as you can—Grand Hotel to-night—to-morrow, the Continental, Paris. Write to-morrow, and send my portmanteau; I'll take my bag. I shall come back if there's any trouble."

" No, no, you mustn't," said Jenny.

" Well, we'll see about that presently. Good-by."

I watched him go into the hall and take up his bag; then I came back to Jenny.

" Now come away," I said, quickly. " You don't want to meet Fillingford, and he may be here any minute. I'll see you safe on the road, then I'll come back to this fellow. We can hush it all up—it's only a matter of enough money."

I heard the wheels of a carriage in the road. Jenny held up her hand for silence. We listened a moment. The carriage stopped at the gate of Hatcham Ford. It was Fillingford—Would he meet Octon? I feared that Octon would take no pains to avoid him.

In that I was wrong. The situation had sobered him. He had seen where lay the best chance for Jenny, and he would not throw it away. When the carriage drove up, he was just by the gate of Ivydene—Lacey, hidden in the shrubberies, saw him there. He drew back into the shadow of the gate and watched Fillingford get out. Fillingford, intent on Hatcham Ford, never glanced in his direction. When Fillingford had gone in, he resumed his way to the station.

When I heard the carriage stop, I cried to Jenny,

"He mustn't find you! Run upstairs somewhere—I'll manage to send him away."

"What's the good?" she asked. "We've got to have it out; we may as well have it out now." She looked at me haughtily. "I'm not inclined to hide from Lord Fillingford."

Powers's hand went up to his throat; he coughed and gurgled again. She looked down at him with a smile. "What's the good of hiding me? You can't hide that!"

"I won't let him in at all!" I cried.

"What's the good? He'll know I'm here if you do that. It's best to let him in. I'm not afraid to meet him, and I'd rather—know to-night."

His knock came on the door. I went and opened it. He started at the sight of me.

"You, Mr. Austin? I was looking for Mr. Octon."

"He's not here," I answered. "He has just left for London."

He seemed to hesitate for a moment. "Then are you alone here?" he asked.

Before I had time to think of my answer, Jenny's voice came from the dining-room. "I am here. Bring Lord Fillingford into this room, Austin."

He did not start now, but he bit his lip. I stood aside to let him pass, and shut the door after him. Then I followed him into the dining-room. Jenny was standing near the fire beside Powers, who kept shifting his head about on the footstool with stiff awkward movements. Fillingford came to the middle of the room and bowed slightly to Jenny; then his eyes fell on Powers and, in sudden surprise, he pointed his finger at him.

"My servant—and your spy," she said. "He has had a narrow escape of his life."

"So it's true," he said—not in question, but to himself, in a very low voice. "True to-night—and true often before!"

She made no attempt at denial. "Yes, I have often been here. I'll answer any question you like to put—and answer it truthfully.

"What I know is enough. I impute no more than I know."

"I thank you for that at least. It's only justice, but justice must be hard to give—from you to me."

"But what I know is—enough."

"You've a perfect right to say so."

Both were speaking calmly and quietly. There was no trace of passion in their voices. Neither took any heed of me, but I stayed—since she had not bidden me go.

He took a letter from his pocket. I recognized the large square envelope as of the shape which Jenny used.

"The letter you were so good as to send me this afternoon," he said, holding it up in his hand.

"Yes."

"I read it with very great pleasure." He tore it into four pieces and flung them on the table before him. They lay there between him and Jenny. He looked at her with a smile. "You're not like Eleanor Lacey for nothing," he said.

She smiled, too, and raised a hand to restrain me,

for at his bitter taunt I had made a step forward, meaning to interpose.

"Probably not!" she answered. Then she turned to me. "You'll look after Powers for me, won't you, Austin? It's only a matter of money with him, as we all know—and Mr. Cartmell has plenty."

"I'll do all I can to prevent your being troubled at all."

"I shan't be troubled—but I shall be grateful to you. Lord Fillingford, in return for your compliment, may I beg a favor of you?" She had given a quick glance at the clock.

"Anything that it's in my power to grant," he answered with a little bow.

"It's nothing great—only the loan of your carriage. I came here on foot—and I'm tired."

"It's quite at your disposal."

"It's not inconvenient? You're not hurried?"

"I can walk, Miss Driver."

"Please don't do that. I'll send it back for you as quickly as possible."

"As you please," he said courteously.

"Good-night, Austin," she said to me, holding out her hand. "Don't come with me. I'd rather find my own way to the carriage, if you and Lord Fillingford will let me."

I took her hand. She gave mine a quick light squeeze. "God bless you, Austin," she said. Then, with a last slight salutation to Fillingford, she walked out of the room—and we heard the hall door shut behind her. Fillingford stood where he was for a moment, then slowly sat down. I went to the table and collected the fragments of Jenny's letter. I made a gesture toward the fire. He nodded. I flung the pieces into the flames.

Powers slowly raised his head, leaning on his elbow. "Where am I?" he muttered.

"Not where you ought to be," I said. He laid his head down again, grumbling inarticulately.

"We want no publicity about this, Mr. Austin," said Fillingford—he spoke quite in his usual reserved and measured way. "I shall be willing to second your efforts in that direction. This man had better be got out of the town quietly—that can probably be managed by using the appropriate means. For the rest, no public announcement having been made, nothing need be said. It will probably be desirable for me to go away for a few weeks—that is, if Miss Driver prefers to remain at Breysgate. Or, if she takes a short holiday, I can remain—just as she wishes."

"I think it can all be managed, Lord Fillingford. We must try to have as little gossip as possible—for everybody's sake."

"You don't want my help to-night?"

"Oh, no. I can get him home. He'll soon be well enough, I hope, to understand that it's his interest to hold his tongue, and I can settle the rest with him to-morrow. If he is inclined to make trouble——"

"I think that we can persuade him between us. If you need my help, let me know."

"I'm much obliged to you for that." I paused for a moment. "You, I suppose, have no business with him just now?"

He looked at me gravely. "I am informed that he has already been paid for his services," he said. "Such services, Mr. Austin, are, as your tone implied, not very pleasant to receive. But the greater fault seems to lie with those whose methods make them necessary." He rose to his feet, saying, "It'll be some time before the carriage gets back. I think I'll start on my way and meet it. You're sure I can be of no use? No? Then good-night, Mr. Austin."

"Good-night, Lord Fillingford."

"You will communicate with me, if necessary?"

"Yes. I don't see why it should be."

With these words we had reached the door, and I opened it. At the moment I saw the lamps of his carriage at the gate.

"Look, the carriage is back already; it can't have taken her half the way!"

He made no reply, and we walked quickly down the path together.

"You took Miss Driver home, Thompson?" Fillingford asked the coachman.

"No, my lord, not to Breysgate. Miss Driver wished to go to the station. I drove there and set her down. She told me to come back here immediately, my lord."

"To the station?" we both exclaimed, startled into an involuntary show of surprise.

The man hesitated a little. "I—I beg pardon, my lord, but I think Miss Driver meant to go by train. She asked me to drive quickly—and she'd just have managed the eight-fifteen."

I looked at my watch, it was just on half-past eight.

"Perhaps she only wanted to see—somebody—off," said Fillingford, soon recovered from his momentary lapse into a betrayal of surprise. He turned to me. "That'll be it, Mr. Austin."

I looked at his face—there was no telling anything from it. It had given no sign of change as he made his reference to Octon. I think that he must have seen something in mine, for he added in a low voice, "Very likely that's all." He seemed to urge this view upon me.

Well, it was not an unlikely view. She had risked much for a last talk with Octon. She might well be tempted to seek another, a final, farewell. But I was very uneasy.

Without more words, merely with a polite lift of his hat, Fillingford got into his carriage and was driven off toward the Manor. I turned and walked slowly back to the house. Lacey came out from the shrubbery on the left of the path. "Well?" he said.

"I want your help inside," I said.

He asked no questions. We went in together and set to work with Powers. With the help of brandy and a shaking we got him on his feet. Soon he was well enough to be led home. His wife was in by now and opened the door for us. I told her that he had had a kind of seizure, but was much better—there was no need of a doctor. I sent her to get his bed ready. Then I had a word with him.

"Can you understand business?" I asked.

"Yes—I feel queer, though."

"Hold your tongue and you shall be well paid. Talk, and you won't get a farthing. Do you understand that?"

"Yes, Mr. Austin."

"Very well, act on it for to-night—and I'll come and see you to-morrow."

I left his wife getting him to bed. I do not think that the story of the seizure imposed on her, but she pretended to accept it. Probably she was accustomed to his having accidents—the risks of the trade he practiced were considerable. Meanwhile Lacey had been over to the Ford again, and left a written message on the table, saying that Octon had been called to town and would not be back that night. All else could wait till to-morrow. Now I wanted to get back to Breysgate. Lacey, too, was for home, which he could reach quicker by the public road than by coming round through our park. He had put to me no question at all up to now. Just as we were parting he did ask two.

"We didn't bring it off, I gather?"

I shook my head. Most certainly we had not brought it off.

"How did the—the governor behave?"

One speech of "the governor's" had been perhaps a little bitter. That was his right; and the bitterness was in the high manner—as Jenny herself had felt.

"He behaved—perfectly." That description was—from our side—only his due.

Lacey looked at me, smiled woefully, and shrugged his shoulders. "Yes—and so he's lost her!" he said. He turned on his heel, and swung off into the darkness. I was left with a notion that we possessed a man more than we had counted in our neighborhood.

I made for the Priory—*ventre-à-terre*. Something had come home to Jenny when Fillingford tore up her letter and told her that she was not like Eleanor Lacey for nothing. Till then she had been negotiating—negotiating still, though ever so defiantly—still trying to find out what he thought, trying to see what view he took, even though she ostentatiously abstained from self-defense. At that action and at that speech she had frozen. "Probably not!" That was her acceptance of his action and his words. She had taken them for her answer—the tearing of the letter and his one bitter speech.

The big house lay hospitably open to the night—lights in the windows, lamps burning in the hall and illuminating the approach. Well, it was early evening yet—only nine o'clock. All might be safe and well within doors, and yet the doors be open. I ran up the steps in a passion of excitement.

As I reached the door, I was met—not by Loft nor by any of the men—but by the trembling figure of a woman. Chat had heard feet on the steps—she had been in waiting! My heart sank as lead. Whom had she been waiting for? Not for me!

"I did my best, I did my best," she whispered, catching me by the lapel of my greatcoat. "I kept him as long as I could. What happened?"

"The worst of luck. Is she here?"

"Here?" She seemed amazed. "No! Did you see her? Where have you left her?"

"Then she's gone," I said.

Chat stood where she was for a second, then dropped into the hall-porter's chair which was just behind her. She began to sob violently, rocking herself to and fro. " I tried, I tried, I tried! " she kept saying through her sobs.

I became suddenly aware that Loft had come into the hall. He appeared not to notice Chat. He stood there, grave and attentive, awaiting my orders.

" Miss Driver has been suddenly called away. I don't think she'll be home to night. If she should come, the night-watchman will let her in, and Miss Chatters will be up. The rest of you needn't wait after your usual time."

" Very good, sir," said Loft. Gravely, with his measured step, he walked away and left us alone together.

Chat stopped sobbing for a moment—to ask me a supremely unimportant question.

" Was she very angry with me, Mr. Austin? "

" She didn't say one word about you."

" Oh, I'm glad of that, I'm glad of that! " Her sobbing again broke the silence of the great empty house.

CHAPTER XV

IN THE DOCK

SHE had gone—and we, her friends, were left to make the best of the situation.

It proved, indeed, easy enough to deal with Powers; the police court was not to be added to our troubles! The man was thoroughly frightened and shaken; confronted with the suggestion that Octon might well return in a few days, he was eager to hide himself. Cartmell took advantage of his mood and pared down his money cruelly; he took what he could get—no doubt he had been well paid from Fillingford Manor—and within two days was out of Catsford with all his belongings. There, one might well hope, was an end of Powers; even Jenny would not call him back again!

But an end of Powers did not much mend matters; even the fact that Jenny's engagement to Fillingford had not been formally announced failed to assist them to any great extent. The engagement had been a subject of general speculation, confidently foretold and almost daily expected. Now the subject of common talk was very different. Jenny was gone, Octon was gone. So far, perhaps, little. One might return, the other had, no doubt, good reasons for departure.

But there were witnesses of their departure together, and of circumstances which made it look strange. Alison the Rector was one of these—a friendly unimpeachable witness. He had been seeing two lads off to London—former members of his choir who had returned to pay a visit to old friends—and he told Cartmell (he did not speak to me, nor, I believe, to anybody but Cartmell) how he had seen Jenny come hurriedly on to the platform; she was veiled, but her face was easily to be distinguished, and her bearing alone would have caused her to be recognized. She stood for a moment looking about her, then caught sight of Octon's tall figure by the bookstall. She went straight up to him. He turned with a start. " The man's face when he saw her was a wonder," said Alison. They talked a little, then walked to the train. Octon spoke to the guard and gave him money. The guard put them into a compartment and turned the key. No sign of companion, maid, footman, or even luggage, appertaining to Jenny! Did Miss Driver of Breysgate Priory travel by night to London in that fashion?

What he had seen others saw—both Jenny and Octon were well known in Catsford—and others were less reticent than the Rector. When no announcement was made of Jenny's return and none of her engagement, when Powers vanished and Ivydene was shut up, then the stream of talk began to flow. Fillingford was loyally silent; his silence seemed only to add significance to the rumors. Lacey abruptly rejoined his regiment, though he had engagements for three weeks ahead—yet another unexplained de-

IN THE DOCK

parture! The whole town—the whole neighborhood—were agog. Human nature being what it is, small blame to them!

Of course his interview with Alison sent Cartmell flying up to me in excitement and consternation. He had become devoted to Jenny; he was devoted also to that fabric of influence and importance which she had been building for herself. He was terribly upset. He had not been so far behind the scenes as I had, or as Chat; the catastrophe came on him with unmitigated suddenness. He had been a great partisan of the Fillingford match; that crumbled before his eyes. But the greater blow was the mystery of her flight with Octon.

"I can tell you nothing. We must wait for a letter." It was all I could say unless and until Jenny gave me leave to speak.

That she did promptly, so far as Cartmell was concerned, thereby enabling me to use his services in regard to Powers. A letter arrived on Saturday morning—the flight had been on Thursday. It was a brief letter, and a businesslike one. It showed two things: that Jenny was, for the moment, in London—she did not say where—and that she was not coming back. It told me to take Cartmell into my full confidence, to tell him all I knew; neither he, nor Chat, nor I, was to say a word to anybody else. "Announce that I am going to winter abroad, and say nothing else—absolutely nothing—no explanations, no excuses, no guesses. Say just what I have told you, and nothing else. Tell Chat that I want nothing sent on. I shall get what I want. I will write at length about business—to you or to Mr. Cartmell—as soon as I have made my plans." Then she bade me go to Hatcham Ford, to pay off Octon's two servants, and have the house put in charge of a caretaker. That injunction was the only reference to Octon; of her own position, feelings, or intentions in respect to him she made no mention whatever.

Cartmell heard the letter, and the story which, in obedience to it, I told him, without signs of very great surprise. He twisted his mouth about and grunted over Jenny's folly and double-dealing—but to his practical mind the present situation was the question; my story seemed to make that more, not less, explicable. Jenny, in honor pledged to Fillingford, found that she wanted to marry Octon; she had not dared to tell Fillingford so; hence all the subterfuges, the secret meetings, the catastrophe, and the flight.

"In a day or two we shall get news of their marriage, no doubt. It's very silly, and not very creditable—but it's hardly a tragedy, Austin. Only—there goes Fillingford Manor forever! And what a master for Breysgate!"

His was as plain and reasonable a view as the situation could be fitted into. Jenny would now marry Octon, wait till the sensation was over, and then come back to Breysgate with her husband. Or perhaps she would not come back to Breysgate; perhaps she would not face the neighborhood with her record behind her—and Octon by her side, ever recalling it. She would break up all the fabric which she had made—and start anew somewhere else. That did not seem unlikely; a suggestion of it filled Cartmell with fresh dismay.

"A pretty thing that!" he said. "After all our tall talk about our love for Catsford, and our Institute, and all the rest of it! How am I to face Bindlecombe, eh? And look at the money she's put into the estate! She'll never get that back on a sale."

I found Cartmell rather comforting—at least he created a diversion in my thoughts. His care for the externals of the position, for the material and even the pecuniary aspects of it, was a relief to an imagination which, all against its will, had been engrossed in the state and the struggle of Jenny's heart—dwelling on her intentions not about her estate and her Institute, but about herself, picturing the strong rush of feeling which had impelled her to her flight, asking whither it would lead or had led her—and asking doubtfully.

Cartmell tapped my knee with the end of his stick. "The sooner we get news of the marriage, the better —though bad's the best!" he said with a solemn nod of his head.

He was right—but most heartily did I echo his "Bad's the best!" Had Jenny herself ever thought differently—at least before that fatal night? What was she thinking now—when the night was past?

Two days later a long letter reached Cartmell; he came up to me with it directly after breakfast, when I was in my office at the Priory. A lonely, weary great place was the house now—no life in it; Chat in bed and probably in flutters—she had taken to both on the night of the disaster, and clung to both; Loft's face and gait was pronouncedly funereal. Visitors, of course, there were none. The establishment seemed to be in quarantine.

Jenny's letter was in her best style—concise, clear—and handsome. Everything was to go on at Breysgate as though she herself were there. Cartmell was given full control of finances—a power of attorney was to follow from London. Chat was to stay till further orders. Nothing was to be shut up, nobody to be dismissed. I was directed to take full charge of the house and grounds, allotted ample funds for the expenses, and intrusted with the care of all her correspondence. Urgent letters were to be sent under cover to her bankers at Paris; there all communications were to be addressed, thence all would come. Money for her own use was to be deposited there also. Finally, the Committee was fully empowered to proceed with the plans and preliminaries of the Institute; they were to be credited with five thousand pounds for this purpose. I was to act on her behalf and report progress to her from time to time. Whatever her feelings were, her brain was active, busy, and efficient.

"It doesn't look as if she meant to give up Breysgate, anyhow," said Cartmell.

"Neither does it look as if she meant to come back," said I.

That, again, was like Jenny. She did not mean to come back, but neither did she mean to let go. She elaborately provided for a long absence, but by careful implication negatived the idea that the absence

IN THE DOCK

was to be permanent. Though she was not there, her presence was to be felt. Though she was away, she would rule through her deputies—Chat, Cartmell, the Institute Committee, myself. She forsook Catsford, but would remain a power there.

With all this, not a word of what she herself meant to do or where she meant to go—no explanation of the past or information about the future. Not a word of Octon—not a word of marriage! The old signature held still, " Jenny Driver." The silences of the letter were even more remarkable than its contents. The whole effect was one of personal isolation. That great local institution, Miss Driver of Breysgate, was all to the fore. Jenny had withdrawn behind an impenetrable veil. Miss Driver of Breysgate was benign, conciliatory, gracious, loyal to Catsford. Jenny was enigmatic, unapologetic, defiant. Jenny slapped while Miss Driver stroked. What would they make out of these contradictory attitudes of the dual personality?

Cartmell put his common-sense finger on the spot—on the very pulse of Catsford and the neighborhood.

" What they'll want to hear about is the marriage. Any irregularity in her position—! " He waved his hands expressively.

Graciousness and loyalty, charities continued and institutes built—excellent in their way, but no real use if there were any irregularity in her position! Cartmell was right—and I am far from wishing to imply that Catsford was wrong, or that its pulse beat otherwise than the pulse of a healthy locality should. The rules must be kept—at any rate, homage must be paid to them. Jenny herself never denied the obligation, whether it were to be regarded as merely social or as something more. It is no business of mine to question it on her behalf—and I feel no call to do it on my own account.

Cartmell's words flung a doubt. Was there much positive reason for that doubt yet? People may get married without advertising the fact. Even although they have departed by the same train for the same place, they may behave with propriety pending arrangements for a wedding. Jenny had great possessions; she was not to be married out of hand, like a beggar-girl. Settlements clamored to be made, lawyers to be consulted. Cartmell cut across these soothing reflections of mine.

"It's a funny thing that I've had no instructions about settlements. She'd surely never marry him without settlements?"

I cut my reflections adrift, it was the only line left open to me. "How could you expect a girl to think about them in such circumstances?"

"I should expect Jenny Driver to," he said.

"She'd be thinking of nothing except the romance of it."

"Is that the impression you get from her letter?"

"There are always two sides to her mind," I urged.

"One's in that letter," he said, pointing to it. "What's the other doing, Austin?"

To ask that question was, as things stood, to cry to an oracle which was dumb. Miss Driver of Breysgate spoke—but Jenny was obstinately mute. Before many days were out, Catsford became one colossal

"Why?" It must have been by a supreme effort, by a heartrending sacrifice to traditional decorum, that the editor of the *Herald and Times* refrained from writing articles or "opening our columns to a correspondence" on the subject.

At last there came a word about herself—to me and to me only. It was contained in the last communication I received from her before she left London; she spoke of herself as being "just off." The letter dealt with nothing more important than the treatment of a pet spaniel which had been ailing at the time of her flight. But there was a postscript, squeezed in at the foot of the page; the ink was paler than in the letter itself. It looked as though the postscript had been added by an afterthought—perhaps after hesitation—and blotted immediately. "I still hold my precarious liberty."

The one sentence answered one question—she was not married. There were things which it left unanswered; her present position and her intentions for the future lay still in doubt. She held her liberty, but the liberty was precarious. Here was no material for a reassuring public announcement; even if I had not been sure that the postscript was meant for me alone —and of that I was sure—I could only have held my tongue; it was charged with so fatal an ambiguity, it left so much in the dark. Yet in its way it was to me full of meaning, most characteristic, most illuminating—and it fitted in with the picture which my own imagination had drawn. Out of a tangle of hesitations and doubts she had plunged into her wild adventure. How far it had carried her it was not possible to say; but here were the hesitations and doubts back again. After the impulsive fervor of feeling had had its way with her, the cool and cautious brain was awake again—awake and struggling. The issue was doubtful; the liberty to which her mind clung was " precarious "—menaced and assailed by a potent influence. Past experience made it easy to appreciate the state in which she was—her wishes on one side, her fears on the other—her strong inclination to Octon against her obstinate independence, her feelings crying for surrender, her mental instinct urging that she should still keep the line of retreat open.

But was it still open in any effective sense? As regards her position, so far as the opinion of the world —of her world—went, every day barred it more and more. She must know that; she must realize how her silence would be interpreted, how no news about her would be confidently reckoned the worst of news. For Octon she had sacrificed so much that there was nothing for it but to give him all—to give him even her liberty, if marriage with him meant the loss of it. There was no other possible conclusion if she would look at the matter as others looked at it, if she would use the eyes and ears of Catsford, and see what they made of her situation. But perhaps she was no readier to surrender herself to them than to Octon himself. She might answer that in her own soul she would still be free, though her freedom were bought at a great price, though in the eyes of the world she had forfeited her right to it.

My memory harked back to a conversation which

I had once held with Alison. A mind that thought for itself in worldly matters, I had suggested to him, would very likely think for itself in moral or religious ones, too—and such thought was apt to issue in suspending general obligations in a man's own case. I had hazarded the opinion that Miss Driver would be capable of suspending a general obligation in her own case—as the result of careful thought about it— as an exercise of power, to repeat the phrase I had used. If that were her disposition now—if what I had foreshadowed as a possibility had become a fact —would Octon save her from the results of it? He was the last man in the world to do that. Skeptic in mind and rebel in temper, he would not insist on obedience to obligations in whose sanction he did not believe, nor be urgent in counseling outward conformity with conventions which he disliked and took a positive pleasure in scorning. On the other hand, he would not be swayed by a vulgar self-interest; he would be too proud to seek to bind her to him that he might thus bind her money also. If she said "I will remain free," he would acquiesce and might even applaud. If she said "I will be free and yet with you," it was not likely that he would offer any strong opposition.

Meanwhile she stood where people who arrogate to themselves the liberty of defying the law cannot reasonably complain of standing—in the dock. That is the fair cost of the freedom they claim. Jenny was arraigned at the bar of the public opinion of her neighbors; unless she could and would clear herself of suspicion, there was not much doubt how the verdict would go. The first overt step in the proceedings took place under my own eyes.

Cartmell had apprised Bindlecombe of Jenny's wish that the work of the Institute should proceed in her absence, and of her financial arrangements to this end. Bindlecombe, as Chairman, convened a meeting of the Committee. Cartmell was out of town that day and did not attend, but I went to represent Jenny's side of the affair. Fillingford and Alison were talking together in low voices when I came in. Fillingford greeted me with his usual reserved courtesy, Alison with even more than his wonted kindness. Bindlecombe was visibly nervous and perturbed as he read to us Cartmell's letter. When he had finished it, he looked across the table to Alison and said, "I understand that you have something to say, Mr. Alison?"

"What I have to say, sir, is soon said," Alison answered. He spoke low and very gravely, like a man who discharges an imperative but distasteful task. "The Institute is very closely connected with the personality of the liberal—the very liberal—donor. In my opinion—and I believe that I am very far from being alone in the opinion—it is inexpedient to proceed with the work until we can feel sure of being able to enjoy Miss Driver's personal coöperation. I move that, while thanking Miss Driver for the offer contained in the letter we have just heard, we express to her our opinion in that sense." He had not looked at any of us, but had kept his eyes lowered as he spoke.

There was a moment's pause. Then Fillingford

said, " I agree, and I second the motion." His voice was entirely impassive. " I don't think it is necessary for me to add anything."

Bindlecombe turned to me with an air of inquiry.

" I can take no part in this," I said. " It is simply for me to hear the decision of the Committee and to communicate it to Miss Driver in due course."

Bindlecombe clasped his hands nervously; he was acutely distressed—and not only for the threatened loss of his darling Institute. He knew how Jenny would read the resolution, and Jenny had been his idol.

" Is—is this really necessary? " he ventured to ask, though Alison's sad gravity and Fillingford's cold resoluteness evidently overawed him. " Perhaps some of the preliminary work could——? "

Alison interposed; " I fear I must ask that my resolution be put as it stands."

Fillingford nodded, drumming lightly on the table with his fingers. Evidently they had made up their minds; if the resolution were not passed, they would secede. That would be worse than the resolution itself, and would make progress just as impossible.

" Then I'll put it," said Bindlecombe reluctantly. " No gentleman desires to say any more? "

No more was said. The resolution was carried, I, of course, not voting.

" And I suppose that we adjourn—*sine die*? " said Bindlecombe.

That followed as of course, and we all three assented. Bindlecombe rose from the chair. There, for the present at all events, was an end of the Institute, there Jenny's first public and official rebuff. Catsford would have to be told what had been decided, why no more was done about the Institute. I had no doubt that Alison had thought of this and had worded his resolution with a view to its publication.

Fillingford and Alison went out of the room together, and I was left with Bindlecombe. (We had met at his house, Ivydene being shut up.) " I'm very sorry for this, Mr. Austin," he said.

I was very sorry, too. The decision would not be a grateful one to Jenny. It was an intimation that her idea of keeping her hold on Catsford, even while she defied it, would not work; the dual personality of munificent Miss Driver of Breysgate and wayward Jenny Driver—of where?—would not find acceptance.

"A winter abroad is not eternity, Mr. Bindlecombe," said I, smiling. "We shall be busy at the Institute again by the spring, I hope." That, of course, was speaking to my cue—Jenny's official version of her departure; she was wintering abroad—that was all.

"I hope so, I hope so," he said, but he hardly pretended that he was imposed upon. He shook his head dolefully and looked at me with a gloomy significance. "The Rector's a hard fellow to deal with. Pleasant as can be, but hard as a brick on—well, where his own views come in. He's not a man of the world, Mr. Austin."

Evidently in Bindlecombe's opinion a man of the world would have stuck to the Institute, even if he could not stick to its donor—stuck to the Institute and carved *Non Olet* on its handsome façade; it would have been in no worse case than many imposing public buildings—to say nothing of luxurious private residences. But Alison was not a man of the world—and in this instance the current of opinion was with him. The two worlds joined in condemning Jenny; neither as an individual nor as a local institution could she be defended. A lurking loyalty in Bindlecombe—if I mistook not, a reluctant admiration in Lacey—were the only exceptions to the general verdict—outside her own retainers. I do not think that we asked ourselves questions about approval or disapproval, condemnation or condonation. We were not judges; we were, in one way, in the fight.

To my surprise Alison was waiting outside the house. When I came out, he approached me.

"Austin, I want you to shake hands with me," he said. "I had to do that, you know. You don't suppose I liked doing it?"

"I'll shake hands," I said. "I'm not particular. But I don't feel called upon to have any opinion as to whether you're right, nor as to whether you liked doing it or not."

"That last bit's unfair, anyhow," he declared indignantly.

"Fair and unfair! Man, man, do you suppose I'm worrying about things like that?"

I had lost control for a moment. He was not angry with me; he seemed to understand, and patted my shoulder affectionately.

"Of course I know you didn't like doing it," I growled. "But does that make things any better?"

"Tell her I didn't like doing it," he said. "If only she understood why I had to do it!"

Well, from neither of the worlds can defiance look for mercy.

CHAPTER XVI

NOT PROVEN

IN the stern condemnation of moral delinquencies, when such are discovered or conjectured, we may be content to find nothing but what is praiseworthy; the simultaneous exhibition of a hungry curiosity about them is one of those features of human nature which it is best to accept without comment—if only for the reason that no man can be sure that he does not in some degree share it. In Catsford at this time it was decidedly prominent. The place went wild on the news that Sir John Aspenick, happening to be in Paris on a flying visit, thought that he saw Jenny go by as he stood outside the Café de la Paix: great was the disappointment that Sir John could not contrive even to think that he had seen Octon with her! Lady Sarah Lacey, working on the feminine clew of Jenny's having departed luggageless, set inquiries afoot among London dressmakers, with the happy result of revealing the fact that Jenny had bought a stock of several articles of wearing apparel: the news worked back to Chat from one of the dressmakers, and from Chat I had it, with more details of the wearing apparel that my memory carries. Mrs. Jepps waylaid Chat—who had timidly ventured into the town under a pressing need of finding some very special form of needle —in the main street and tried the comparative method, not at all a bad mode of investigation where manners forbid direct questions. She told Chat numbers of stories of other "sad cases" and looked to see how Chat "took" them—hoping to draw, augur-like, conclusions from Chat's expression. I myself— well, I would not be uncharitable. My friends were all honorable men; they might naturally conclude that I was depressed and lonely; why look farther for the cause of the frequent visits from them which I enjoyed? Bindlecombe and a dozen more so honored me, and Cartmell told me that only the severest office discipline kept his working hours sacred from kind intruders.

Moreover, a little problem arose, not in itself serious, but showing the extreme inconvenience which results when people who are in a position to confer pleasant favors so act as to make it doubtful whether favors can properly be accepted from them. Such a state of affairs puts an unfair strain on virtue, inconsiderately demanding martyrdom where righteousness only has been volunteered. As may have been gathered, Jenny's neighbors were in the habit of using the road through her park as an alternative route to the high road in their comings and goings to and from Catsford. For some it was shorter—as for the Wares, the Dormers, and the Aspenicks; for all it was pleasanter. What was to be done about this now? Fillingford had no doubt; neither he nor Lady Sarah used the park road any more; but then the road was no great saving of distance for the folks at the Manor—their martyrdom was easy—whereas it was very materially shorter for the Wares, the Dormers, and, above all, for the Aspenicks. The question was so acute for the Aspenicks that I heard of Lady Aspenick's collecting opinions on the subject from persons of light and leading. She did not consider Fillingford's course impartial—nor decisive of the question; it was easy for him to take the virtuous line; it did not involve his going pretty nearly two miles out of his way.

Discussion ran high on the question. Mrs. Jepps declared against using the road, though her fat pair of horses had been accustomed to get what little exercise they ever did get along it three afternoons a week.

"If I use the road, and she comes back and finds me using it, where am I?" asked Mrs. Jepps. "I can't cut her when I'm driving in her park by her permission. Yet I may feel obliged to refuse to bow to her!"

The attitude had all Mrs. Jepps's logic in it; it was unassailable. Very reluctantly old Mr. and Mrs. Dormer gave in to it—they would go round by the King's highway, longer though it was. Bertram Ware, lawyer and politician, stole round the difficulty—and along the park road—by adopting a provisional attitude; until more was known, he felt justified in using—and in allowing Mrs. Ware to use —the road. He reserved liberty of action if more facts condemnatory of Jenny should appear.

The Aspenicks remained—to whom the road was

more precious than to any of the others. Sir John would have none of Ware's provisional attitude—it was not what he called " straight "; but then he had a prejudice against lawyers, and held no particularly high opinion of Bertram Ware.

" Make up your mind," he said to his wife. " Either we use it or we don't. But if we use it, it's taking a favor from her, and that may be awkward later on."

Now Lady Aspenick wanted to use the road very much indeed—and not merely the road for her tandem, so sadly famous in history, but also the turf alongside it for her canters. But in the first place Lady Aspenick was herself a model of propriety, and in the second—it was an even weightier consideration—she had a growing girl; Eunice Aspenick was now nearly sixteen—and rode with her mother. Supposing Lady Aspenick and Eunice used the road, supposing Jenny were guilty of enormities, came back guilty of them, and discovered Lady Aspenick, with Eunice, on the road! Lady Aspenick's problem was worse than Mrs. Jepps's—because of Eunice on the one hand, and of Lady Aspenick's remarkably strong desire to use the road on the other.

This question of the road—work on the Institute at a standstill—no more parties at Breysgate (what of the Flower Show next summer?)! Verily Jenny was causing endless inconvenience!

It would not be just to say that this difficulty about the road—and Eunice—determined Lady Aspenick's attitude toward Jenny; it is perhaps permissible to conjecture that it led her to reconsider it.

After the lapse of a fortnight she came out on Jenny's side, and signified the same by calling on Chat at Breysgate Priory. Chat and I sometimes consoled one another's loneliness at afternoon tea; I was present when Lady Aspenick arrived.

We had our lesson pat—so long as we were not cross-examined. Jenny was wintering abroad; Chat's health (this was our own supplement) had made traveling inadvisable for her, and Jenny had found other companions. Lady Aspenick was most affable to the story; she admitted it to belief at once. Sympathy with Chat, pleasure at not being deprived of Chat's society, kind messages through Chat to Jenny—all came as easily and naturally as possible. Not an awkward question! It was with real gratitude that I conducted Lady Aspenick to her carriage. But she had a word for me there.

"I didn't want to talk about it to that poor old thing," she said, "but have you any—news, Mr. Austin?"

"None, except what I've told you. She isn't a great letter-writer."

"They're saying horrid things. Well, Sarah Lacey would, of course. I can't see any reason for believing them. I'm on her side! One may wonder at her taste —one must—but she has a right to please herself, and to take her own time about it. Of course that night journey—!" Lady Aspenick smiled in a deprecating manner.

"Impulsive!" I observed.

Lady Aspenick caught at the word joyfully. "That's it—impulsive! That's what I've always said.

Dear Jenny is impulsive—that's all!" She got into her carriage and ordered the coachman to drive her to Mrs. Jepps's. She was going to tell Mrs. Jepps that Jenny was impulsive—going by the road through the park to tell Mrs. Jepps that it was no more than that.

Her own line taken, Lady Aspenick gathered a tiny faction to raise Jenny's banner. They could not do much against Lady Sarah's open viciousness, Fillingford's icy silence, the union of High Church and Low in the persons and the adherents of Alison and of Mrs. Jepps. But Sir John followed his wife, Bindlecombe took courage to uplift a friendly voice, and old Mr. Dormer began to waver. His memories went back to George IV.—days in which they were not hard on pretty women—having, indeed, remarkably little right to be. Mr. Dormer was reported to be inclined to think that the men of the surrounding families might ride in Jenny's park—about their ladies it was, perhaps, another question. It was understood that Lady Aspenick's faction gave great offense at Fillingford Manor. The alliance between the two houses had been close, and Fillingford Manor saw treachery to itself in any defense of Jenny.

So they debated and gossiped, sparred and wrangled—and no more news came. At the Priory we began to settle down into a sort of routine, trying to find ourselves work to do, trying to fill the lives that seemed now so empty. Our position—like Bertram Ware's attitude about the park road—was provisional—hopelessly provisional. We were not living;

we were only waiting. Not the actual events of to-day, but the possible event of to-morrow was the thing for which we existed. It was like listening perpetually for a knock on the door. Little could be made of a life like that. Well, we were not to sink into the dullness of our routine just yet.

In my youth I have heard a sage preach to the young men, his hearers and critical disciples, on the text of the certainty of life; discarding, perhaps thinking trite, perhaps deeming misleading, the old *Memento mori.* He bade them recollect that for practical purposes they had to reckon on—and with—thirty, forty, fifty, years of life and activity. That was a long time—order the many days! You could not afford to calculate on the accident of an early death to end your responsibility. It was well said; yet not even the broadest sanest argument can altogether persuade Death out of his traditional rôle, nor induce Atropos to wield her shears always without caprice. Yet again, in this case there seemed little caprice; the likely ending came rather quickly—that was all; it was just such an ending as, in some form or other, might have been expected—just such as once, in talk with me, the man himself had, hardly gravely yet quite sincerely, treated as likely, almost as inevitable.

I was the first to get the news—at breakfast time one November morning. A telegram came to me from Jenny; it was sent from Tours. " Leonard has died from wound received in a duel. Do not come to me. I want to be alone.—JENNY DRIVER."

He had insulted somebody—in a country where

men still fought on the point of honor. The conclusion sprang forward on a glance. He had passed much time abroad, I knew—the code was not strange to him, nor the use of his weapons. Though both had been strange, little would he have shunned the fight! He would take joy in it—joy in shedding the advantage of his mighty strength, glad to meet his man on even terms, eagerly accepting the leveling power of a bullet. He had made himself intolerable again; some one had uprisen and done away with the incubus of him. The whole affair seemed just what might be looked for; he had died fighting —for him a natural death.

So the life was out of the big man—and he had been so full of it. That was strange to think of.

Somehow he seemed incompatible with death. I remember drawing a long breath as I said to myself "Dead!" and thought grewsomely of the carrying out of that great coffin—with all the mighty weight of him inside; even dead he would oppress men by size, insolently crushing their shoulders with his bulk. "Part of the objection to me is because I'm so large," he had said. Even the undertaker's men would share in that objection. "I shall certainly be stamped out." Ah, well, small wonder—and what a pity!"

He had a power over me; something of his force had reached me, too—or my thoughts would not have dwelt on him so long; they would have turned sooner to Jenny. To what end? Her message forbade the one thing which it was in my mind to do—go to her directly. She would not have it; she would be—

as she was—alone. I had no thought of disobedience —only a great sorrow that I must obey. I read the telegram again. " Jenny Driver!" She had hesitated too long. Ways could not be kept open forever. Mr. Powers had taught her this truth once, and she had not hearkened. Death himself came to enforce the lesson. She stood no longer between the fascination that she loved and feared and the independence which she cherished and yet wearied of. She was free perforce; the tenure of her liberty was no longer precarious; and the joy of her heart was dead. Her equipoise—another of her delicate balancings—was hopelessly upset; when Death flung his weight into one of her scales, the other kicked the beam.

So long as I was alone, it did not occur to me to think of the bearings of the event—and of its announcement—on her outward fortunes. My mind was with herself—asking how she faced the thing, in what mood it left her; nay, going back to the days before it, viewing them in the alien light of their sudden end. Not what would be said or thought, but what was, engrossed my meditation. Death brings that color to the mind; it takes us " beyond these voices." But they who live must soon return within hearing.

I did not hear Cartmell come in—I had been out before breakfast, and I believe I had left my door ajar. His hand was on my shoulder before I was aware of his presence. He held a morning paper in his hand, but he did not show it to me directly. He looked down in my face as I sat in my armchair and then said, " You've heard, haven't you?"

"Yes," I answered, giving him Jenny's telegram.

He read it. "This must be between you and me, Austin. So far, there's nothing in the paper to show that she was there—to show who the woman was, I mean."

"The woman?"

"The woman mentioned in the paper. Read it." He pushed it into my hand. His practical mind did not waste itself in memories or speculation; it flew to the present need. I had lost myself in wonderings about the man and the woman; he was concerned solely with our local institution—Miss Driver of Breysgate. He was right.

The telegram in the paper came from Reuter's news agency. "A quarrel in the Café de l'Univers last night resulted in a duel this morning, in which an Englishman named Octon was mortally wounded at the first fire. He subsequently expired at the house of a lady, understood to be Mrs. Octon, in the Rue Balzac, to which he had been carried at his own request."

Beneath was a short paragraph stating that it was conjectured that the "deceased gentleman" was "Mr. Leonard Octon, the well-known traveler and entomologist." On inquiry at his publishers', those gentlemen had stated that Mr. Octon was, to their knowledge, traveling in France.

"Not much harm done if it stops there," said Cartmell, thoughtfully rubbing his hands together.

"How can it? There'll have to be an inquest—or something corresponding to it, I suppose?"

"She's very clever."

"Will she care about being clever?" I asked, studying the paragraph again. "Understood to be Mrs. Octon" had a smack of Jenny's own ambiguity and elusiveness. And it hardly sounded as though the house to which he had been carried at his own request were the house where he himself had been lodging.

"Of course it'll be all over Catsford in an hour. There's no helping that. But, as I say, there's no particular harm done yet."

"They'll guess, won't they?"

"Of course they will; but there's all the difference between guessing and having it in print. We must wait. I've got to go out of town—and I'm glad of it."

I did not go away, but I hid myself. The only person I saw that day was Chat: she was entitled to the news.

Telling her was sad work; her devotion to Octon rose up against her accusingly. She railed at herself for all her dealings with Jenny; old-time delinquencies in duty at the Simpsons' dressed themselves in the guise of great crimes; she had been a guilty party to Jenny's misdemeanors; they had led to this.

"I shall have to render an account for it," said poor Chat, rocking her body to and fro, as was her habit in moments of agitation: her speech was obviously reminiscent of church services. "If I had done my duty by her, this would never have happened." I am afraid that "this" meant the scandal, rather than any conduct which gave rise to it. But if Chat were going to be so aggressively penitent as this, the case was lost.

"We must hope for the best—and, anyhow, put the best face on it," I urged.

Chat cheered up a little. "Dear Jenny is very resourceful." Cartmell had observed that she was clever. I was waiting with a vague expectancy for some move from her, some turn or twist in her favor. We had not lost faith in her, any of us; the faith had become blind—if you will, instinctive — surviving even the Waterloo of her flight and this calamitous tragedy.

Were we wrong? Only the future could show that; but the next day brought us some encouragement. There was a fuller paragraph, confirming the conjectured identification of Octon, giving a notice of his work, and the name of his opponent in the duel —an officer belonging to an old family distinguished for its orthodox Catholic opinions. "The quarrel is said to have originated in a discussion of religious differences." That sounded quite likely, and relieved the fear that it might have sprung from a more compromising origin. Then came—well, something very like an apology for that phrase about the lady "understood to be Mrs. Octon." The lady was not, it now appeared, Mrs. Octon; she was "a Miss Driver" (*A* Miss Driver—that would sound odd to Catsford!) to whom the deceased gentleman was engaged to be married. This Miss Driver had taken a house in the Rue Balzac, where she was residing with another lady, her friend: the deceased gentleman had recently arrived at the Hôtel de l'Univers; notice of their intended marriage had been given at the British Consulate three days before the fatal occurrence. A few days more would have seen them man and wife. " Much sympathy is felt for the lady under the very painful circumstances of the case. It is understood that she will leave Tours immediately after the funeral."

It would hardly be doing Cartmell a wrong to describe him as gleeful; the statement was so much less damaging than might have been expected. To the world at large it was, indeed, not damaging at all; it rather appealed to sympathy and invested Jenny with a pathetic interest. In Catsford the case was different: there was the flight, the silence, the interval. But even for Catsford we had a case—and the difference between even a bad case and no case at all is, in matters like this, enormous.

What was the truth of it? It was not possible to believe that the notice to the Consulate was a mere maneuver, a pretense, and a sham. She was neither so cold-blooded nor so foolish as that—and Octon would have ridiculed such a sham out of existence. The notice to the Consulate showed that her long hesitation had at last ended—possibly on Octon's entreaties, though I continued to doubt that—possibly for conscience' sake, possibly from regard for the world's opinion. She had made up her mind to let go her " precarious liberty." But for this stroke of fate she would have become Octon's wife.

How did the stroke of fate leave her? Or, rather, leave her fame? Of herself I knew nothing—save that she would be alone. She loved an equipoise. Her fame was balanced in one now. Fillingford and Lady Sarah, Mrs. Jepps and Alison, would think still what they had thought; probably the bulk of opinion would be with them. But we had a case. We could brazen it out. Bertram Ware could still be provisional, Lady Aspenick could use the road through the park—even Eunice might ride with her; and old Mr. Dormer would scarcely strain the proprieties to breaking point if he permitted himself to be accompanied by his wife. The verdict could be " Not Proven."

A week later the French authorities forwarded to me a letter from Octon—found on his table at the hotel and written the evening before the meeting:

" My Dear Austin—I have to fight a fellow tomorrow—a very decent fellow—on the ostensible ground of my having spoken disrespectfully of the Pope, which naturally is not at all the real cause of quarrel. I rather think I shall be killed—first, for the sensible reason that he is angry (I hit him. ' Of course you did,' I hear you say) and a good shot; secondly, because she has at last elected to settle things and that offers a temptation to chance—not such a sensible reason — indeed an utterly nonsensical one, which accordingly entirely convinces me. I leave her to you. Don't try to marry her—it only worries her —but serve her well, and as you serve her, so may God Almighty, in whom I believe though you think I don't, serve you. You couldn't spend your life (you're not a great man, you know) to better account. How I have spent mine doesn't matter. I have on the credit side of the balance the discovery of five new insects. It is to be hoped that this will not be overlooked.—Yours, L. O."

New insects—five! Private faults—how many? What is the Table of Weights? That must be known, to strike the balance of Leonard Octon's life.

CHAPTER XVII

ONE OF TWO LEGACIES

THE clouds settled down over Jenny; a veil of silence obscured her. Business letters were still exchanged through the bankers at Paris, but hers bore no postmarks; they must have arrived in Paris under cover; they came under cover to Breysgate, and thus gave no indication of her whereabouts. She was in constant communication with Cartmell about her affairs; to me she wrote much seldomer and only on necessity; to Chat she never wrote at all. To none of us, I believe, did she say a word about what had happened—and she certainly said no word to Catsford. Nor did we; her orders stood—no excuses, no explanations, no guesses. Thus starved of food, Catsford's interest at last languished; they did not forget Jenny, but talk about her catastrophe and Octon's death died down. Nobody having anything fresh to tell or any guess to make that had not been made already, the topic grew stale.

The long wait began—it was a wait to me, for I knew that she meant to come back in the end—and lasted for nearly three years. I employed an ample leisure in writing my essay on "The Future of Religious and Ethical Thought." It brought me some

ONE OF TWO LEGACIES

credit in the outside world—or rather the small part of it that cares for such speculations; but indifference was the best I hoped from Catsford—and I did not altogether achieve that. Friendship sometimes gives a writer what I may term unnatural readers—and not with the happiest results. Alison continued to be kind and cordial to me, but he would not talk about my book. Mrs. Jepps—what business had she with such a book at all?—shook her head over it, and over me, very solemnly, and, as I heard, was not slow to trace a connection between Jenny's acts and my opinions. I did the local reputation of Breysgate no good by that book, though its reception in the Press flattered my vanity considerably.

More important things happened in the neighborhood—for three years make differences in a little society. Old Mr. Dormer died, carrying off with him into the inaudible much agreeable anecdote; his cousin, a young man of thirty, reigned at Hingston in his stead. Bertram Ware was no longer M.P.; the domestic dissensions, in which Jenny had once seen an opportunity for herself, had ended in his retiring at the General Election; he was said to be sulky, and to be talking of selling his place and going away. Lacey, his majority just attained, had been put forward in his stead, and elected after a stiff fight with an eloquent stranger from London—(Bindlecombe reserved himself till Catsford should be given a borough member!)—I did not follow closely Lacey's doings—or anybody's—at Westminster, but he was assiduous in his social duties in the constituency. There was no change at Fillingford Manor, save that its master looked more definitely middle-aged, and its mistress riveted on our necks the power which Jenny's rise had threatened. Finally, Lady Aspenick's growing girl had grown, had "come out," and was a personage in our society. She was a rather pretty, tall, fair girl, great at all outdoor pursuits. The gossips had already begun to say that she would make a capital bride for Lacey—if only there were more money! The little cloud which had arisen between the two households over Jenny had naturally passed away, when absence and silence removed Jenny from the arena of discussion. None the less Lady Aspenick still used our road—and still Fillingford Manor did not.

Such was the petty chronicle. The Institute found no place in it. There nothing was done; even Bindlecombe seemed no longer sanguine. Hatcham Ford, with its windows shuttered and its gravel-path grass-grown, witnessed to a project apparently still-born, no less than it recalled the catastrophe of that last night. When I passed by, I could not help expecting to see Octon's great figure come out and slouch across the road—to smoke a pipe with Mr. Powers! He did not come, and a most respectable insurance agent now dwelt where Mr. Powers had played his unedifying game. Nor was the Flower Show any longer part of our Breysgate programme. Cartmell had offered the grounds, but the Committee preferred to accept a proposal from Fillingford. For the last two years it had been held at the Manor, and was to be held there again this year—this the third summer since Jenny left us.

ONE OF TWO LEGACIES

Then she came back. Her return was as sudden and as unannounced as her departure, but otherwise marked by considerably more decorum.

I was writing one morning after lunch, and had wandered to the window, to seek from the empty air an improbable inspiration. Suddenly I saw the unparalleled spectacle of Loft running. Loft running! I had never associated him with running, and should about as soon have expected to see St. Paul's Cathedral dancing a fling down Ludgate Hill. But there he came, down the path from the Priory. As soon as he got near me, he shouted excitedly, "She's come back, sir, she's come back!" Then he came to a stand outside the window, and recovered his professional demeanor at the cost of some confusion. "I beg your pardon, sir, but Miss Driver orders me to tell you that she has just returned, and will be glad to see you in half an hour."

"When did she come?"

"Just in, sir—the 2.45 from London, it must be."

"How does she look?"

"Much the same as usual, sir—a little thinner in the face perhaps."

I looked at Loft; he was grinning. So, I suppose, was I. "This is good, Loft."

"You may say that, sir!"

"Did she come alone?"

"No, sir. Her maid—a Frenchwoman, I think, sir —and a young lady. If she'd brought twenty, she'd have found the house all ready for them."

"I'm sure she would. Tell her I'll come up in half an hour."

Her coming transformed everything for me; it seemed to put life into the place, life into the big dull house on the hill, life into my little den, life into that summer's day. It was the breaking of a long frost, the awakening from a stupor. The coming that I had always believed in began to seem incredible only now, when it had happened; incredible it seemed that by just walking up the hill I could see Jenny again and hear her voice. Absence and silence had rendered her so distant to sight or sound, so intangible and remote. My last clear memory of her was still at Hatcham Ford—as she asked Fillingford for the loan of his carriage, and, with "God bless you, Austin," vanished into the night. A man can, I suppose, get on without anyone, if he must; but he cannot always make out how he has managed to do it.

I found her sitting in her old place in the big drawing-room; she wore—whether by purpose or not what was in effect slight mourning, a white summer frock with touches of black. Yes, her face was a little thinner, but it had not lost its serenity. She was less a girl, more a woman—but not a woman prematurely aged.

"Dear Austin!" she said, as I kissed the hand she held out to me. "You've waited a long while—here I am at last! You've become famous in the interval—yes, you have. I've seen your book, and I wish Leonard could have read it. He'd have liked it. But though you're famous, still you waited for me!"

"I don't think you expected me to do anything else."

She smiled at me. "Perhaps not. But, do you

ONE OF TWO LEGACIES 259

know, I'm afraid you've done something else than grow famous. Have you grown into an old bachelor? You look rather like it."

"I expect I have," said I ruefully, and with an anxious gaze at my coat. "It's rather an old coat, isn't it?"

"And the knees of your trousers!" pursued Jenny remorselessly.

They were atrocious—there was no denying it. "There's been nobody to dress for. I'll order a new suit to-morrow."

"Things begin to move directly I come back, don't they? Is there any news in the neighborhood?"

I told her my little budget, sketching it in as lightly as I could and with as little reference to herself. She fastened on the news about Eunice Aspenick.

"Grown up, of course, by now, isn't she? And you say she's pretty. Very pretty?"

"Not so very, in my judgment. Very fresh and healthy, and rather handsome."

Jenny smiled mysteriously. "Oh, that doesn't matter—if it comes to no more than that," she said contemptuously. She saw me smiling. "Oh, yes, I'm scheming again!" she declared with a laugh. "Not for myself, though. I've done with schemes about myself."

"At five-and-twenty?"

Jenny grew grave. "Things count, not years—or, anyhow, sooner than years. Have I any friends left?"

She smiled again when I told her of Lady Aspenick's faction, and how Lady Aspenick still used the road. "Come, that's not so bad," was her comment, rather playfully than seriously given. "And you ask me no questions?" she said the next moment, rather abruptly.

"No, I don't want to ask you any questions. I was very much grieved for him."

She nodded. "When I went away with him," she said, "I burned my boats. I wanted them burned, Austin. I was so sick of doubts—and of tricks and maneuvers. Recklessness seemed fine; and everything seemed to have gone out of the world—except me and him. There was some business to be done and I did it—with the surface of my mind; it made no real part of my thoughts. There I was all hatred for what I had been doing—yes, and horrible hatred of having been found out—I'd better be frank about that. I'd been tricking—I wanted to defy. Leonard didn't mind defying either, did he? That lasted a week—ten days, perhaps. Then the old thing came back—the fear of him, the fear of it. I couldn't help it—it's so deep in my blood, Austin. He told me I ought to marry him for my own sake—for his own he was indifferent. I think he really was. I was terribly afraid but, as you must know from the papers, I agreed, and everything was in train when—he died. That was my fault partly—but only partly. The young man did—make a mistake about me—but he apologized most humbly and courteously. But Leonard wouldn't take it properly, and picked a quarrel with him the next evening."

"Then it doesn't seem to have been your fault."

"My being — vulnerable — made Leonard more,

even more, than usually aggressive. That's all. They brought him back to me dying. He lived only about half an hour. We were curiously happy in that half hour—but it was terrible afterwards." She fell into silence, her eyes very sorrowful. Then she turned to me, with a gesture of her hands. "That's all the story—and it's for you alone—because you're Austin."

I took her hand for a moment and pressed it. "For me alone—I thank you."

"A thing like that seems to sweep across life like a hurricane, doesn't it? Leveling everything, destroying such a lot!"

"You've come back to build it all up again."

She smiled for a moment. "So you've found that out? But I can't build it all up. Some things I shall never try to build again. The track of the hurricane will always be left."

"Time, time, time!" said I.

"Not even time. Life's not over—but it's life with a difference. I don't complain. I accept that readily. I almost welcome it. I may cheat the world, but I won't cheat myself. I'm not at my old trick of having it both ways for myself, Austin."

She was determined to see clearly herself, but admitted no obligation to allow outsiders a view. She would not minimize the thing for herself, but was quite ready to induce the rest of the world to ignore it. It was her affair. To her the difference was made, over her life the hurricane had swept.

"I have no kith or kin; nobody is bound to me. The love of my friends is free—free to withhold, free to give. I did it for myself, open-eyed. There is nobody who has a right to harbor it against me."

And she meant that there never should be? It sounded like that.

"As a private offense against him, or her, I mean—as a personal offense. Of course they've a right to their opinions—and with their opinions I expect I should agree."

She would agree with the opinions, but did not feel bound to furnish material for them. She could hardly be blamed there. The candle and the white sheet—in open congregation—have fallen into such general disuse that Jenny could not be asked to revive them. So far she might be excused—people do not expect confessions. But she seemed to underrate what she termed "opinions" even though, as opinions, she thought that she would agree with them. On this subject neither Alison nor Mrs. Jepps would talk of "opinions"; they would use other words. When she said that there was nobody who had a right to harbor the affair against her, it was easy to understand her meaning; but her meaning did not exhaust the case. Society claims the right—and has the power—to harbor things against us; hence the gallows, the prisons, and decrees of social banishment. However, this sort of talk was confidential—between her and me only. If society were disposed to give her the benefit of the doubt, it would be very unlike Jenny not to make the thing as easy as possible for society. Often society has no objection to being " cheated "; it will let you shut its eyes to what you have done—strictly on condition that you do not so much as hint that you had any right to do it. But it was doubtful whether Jenny would find all Catsford in this accommodating temper.

"What's your opinion?" she asked abruptly.

"If I understand you rightly, you did a serious thing; on any theory and to anybody who thinks—never mind his precise views—a very serious thing. But you seem to know that well enough, and more talk about it won't mend matters."

"It was a wonderful time—my time of defiance—my time of surrender. At least I tried to make it surrender—and my greatest surrender was to consent not to go on defying. While I defied, I could surrender—because I could lose sight of everything in him. He was big enough, Austin! I seemed then to be putting the world—both worlds, if you like—quite out of sight, annihilating them for myself, saying I could get on without them if only I had Leonard—or, rather, if only Leonard would—would swallow me up!" She looked at me with one of her straight candid glances. "Well, he had no objection to that." Her lips curved in a reluctant smile. "You wouldn't expect him to have, would you? We made a plan. We were to go to Africa—somewhere in British East Africa—and live there—away from everything. Not because of fear or anything of that sort, you know—but because we felt we could get on better there. I wanted to strip myself of everything that made me distinct from him—of all I had or was, apart from him. I knew all the time that here, at home, we should be impossible together; you know I felt that because you watched the whole thing, Austin, and must have known that only that feeling could have kept me from him. Well, I could only try to drive out that fear of him by accepting all it meant—by being quite natural about it—by saying, ' I've an instinct that you'll absorb me; I yield to it—only make it easy—give it the best chance—don't keep me where all sorts of things compel me to struggle against it. Struggling isn't a possible life; perhaps surrender is. Let's try.' All this was the underlying thing—the real thing that was going on. On the top we were doing all sorts of interesting outside things—he was a wonderful companion—but this was what we were battling out all the time—how to make it work—how we could give our lives a chance of working together. We both wanted that—and we both knew that it was horribly difficult. The greatest thing about him is that he knew my side of the difficulty so extraordinarily well. Isn't that rather rare?"

"To his mind you were a great woman. He called you so to me. That accounts for it."

"How difficult it all is! The more the thing is worth while, the more difficult! Well, we were to try—to be married and go to Africa and try. Leonard didn't press marriage on me, but he admitted that he'd prefer it—for a particular reason that I'll tell you about presently. And I agreed; but neither of us made a great thing of that. Marriage may be a great thing, but I can't think that marrying just to mend matters is anything very great and sacred, can you? And that was all ours would have come to, of course. It would have been by way of apology."

She had a remorseless mind—most remorseless for herself and her motives. Yet a man might be a bit puzzled how to meet her reasoning.

"We're getting into the sphere of those opinions," I said. "We shall be up against Alison and Mrs. Jepps in a moment!"

"I know, and I'm only trying to tell you what happened—how we felt about the thing. And then— we needn't have troubled! A gay young gentleman, a little merry with wine—a lady in a café—a hot-tempered man particularly jealous to exact respect for her—what a simple, obvious, silly way to bring everything to dust!"

"You said you were happy at last."

"Our fight was done; our love was perfect. Oh, but we managed a quarrel; I wanted to die, too, and that made him terribly angry." She laughed—and the tears rolled down her cheeks. "Dear, dear Leonard—he said that, if he'd known I should talk such nonsense, he'd have thrown the Frenchman into the Loire and had no more trouble about it. So he died —his crossness with me just over!"

"Well over, I think," I said gently.

"He gave just one turn of his great great body, laid his head on my breast, swore at a fly that settled on his nose—oh, Austin!—and went to sleep there like a little child. It was above two hours before I could bear to call anybody. Then—they took him away."

After a long pause, which I had no inclination to break, she went on: "I daresay you wonder why I came back here?"

"I thought you'd come back. Things never seem irremediable to you; you never like to let go finally."

"That's true, I suppose. But I've a more special reason than that. Leonard left me a legacy—that brings me here—but don't let's talk about that for a minute. Is it true that Bertram Ware talks about selling Oxley. Mr. Cartmell said something about it in one of his letters."

"He's understood to be open to a good offer, I fancy."

"Then we'll make him one."

"You're at work already!"

"A pretty place and a nice little estate—just between Fillingford Manor and Overington!" Was the inherited liking for "driving wedges" still in force? She had lost Fillingford Manor, but Oxley Lodge would make a useful wedge. "I wonder if there's any chance of that new man at Hingston selling! I don't want the house, but those farms round Hilton Heath would round us off nicely."

"Buy the county and the town! Isn't that what you want?"

"I don't want one single thing, Austin—for myself. But I have a little plan in my head. Well, I must do something with my life, mustn't I—and with all this money?"

"Build the Institute!"

"I really think I shall be able to manage that. Mr. Bindlecombe's my friend still?"

"He has plucked up courage—under the influence of Lady Aspenick."

"Ah, yes," said Jenny, "I must try not to lose

Lady Aspenick." She looked thoughtful. " Yes, I must try." She seemed to anticipate some difficulty.

Her plan of campaign was indicated, if not revealed. She had come back; she was going to try to " get back." What had happened was to make a difference only just where, and in so far as, she herself decided that it must. About that she had not been explicit, but it was evidently a great point with her—a thing which profoundly affected her inner life. But her outer life was not to be affected—her external position was not in the end to suffer. And this ambition, this plan, was somehow connected with her " legacy " from Leonard Octon.

Suddenly she spoke again. " When a mask is on, you can't see the face. I shall wear a mask—don't judge my face by it. I've taken it off for you to-day. I have given you the means of judging. But I shall wear it day by day—against everybody; even against you generally, I expect, though I may sometimes lift a corner up for you."

What had I seen while the mask was off? A woman profoundly humiliated in herself but resolute not to accept outward humiliation? It was hardly that, though that had an element of applicability in it. A woman ready—even determined—to pay a great penalty for what she had done, but resolved to evade or to defy the obvious and usual penalties? There was truth in that, too. But more remained. It seemed as though, with the hurricane of which she spoke, there had come an earthquake. It had left her alive, and in touch with life; life was not done. But it was different—forever and irrevocably different. Her relations to life had all been shifted. That was the great penalty she accepted—and she was prepared to accept its executions, its working-out, seeing in that, apparently, the logically proper, the inevitable outcome of her act. The obvious penalties were not to her mind inevitable; she would admit that they were conventionally proper—but that admission left her free to avoid them if she could. The outward punishment she would dodge; before the inward she would bow her head. And the sphere of the penalty must be the same as the sphere of the offense. Her intellect had not offended, and that was left free to work, to expatiate, to enjoy. On her heart fell the blows, as from her heart had come the crime. There it was that the shifting of relations, the change of position, the transformation of feelings, had their place.

An intelligible attitude—but a proud, indeed a very arrogant, one. Only Jenny should punish Jenny—that was pretty well what it said. She herself had decreed her penalty. It might be adequate—perhaps she alone could know the truth of that—but it was open to the objection that it was quite unauthorized. Neither in what it included nor in what it excluded did it conform to any code of religious or social obligation. It was Jenny's sentence on Jenny—and Jenny proposed to carry it out. Centralization of power seemed to shake hands with anarchy.

Jenny's mood grew lighter on her last words. "To-night we'll send a paragraph to the Catsford paper to announce my return," she said, smiling. "I'm not skulking back!"

"It will occasion interest and surprise."

"It's not the only surprise I've got for them," laughed Jenny. Then, suddenly, she held up her hand for silence. From the terrace outside the window I heard a merry sweet-toned laugh. Jenny rose and went to the window, and I followed her.

Old Chat was on the terrace, and beside her stood a girl, not tall, very slender. Her arm was through Chat's, her back toward us, her face in profile as she turned to talk—and she was talking briskly and in excited interest—to her companion. The profile was small, regular, refined; I could not see the eyes; the hair was a golden brown, very plentiful.

"Who's that pretty girl?" I cried.

Jenny copied the attitude of the pair on the terrace; she put her arm through mine and said with a laugh, "She is pretty, then?" The laugh sounded triumphant. "Why, as pretty a little thing as a man could find in a lifetime!" I cried in honest enthusiasm.

"Oh, come, you're not such a hopeless old bachelor after all," said Jenny. "Not that I in the least want you to fall in love with her—not you, Austin."

"I think I am—half!"

"Keep just the other half for me. Half's as much as I want, you know." Her voice sounded sad again, yet whimsically sad. "But I do want that from you, I think." She pressed my arm; then, waiting for no answer, she went on gayly, "I think I shall surprise Catsford with that!"

"She's going to pay you a visit?" I asked.

"She's going to live here," Jenny answered. "That's my legacy, Austin."

I smote my free arm against my thigh. " By Heaven, the girl on the mantelpiece at Hatcham Ford! " I cried.

At the moment the girl on the terrace turned round, saw us, and waved her hand merrily to Jenny. Certainly the prettiest little creature you ever saw—in the small, dainty, delicate, roguishly appealing way: and most indubitably the original of that picture which I had seen at Hatcham Ford, which vanished on the night when Octon went forth alone—little thinking that Jenny would follow him.

I turned from her to Jenny in astonishment. " But I'd made up my mind that it was his wife."

" I'm glad he told you he was married. He told you the dreadful thing about it, too, didn't he? It wasn't a thing one could talk about—he'd never have allowed that for a minute—but I wish everybody could have known. It seems a sort of excuse for what they all quarreled with in him. He'd been made to feel the world his enemy when he was young; that must tell on a man, mustn't it? "

" This is a daughter? He never said anything about a daughter."

" Well, I suppose you didn't happen to get on that—and you didn't ask. A woman would have asked, of course, whether there were any children—and how old they were, and what was the color of their hair."

" Upon my soul, it never occurred to me! "

" It wouldn't," she remarked, smiling. " But this is Margaret."

" Where's she been all the while? "

"Oh, only at school—there's no mystery. He was only at Hatcham Ford four years—just her school years. He didn't bring her there in the holidays, because that would have meant a chaperon — he couldn't have looked after a girl—and he hated the idea of that. And I think he was afraid, too, that the people wouldn't be nice to her. He was very sensitive for her, though he wasn't at all for himself." She paused a moment. "Does that explain anything else I've said?"

I thought, for a moment, over our talk. "About the marriage?"

"Yes," said Jenny. "It didn't seem fair to her without that. That weighed with him more than anything else—and with me, too, a good deal. I don't think I need be ashamed of that."

"Certainly you needn't — quite the contrary in fact."

"We should have wanted her to be with us—to pay us visits anyhow—at least until she married. Yes, it wouldn't have been just." She frowned impatiently; still more than anything else, Margaret Octon seemed to bring home to her the difficult side—the side most hard to defend—of what she had done and contemplated. She passed away from it without more words.

"When he was dying he gave her to me. That put an end to the quarrel I told you about. It gave me back some of him and gave me something to live for. 'I know you'll do the handsome thing by her, Jenny,' he said. I mean to try, Austin."

"I'm sure you do, but "—I could not help blurting it out—"won't her being here make matters worse?"

"Worse or better, better or worse, here she's going to be," said Jenny. "She's been with me nearly a year already. She's one of the two things he's left behind him—to stay with me."

I did not ask what the other thing was.

"Is she to bear his name?"

"Of course she is. She's my friend and ward—and Leonard Octon's daughter."

"Rather a pill for Catsford! Dear me, what a pretty little thing it is!"

"I'm very glad she's like that. It makes so much more possible. This is a good gift that Leonard has left me. She's my joy—you must be my consolation. I can't give you anything in return, but there's something I can give her—and I'll give it full measure, for Leonard's sake." She laughed, rather reluctantly, squeezing my arm again. "Oh, yes, and I'm afraid a little bit because Jenny Driver still likes her own way! And, above all, her own way with Catsford! Shall we see if she can get it?"

CHAPTER XVIII

THE NEW CAMPAIGN

JENNY had come back with her courage unbroken—and with her ambitions unappeased, though it seemed that their direction had been in some measure changed. Somehow Margaret Octon was now one of their principal objects. It was not possible just now to see further into her mind, even at a tolerably close view—a much closer one than her neighbors were permitted to enjoy. It was even an appreciable time before Catsford heard of Margaret Octon at all. The presence of the girl was not obtruded, much less her name; nothing was said of her in the paragraph that went to the paper. Jenny left Catsford to digest the fact of her own return first.

It was enough to occupy the neighborhood's digestive faculties for many days. It raised such various questions, on which different minds settled with differing degrees of avidity. Questions of morality, of propriety, of conventionality on the one hand—questions of charity, of policy, of self-interest on the other. There were the party of principle and the party of expediency, cutting across the lines of the party of propriety and the party of charity. Some quoted Cæsar's wife—when do they not? Others maintained that an Englishman was innocent till he was proved guilty—and *a fortiori* a handsome, attractive, interesting, and remarkably rich Englishwoman. It was contended by one faction that a self-banishment of nearly three years was apology enough—if apology were needed; by the other that Jenny had insolently spurned any effort to "put herself right" with public opinion. To add to the complication, people shifted their attitudes from day to day—either under influence, as when they had been talked to by Mrs. Jepps or by Mr. Bindlecombe as the case might be, or from the sheer pleasure of discussing the matter over again from another point of view, and drawing out their neighbors by advocating what, twenty-four hours earlier, they had condemned.

The climax came when the news of Margaret leaked out, as it was bound soon to do, if only through the mouths of the servants at the Priory. There was a pretty girl there, a girl of seventeen—whose name was Octon—daughter, it was understood, of the late Mr. Leonard Octon of Hatcham Ford; she was living with Miss Driver, as her friend or her ward—at any rate, apparently, as a fixture. Some found a likeness between Margaret's sudden appearance and Jenny's own, and this element added a piquancy to the situation, even though the similarity was rather superficial than essential. Old Nicholas Driver had every reason to produce his daughter and invest her formally with the position of heir-apparent to his great possessions, to his over-lordship of the town. Octon had been merely the temporary tenant of a hired house—a mere bird of passage—and a solitary bird besides, neither giving nor receiving confidences. Why should he have talked about his dead wife and his young daughter to ears that cared not a straw about either of them? The coincidence was noted, but it was soon swallowed up in the new issue as to Jenny's conduct which the appearance of Margaret raised. Bluntly—for which party was this a score? Jenny's opponents saw in it a new defiance—a willful flaunting of offense; her friends found in it a romantic flavor which pleaded for her.

On the whole, so far as could be judged from Bindlecombe's accounts—he was my constant reporter—Jenny's adherents gained ground in the town—partly from her personal popularity, partly from the old power of her family, in part, perhaps (if one may venture to say so from the safe obscurity of a private station), because our lords the masses are not in a matter of this sort very unforgiving—in which they touch hands with the opposite end of society. Self-interest probably aided—Catsford had of late basked in the somewhat wintry favor of Fillingford Manor; the beams were chilly; Breysgate would emit a kinder glow. It "paid" so many people in the town to have Jenny back! The feeling in the county was preponderatingly against her. There Fillingford Manor was a greater power; its attitude was definite, resolute, not to be misunderstood. Outside the town Jenny could look at present for little support. Old Mr. Dormer with his pliant standards was dead.

There were only the Aspenicks—Lady Aspenick must be civil—owing to what she had done about the road; but her influence, even if cordially exercised, would not be enough.

Following the example of great commanders, Jenny massed her forces on the most favorable point. She flung herself on the workingmen of Catsford. Hesitating, probably, to expose Margaret to the chances of the campaign, she left her at home, but she requisitioned Cartmell and myself, and we drove down in full state into Catsford at noon on the fourth day after her return. Our ostensible purpose was to go to Cartmell's office, to transact some legal business; as he could easily have brought his papers up to the Priory, this did not seem very convincing. Our way took us past the great Driver works—conducted now by a limited company, in which Jenny held a controlling interest. In front of the big building was a large open space, still known as "The Green" though constant traffic of feet had worn away all trace of grass. Here was the forum of Catsford, where men assembled for open-air meetings and, less formally, for discussion, gossip — even, it was said, for betting—in their spare moments, and especially in the dinner-hour. It happened to be the dinner-hour now—as Jenny observed innocently when we found the place full of Driver employees who had swallowed their meal and were talking together or lounging about, their pipes in their mouths. Cartmell gave a grim chuckle at Jenny's artless surprise. He had taken her return very quietly, loyally accepting his position as her man of business, but

THE NEW CAMPAIGN

hardly welcoming her with real cordiality. I fancy that he found it hard to forgive; was not Fillingford Manor gone forever?

We had not progressed many yards before she was recognized. She courted recognition, stopping to speak to an old artisan who had once been introduced to her as a contemporary of her father's. Men gathered round her as she sat chatting with the veteran. She seemed unconscious of being gradually surrounded. At last, with a most gracious good-by, she said, " Now drive on, please," then looked suddenly round, saw all the folk, and bowed and smiled. One fellow started, " Three cheers for Miss Driver! " That set the thing going. They gave her cheer on cheer. Jenny sat through it smiling, flushed, just once glancing across to me with a covert triumph. The cheers brought more men running up; there were two or three hundred round us. " Welcome home! " they cried. " Welcome home! " Then somebody called, " Speech, speech! " The cry was taken up with hilarious enthusiasm, and the crowd grew every minute.

Suddenly on the outskirts of the throng I saw a man on horseback. He had stopped his horse and was looking on. There was no mistaking Lacey's handsome face and trim figure.

Jenny rose to her feet and held up her hand for silence. She spoke her few words in a ringing voice. " My friends and neighbors, thank you for your welcome home. I am glad from my heart to be in Catsford again. That's where Nicholas Driver's daughter ought to be. So I've come back." She kissed her hand to them two or three times, standing there in the carriage. Then I saw that she caught sight of Lacey. The flush on her cheeks deepened. For a second she stood, looking at him her lips just parted in a smile; but she did not incline her head. He lifted his hat and bowed low from his saddle. Then she gave him her most radiant recognition—and sank down on the cushions of the carriage with a sigh.

Jenny could not have reckoned on that encounter —though it seemed all to the good. We were to have another, on which she had not counted either when she chose so cleverly the scene of her public reappearance. When at last they made a lane for our horses to pass, some taking leave of us with fresh cheers, others escorting us on either side, with jokes and horseplay among themselves, we met a little procession. It was Alison's custom to hold a short out-of-door service three times a week during the men's dinner-hour; the Green was his chosen pulpit, as it had been Jenny's chosen scene. He came toward us now in all his ecclesiastical panoply, attended by two or three of his (if Mrs. Jepps will allow me the term) assistant priests and by a band of choir boys, all in their robes. Jenny caught sight of the procession and leaned forward eagerly. I looked back. Lacey was still there; a man was by his horse, talking to him no doubt, but his eyes were following our progress.

I do not happen to know whether it be etiquette to offer or return the ordinary signs of recognition when one forms part of a procession, either secular or ecclesiastical. In the case of the latter, at all events, probably it is not. This perhaps got Alison out of a difficulty—while it left Jenny in a doubt. But I think that it must be permissible to look rather more benevolent, rather less sternly aloof, than Alison's face was as she passed, escorted by her jesting adherents. To say that he took no more notice of us or of them than if we had not been there is inadequate. His ignoring of us achieved a positive quality. He passed by with his eyes purposely, aggressively, indifferent. The boys and men looked after him and his procession, and nudged one another with smiles.

Jenny's face told nothing of her view of this little incident. She was still smiling when we quickened up and, with final hand-wavings, shook ourselves clear of our adherents. At Cartmell's office her head was as clear and her manner as composed as possible. The business that brought us having been transacted, she opened fire on Cartmell about Oxley Lodge and the outlying farms of Hingston. Verily she was losing no time in her campaign!

Cartmell was obviously amused at her. "That's making up for lost time with a vengeance, Miss Jenny! Hingston and Oxley all at once!" As soon as they got on to business—got to work again—his old pride and pleasure in her began to revive.

"Only a bit of Hingston!" Jenny pleaded with a smile.

"There's plenty of money," he said thoughtfully. "In spite of keeping things going here as you ordered—much too lavishly done it was, too, in my opinion—it's been piling up since you've been away. If they're willing to sell—I hear on good authority that Bertram Ware is if he can get his price—the money's not the difficulty. But what's the good?"

"The good?" asked Jenny.

"Surely you've got plenty? What's the good of a lot more? Isn't it only a burden on you?"

She answered him not with her old impatience, but with all her resoluteness—her old certainty that she knew what she wanted, and why she wanted it—and that it was quite immaterial whether anyone else did.

"You look after the money, Mr. Cartmell; you can leave the good to me—and the burden!"

"Yes, yes, you and your father!" he grumbled. "No good advising—not the least! 'Slave-Driver' I used to call him over our port after dinner sometimes. You're just the same, Miss Jenny."

"All that just because I want to buy a pretty house!" said Jenny, appealing deprecatingly to me.

She would not go away without his promise to press both matters on. Having extracted this, she went home—and ended her first day's campaign by issuing an ukase that all the Driver workmen should, at an early date, have a day's holiday on full wages, with a great feast for them, their wives, children, and sweethearts in the grounds of Breysgate—wages and feast alike to be provided out of the privy purse of Miss Driver. Catsford was behaving well and was to be petted! Jenny did not mention whether she intended to invite its chief spiritual director.

I dined at the Priory that night—a night, on the whole, of distinct triumph—and made acquaintance with Margaret Octon. Strange daughter of such a father! Mrs. Octon must—one was inclined to speculate—have been marvelously different from her husband—and from Jenny Driver. Imagination began to picture something ineffably timid, shrinking, gentle —something which, blending with Octon's strong rough strain, would issue in this child. She seemed all things in turn—except self-confident. Evidently she was devoted to Jenny; perpetually she referred all she did to Jenny's approval—but that " all " included many varieties. Now she would be demure, now venturesome, now childishly merry, now assuming a premature sedateness. She played tricks with Jenny, her brown eyes always asking whether she might play them; she enjoyed herself immensely—by Jenny's kind permission. This constant reference and this constant appeal found no warrant in anything in Jenny's manner; the child was evidently a privileged pet and could do just as she pleased—Jenny delighted in her. It was then in the girl's nature itself. She was grace and charm—without strength. It would be very appealing, if one were the person appealed to; it would be most attractive, most tempting, when seconded by her frail fairy-like beauty. For it was a joy to look at her; and if she looked at you, asking leave to be happy, what could you say but—" By all means—and pray let me do all I can to help! "

Jenny seemed to watch her gayeties and her demureness, her ventures and retreats, with delight indeed, but also with a more subtle feeling. She not only enjoyed; she studied and pondered. She gave the impression of wanting to know what would be thought by others. This with Jenny was unusual; but her manner did unmistakably ask me my opinion several times, and when, after dinner, Margaret had waltzed Chat out of the room for a stroll in the garden, she asked it plainly.

"Isn't she just as charming as she looks?"

"She worships you," I remarked.

"That's nothing—natural just at first, while she's so young. But don't you find her charming?" Jenny persisted.

"I don't know about women—but if that form of flattery were brought to bear on any man, I don't see how he could possibly resist."

"It's quite natural; it's not put on in the least."

"I'm sure of it. That's what would make it so dangerous. To have that beautiful little creature treating one as a god—who could refuse the incense, or not become devoted to the worshiper?"

Jenny nodded. "You understand it, I see. Men would feel that way, would they?"

"Rather!" I answered, with a laugh. Jenny was leaning her head on her elbow, and looked across the table at me with a satisfied mocking smile. I could see that I had given an answer that pleased her —but she was not minded to tell me why she was pleased.

Half chaffing her, half really wondering what she would be at, I asked, "Do you want Oxley Lodge for Margaret?"

"For her?" exclaimed Jenny, smiling still. "Why? Isn't this house big enough for the mite?"

"Suppose you both marry—or either? You're both eminently marriageable young women."

"Are we? Eminently marriageable? Well, I sup-

THE NEW CAMPAIGN

pose so." She laughed. "Even if one doesn't marry, it's something to be marriageable, isn't it?"

"A most valuable asset," said I. "Then you'd want two houses."

"I suppose we should. But how far you look ahead, Austin!"

"If that isn't Satan reproving sin—!" I cried.

"What do you suspect me of now?" she asked, still mocking, but genuinely curious, I think, to fathom my thoughts.

"No, no! You'll be off on another tack if you think you've been sighted."

She laughed as she rose from the table. "Oh, come out and walk! At any rate, my getting Oxley would annoy Lady Sarah, wouldn't it?"

"You can annoy her cheaper than that!"

"There's plenty of money, Mr. Cartmell says," she answered, smiling over her shoulder as she led the way.

I had a talk with Margaret, too, a little later on. Jenny sent us for a moonlight stroll together. Young as the child was, she was good company, independently of her place in Jenny's mind, which for me gave her an adventitious interest. But what a contrast to Jenny, no less than to Octon—and perhaps a more profound one! The fine new surroundings, the enlarged horizon which Jenny's friendship opened to her, were still a delightful bewilderment; she enjoyed actively, but she accepted passively; she applauded the entertainment, but never thought of arranging the bill of the play. Jenny could not have been like that—even at seventeen; she would have itched to write some lines in the book, to have a word to say to the scenes. Margaret's simplicity of grateful responsiveness was untouched by any calculation.

"It's all just so wonderful!" she said to me, her arms waving over the park, her brown eyes wide with surprised admiration.

She came to it only on an invitation. Jenny had come as owner. But Jenny had not been overwhelmed like this. Jenny had kept cool, had taken it all in—and been interested to survey, from Tor Hill, the next estate!

"To happen to me—suddenly! Ah, but I wish father had lived. If he could have lived to marry Jenny! They were engaged when he—was killed, you know."

"Yes," I said, "I know. But don't be sad to-night. Things smell sweet, and there's a moon in the sky."

She laughed—merry in an instant. "Jenny says we're going to do such things! As soon as she's settled down again, you know." She paused for a moment. "Did she love my father very much?"

"Yes, I think she did," I answered, "and I think she loves you."

"To me she's just—everything." Her eyes grew mirthful and adventurous; she gave a little laugh as she added, "And she says she'll find me a fairy prince!" At once she was looking to see how I liked this, not with the anxiety which awaited Jenny's approval, but none the less with an evident desire for mine.

"That's only right," I answered, laughing. "But

THE NEW CAMPAIGN

she needn't hurry, need she? You'll be happy here for a bit longer?"

"Happy here? I should think so!" she cried. "Ah, there's Jenny looking for me!" In an instant she was gone; the next her arm was through Jenny's, and she was talking merrily.

I became aware of Chat's presence. She came toward me in her faded, far from sumptuous, gentility. She had a little gush for me. " So happy it all seems again, Mr. Austin!" she said.

"We seem to be starting again very well indeed," I assented.

"Dear Jenny has behaved so splendidly all through," Chat proceeded. "How did they dare to be so malicious about her? But I've known her from a girl. I always trusted her. Why, I may say I did a good deal to form her!"

A vivid—and highly inopportune—picture came back into my mind, a picture dating from the night of Jenny's flight—of Chat rocking her helpless old body to and fro, and saying through her sobs, " I tried, I tried, I tried!" What had Chat meant that she tried to do? To keep Jenny out of mischief? Hardly that. To save her from the danger of it had been the object. As for forming her—Chat had made other confessions about that.

However—as things stood—Chat had always trusted Jenny. It was impossible to say how far—at this moment—Jenny had trusted Chat. Not very far, I think. Jenny probably had said nothing which could make it harder for Chat to say what she would want to say; both reticence and revelation would have been bent to that object—and Jenny was an artist in the use of each of these expedients. Doubtless Chat had been given her cue. Nevertheless, there was something unusual in her air—something very friendly, confidential, yet rather furtive, as she drew a little closer to me.

"But the dear girl is so impulsive," she said. "Of course, it's delightful, but—" She pursed her lips and gave me a significant look. "This child!" said Chat.

"Oh, you mean Margaret Octon? Seems a very nice girl, Miss Chatters."

"Jenny's heart's so good—but what a handicap!"

Chat was of that view, then, concerning the coming of Margaret. Well, it was not uncommon.

"We shall never get back to our old terms with Fillingford Manor as long as she's here," said Chat.

"Were you so much attached to Fillingford Manor?" I ventured to ask.

"That would end all the talk," she insisted with an agitated urgency. "If only Lord Fillingford would overlook—" She stopped in a sudden fright. "Don't say I said that!"

"Why, of course not," I answered, smiling. "Anything you want said you can say yourself. It's not my business."

"One can always rely on you, Mr. Austin. But wouldn't that be perfect—after it all, you know?"

It certainly would be picking up the pieces—after a smash into utter fragments! But it is always pleasant to see people contemplating what they regard as perfection; and no very clear duty lies on a private individual to disturb their vision. I told Chat that the idea was no doubt worth thinking over, and so, in amity, we parted.

That was Chat's idea. Octon was gone with his fascination—not unfelt by Chat. Now it would be perfection if Lord Fillingford would overlook! But with that goal in view Margaret Octon was a heavy handicap. Undoubtedly—so heavy, so fatal, that the goal could hardly be Jenny's. Chat, who had done so much to form Jenny, might have given a thought to that aspect of the matter. If one thing were certain, it was that Jenny, when she accepted her legacy from Octon and brought Margaret to Breysgate, thereby abandoned and renounced all thought of renewing her relations with Fillingford. I was glad to come to that conclusion, helped to getting at it clearly (as one often is) by the opposite point of view presented by another. I had never been an enthusiastic Fillingfordite; I had accepted rather than welcomed. And I could bear him better suing than overlooking. Having things overlooked did not suit my idea of Jenny—though I could enjoy seeing her riding buoyant over them.

Jenny and Margaret came along the terrace toward us, arm in arm, their approach heralded by merry laughter. "We've been building castles in the air!" cried Jenny.

"May you soon be living in them!"

She shook her head at me in half-serious rebuke. "They were for Margaret!"

Jenny might deny herself the sky; but she would have castles somewhere—founded solidly on earth. It was the earth she trusted now. You cannot fall off that.

CHAPTER XIX

A CASE OF CONSCIENCE

"AND now about the Institute!" said Jenny the next morning. Cartmell had obeyed her summons to come up to the Priory, and the three of us were together in my office there.

She was not wasting time. Matters were to move quick. She had come home with her plans matured, ready for execution. The enemies might hesitate, losing themselves in debate. She would not hesitate, nor take part in the debate about herself. Acting and acting quickly, she would carry the position while they still discussed how—or even whether—it should be defended.

"The Committee stands adjourned *sine die*," said Cartmell. "You'd convene a meeting?"

Jenny would have none of convening the Committee. It would be awkward if some of the members did not come—and still more awkward if all of them attended!

"I regard the Committee as having abdicated," she told us. "They chose to adjourn—let them stay adjourned. I shall go over their heads—straight to the Corporation. Let's see if the Corporation will refuse! If they do, we shall know where we are."

A CASE OF CONSCIENCE 289

Of course she did not think that they would refuse, or she would never have risked an offer which forced the issue into the open. Fillingford had his feelings, Alison his scruples. Both scruples and feelings were intelligible. But was the Borough Council going to refuse a hundred thousand pounds freely given for the borough's benefit?

" Hatcham Ford as it stands—and a hundred thousand pounds, please, Mr. Cartmell."

" With the town spreading out as it is in that direction, that's more like a hundred and fifty in reality," he grumbled.

" I'm going to bleed you sadly! " Jenny assured him gayly. " We'll send for Mr. Bindlecombe and get this in hand at once. We'll see the Institute growing out of the ground within the year! "

Bindlecombe, too, was all for a dashing strategy—though I think that he would have been for anything that Jenny wanted. The letter to the Mayor (Bindlecombe no longer filled that office, though he was still a leading member of the Corporation) was written; it appeared in the paper; a meeting to consider it was called for the next week. In the same issue of the paper appeared an account of Jenny's reception in Catsford, and an announcement of the impending holiday and feast. That issue might fairly be called Jenny's number. Her friends were jubilant; her enemies were bewildered by the audacity of her assault.

But Jenny did not come off without loss. Not only did she confirm the disapproval of those who were resolute against her—I heard much of Mrs. Jepps's outspoken and shocked comments, something of Alison's stern silence—but she lost or came near to losing an adherent of undoubted value.

Dash and defiance were not Lady Aspenick's idea of the proper way of proceeding; and another thing offended her no less. She had, I think, on the news of Jenny's return, devised a scheme by which she was to be Jenny's protector and champion; she would throw the ægis of Overington Grange's undoubted respectability over Jenny's vulnerable spot; her influence, tact, and diplomacy would gradually smooth Jenny's path back to society; Jenny would be bound to gratitude and to docility. The dashing strategy upset all that; the appearance of Margaret Octon upset it still more.

She paid her call on Jenny—her previous position committed her to that. She drove over—not in a tandem—on the same day on which all the news about Jenny was in the paper. I met her as she went away, happening to come up to the Priory door just as she was coming out—Jenny not escorting her. She was looking black.

"It's pleasant to welcome you to a cheerful house once again, Lady Aspenick. We've had a long dull time at the Priory."

"You won't be dull now, anyhow," she rejoined with some acidity. She dropped her voice that the men might not hear. "Oh, how unwise! All this parade and splash! I can't tell you how I feel about it—and Jack, too! And poor Mr. Alison! And, to crown all, she flings the thing in our faces by bringing this girl with her!"

"She's a very nice girl," I pleaded meekly.

A CASE OF CONSCIENCE

"I know nothing about that. She's that man's daughter. Surely Jenny Driver might have known that her chance lay in having it all forgotten and—and in being—well, just the opposite of what she is now? She goes on as if she were proud of herself!"

As a criticism on Jenny's public attitude, there was some truth in this. I could not tell Lady Aspenick about her private attitude—nor would it make matters better if I did.

"She makes it very hard for her friends," continued the aggrieved lady. "We were anxious to do our best for her. But really—!" Words failed. She shook her head emphatically at me and walked off to her carriage.

I found Jenny in a fine rage as the result of Lady Aspenick's expression of her views—which had apparently been nearly as frank to her as to me. Yet she protested that she had behaved with the utmost wisdom and meekness—for Margaret's sake.

"I stood it, Austin," she declared, with a little stamp of her foot. "How I stood it I don't know, but I did. She lectured me—she told me I ought to have been guided by her! She said I was going quite the wrong way about it with the Institute and that she deeply regretted the 'scene' in Catsford. The scene! She threatened me with the parsons and the Puritans!"

How very angry Jenny was! Parsons and Puritans!

"And ended up—yes, she dared to end up—by telling me I must send Margaret away. She'll see more of Margaret than she thinks before she's done with her!"

"And you were very meek and mild?"

"I know you don't believe it. But I was. I was absolutely civil and thanked her for her kindness. But of course I said that I must judge for myself—and that the question of Margaret lay absolutely outside the bounds of discussion."

"To which Lady Aspenick——?"

"She got up and went. What did she say to you?"

"Much the same—that you were making it very difficult for her."

"I've gained more than I've lost in Catsford," Jenny declared obstinately and confidently. Then her voice softened. "As for poor little Margaret—it's not a question of my gain or my loss there. You do know that?" She was appealing to me for a kind judgment.

"I'm beginning to understand that."

"I stand or fall with Margaret; or I fall—if only she stands. That's final." She broke into a smile. "So, in spite of what you think, I drove myself to be civil to Susie Aspenick. But let her wait a little! Send Margaret away!" Jenny looked dangerous again.

Jenny could have forgiven the criticism of her Catsford proceedings—though not over easily; the attempt to touch Margaret rankled, and, if I mistook not, would rankle, sorely.

It is pleasant to record that Jenny's chivalrous devotion to her "legacy" found appreciation elsewhere; it softened an opponent, and stirred to enthusiasm one already inclined to be a friend.

I had a note from Alison: "I can't countenance her

goings on in Catsford—her courting of publicity and applause, her holidays and picnics—no, nor—at present—her Institute either. If she is entitled to come back at all, she is not entitled to come in triumph—far from it. But I like and admire what she is doing about Miss Octon, and I have scandalized Mrs. Jepps and many other good folk by saying so. In that she's brave and honest. I shouldn't mind if you could let her know how I feel on this second point; my views on the first she'll know for herself."

I did take occasion to let Jenny know what Alison wished to reach her. "He may think what he likes about Catsford, if he's on my side about Margaret," she declared with evident pleasure. Then her eyes twinkled. "We'll have him yet, Margaret and I between us!" she added.

The next Sunday she attended Alison's church—she, Chat, and Margaret Octon. I hope that she was not merely "doing the civil thing," like the duchess in the story. After all she had always been one of his bugbears—one of the people who went "fairly regularly."

That same Sunday, in the afternoon, Lacey came to see me. He drove up in his dog-cart, handed the reins to a good-looking dark man, with upturned mustaches, who sat by him, and came to my door. Having seen their arrival, I was there to open it and welcome him.

"Won't your friend come in, too?" I asked.

"He's all right; he's in no hurry, and he's got a cigar. I want to speak to you alone for just a minute."

He followed me in and sat down. His manner was thoughtful and a little embarrassed.

"I saw you down in Catsford the other day," I remarked. "They were very kind to us!"

"I want to ask you a question, Austin," he said. "Do you think that Miss Driver would wish to receive a call from me?"

"I'm sure she'd be delighted."

"Wait a bit. You haven't heard the whole position. You saw me in Catsford? You saw me bow to her?"

I nodded assent.

"Then I think I ought to go and pay her my respects—if it's not disagreeable to her to receive me."

"But why should it be?"

"I belong to Fillingford Manor. I'm living there now. Neither the master nor the lady of the house will—neither of them shares my views."

That did, on reflection, make the matter a little less simple than it had seemed at first.

"I don't suppose we either of us want to discuss their reasons—or wonder at the line they take. I had a little talk with my father about it. He's always very fair. 'You're a man,' he said. 'Decide for yourself. If after the recognition that passed between you—and on your initiative, as I understand—you feel bound—as you say you do—as a gentleman to go and pay your respects, go. But I shall be obliged to you if you will make the relations between that house and this as distant as is consistent with the demands of courtesy.'"

"In view of that I don't think you're in any way

bound to call: I'm not at all sure you ought to. Lord Fillingford's wishes are entitled to great weight—especially while you're living in his house."

He was a man now—and a fine specimen of one—but his boyish impetuosity had not left him. "By Jove, I want to go, Austin!" he exclaimed.

"Well, I thought that perhaps you did."

"I want to go and see her—and I should like to tell her, if I dared, that there's not a man in the service to touch her. I don't mean her driving through Catsford—though she took a risk there; some of those chaps aren't mealy-mouthed. I mean what she's done about this little Miss Octon. That's what I like. Because the girl's her man's daughter, she snaps her fingers at the lot of us! That's what I like, Austin—that's why I want to go and see her. But I couldn't say that to the governor."

"You'll never be able to, any better. So you must consider your course. Is it—loyal—to your father?"

He knit his brows in perplexity and vexation. "Was I loyal to him that night we went to Hatcham Ford? You didn't make that objection then!"

"I don't think I should have taken any objection to anything that gave a chance then. I can look at this more coolly. Why not wait a little? Perhaps Lord Fillingford will come to the conclusion that bygones had best be bygones."

"And Aunt Sarah?"

"Is that quite so essential?"

He sat struggling between his scruples and his strong desire—loyalty to his father, admiration of Jenny and attraction toward her.

"I might manage to give her a hint of how you feel—and about the difficulty."

"That'd be better than nothing. Then she'd understand——?"

"She'd understand the whole position perfectly," I assured him.

He was plainly discontented with this compromise, but he accepted it provisionally. "You give her that hint, anyhow, like a good fellow, Austin—and I'll think over the other matter." He rose from his chair. "Now I mustn't keep Gerald Dormer waiting any longer."

"Oh, that's Gerald Dormer, is it—the new man at Hingston?"

"Yes, he's not a bad fellow—and he doesn't think he is, either." With this passing indication of Mr. Dormer's foible, he led the way out of doors and introduced me to the subject of his remark. Gerald Dormer's manner was cordial and self-satisfied. We stood in talk a minute or two. The news of the holiday and of the feast in our park had reached Dormer, and he laughingly demanded an invitation. "I'm pretty hard up, and nobody gives me a dinner!" he protested.

"I'll make a note of your hard case and submit it to Miss Driver. But you're not a Driver employee, you know."

"Oh, but I'm quite ready to be—for a good screw, Mr. Austin."

"Here she comes, by Jove!" said Lacey in a quick startled whisper.

Yes, there she was, within thirty yards of us, com-

A CASE OF CONSCIENCE

ing down the hill from the Priory straight toward my house. Lacey glanced at the dog-cart, seeming to meditate flight; then he pulled off the right-hand glove which he had just put on and buttoned.

"Is that Miss Driver?" whispered Dormer. I nodded assent.

Jenny was in great looks that day, and, it seemed, in fine spirits. Her head was held high, her step was buoyant, there was a delicate touch of color in her cheeks as she came up to us. She met the gaze of all our eyes—for all, I am sure, were on her—with a gay smile and no sign of embarrassment.

"Why, I'm so glad to see you again," she cried to Lacey as she gave him her hand. "You can't think how often I've dreamed of our rides since I've been away!"

"I'm very glad to see you, Miss Driver. May I introduce my friend, Mr. Dormer—of Hingston?"

She bowed to him very graciously, but turned back directly to Lacey. I saw Dormer's eyes follow her movements with an admiring curiosity. Small wonder; she was good to look at, and he had, no doubt, heard much.

"You must come and see me," said Jenny. "Now when shall it be? Lunch to-morrow? Or tea? Not later than the next day, anyhow!"

At that point she must have seen something in his face. She stopped, smiled oddly, even broke into a little laugh, and said, almost in a whisper, "Oh, I forgot, how stupid of me!"

Her tone and air, and the look in her hazel eyes, were nicely compounded of humility and mockery.

Confessing herself unworthy, she asked the man if he were afraid! Didn't he dare to trust himself—was he so careful of his reputation?

Lacey had promised me that he would "think over" the question of his relations toward Breysgate Priory. I suppose that he thought it over now—under Jenny's humble deriding eyes.

"Lunch to-morrow—I shall be delighted. Thanks awfully," he said.

So ended that case of conscience. Jenny said no more than "One-thirty"—but her lips curved over that prosaic intimation of the hour of the meal. She turned to Dormer.

"Could I persuade you to drop in, too, Mr. Dormer? We're neighbors, you know."

"It's most kind of you, Miss Driver. I shall be delighted."

No scruples there; yet he, too, was, as he had chanced to mention, a guest at Fillingford Manor.

"Besides, I want to get something out of you," Jenny went on, "and I'm much more likely to do that if I give you a good lunch."

"Something out of me? What, Miss Driver?"

"Ah, I shan't tell you now. Perhaps I may—after lunch."

He leaned down toward her and said banteringly, "You'll have to ask me very nicely!"

"You may be sure I shall!" cried Jenny, with a swift upward glance.

Jenny was flirting again—with both of them—perhaps with me also, for her side-glances in my direction challenged and defied my opinion of her proceedings. I was glad to see it; I did not want her abnegations to go too far, and it is always a pity that natural gifts should be wasted; one might, however, feel pretty sure that any Lent of hers would have its *Mi-Carême*.

But if flirting—a thing pleasant in itself, an exercise of essentially feminine power—it was also purposeful flirting. She conciliated the new owner of Hingston, who had his position—who also had his outlying farms; and again she drove a wedge—this time into Lord Fillingford's house-party.

"I'm so glad you can come," she said to Lacey. "I want you to meet Margaret so much." She paused for a second. "Miss Octon, you know." She looked him very straight in the face as she spoke.

"It's very good of you to let me," he said. "I hear she's charming."

"I'm sure the Priory needs no additional attraction." This from Dormer in the dog-cart.

To one who knew Jenny well it was possible to see that this speech was not wholly to her liking—but Dormer was not allowed to see it. He received a passing but sufficient smile of graciousness before she gave the hearty thanks of her eyes to Lacey. "She is charming—you'll think so." A second's pause again, and then—"It's really very good to see you. Some day—a ride? Margaret's having lessons down in the town. Austin can ride still, although he has taken to writing books. We shall make quite a cavalcade."

"I say, don't leave me out, Miss Driver." This, again, from Dormer in the dog-cart.

"You live too far off."

"You try me and see!" he protested. Evidently he was very well pleased with the progress which his short acquaintance was making.

Lacey shook hands with her again. "To-morrow at half-past one, then—both of you!" she said. He turned away—was it reluctantly?—and got into the cart. With wavings of hands and hats the two young men drove off. Jenny stood looking after them.

"What brought you here?" I asked.

"The sight of those young men," answered Jenny, smiling. "May I come into your house? Do you remember how I came in first?"

"I remember; we had parted forever in the afternoon."

"Things are generally like that. The people who seem transient stay, the people who seem permanent go. I'm glad you seemed transient, Austin." She was in my room now, thoughtfully looking round it as she talked.

"Lacey came here to ask whether you would like him to call."

"Of course I should like him to call."

"Against his father's wishes. Lord Fillingford did not forbid him to come, but expressed his hope that the relations between the two houses would be kept as distant as courtesy allowed. I told Lacey that, in view of his father's wish, it would be better for him not to call. He said he'd think it over. It was a question between loyalty to his father and admiration of you."

"Admiration?" Jenny was listening with a slight smile.

"Rather, of your behavior—especially about Margaret. He's enthusiastic about that—he thinks it splendidly brave. In case he decided against calling, he wanted you to know that."

"He would have decided against it?"

"I can't tell. He meant to think it over."

"I came down just by accident. I was going for a stroll when I saw you. And I came down on the chance—the chance of something amusing, Austin." She frowned a little. "I don't think I much like Mr. Dormer."

"Rather a conceited fellow."

She broke into a smile again. "But he may come in very convenient."

"To his own profit and comfort?"

"I think conceited people must take the chance of that. They expose themselves."

"To being robbed of their farms by deceitful wiles?"

"He'd get a very good price for his farms," said Jenny. I do not think that her mind had been occupied with the question of the farms. She was looking thoughtful again. "I don't think I quarrel with what Lord Fillingford said," she added.

"Not unnatural perhaps."

"I've never had any quarrel with Lord Fillingford," she said slowly. "Or only one—a woman's quarrel. He never fell in love with me. If he had, perhaps—!" She shrugged her shoulders. "But all that sort of thing is over now."

"Did it look so like it this afternoon?"

"Didn't we agree that I was — marriageable? Didn't you say that being marriageable was an asset —even though one didn't marry?" She came suddenly closer to me. "I've no right to ask you to trust me. I didn't trust you—I deceived you deliberately, carefully, grossly—and yet I expected you to help me—and took your help with very little thanks. Still—you stayed. Stay now, and don't think too badly."

"I don't think badly at all—why, you know it! But I must have my fun out of it."

"So you shall, Austin!" she laughed, with one of her sudden transitions to gayety. "I'm the fox, and you're the huntsman! Well, I'll try to give you a good run for your money—if you can follow the scent!"

"Through all your doubles?"

"Through all the doubles that lead me to my— earth!"

A dainty merry little face looked in at my window. "Oh, I've tracked you at last, Jenny!"

"Is everybody tracking me?" asked Jenny, her eyes mischievously mocking. "Run round to the door and come in, Margaret." She added quickly to me, "I'm glad she didn't come when they were here. I'm saving her up till to-morrow!"

The child came in and ran to Jenny. "Oh, what a delightful little room, Mr. Austin! Did my father ever come here?"

"Yes, pretty often," I answered. "We were friends, you know."

"Yes, and he hadn't many friends. Had he, Jenny?"

Jenny stooped down and kissed her. "Come, we'll go for our walk—to look at Hatcham Ford," she said.

"Shall we go inside?"

"It's all shut up," said Jenny.

CHAPTER XX

LIVING PIECES

JENNY had now on the board all the pieces needed for her great combination—embracing, as it did, the restoration of her own position, the regaining of Catsford's loyal allegiance, the extension of her territory and influence in the county, and " doing the handsome thing by " Margaret. Nobody who watched her closely—both what she did and the hints of her mind which she let fall—could long doubt which of these objects was paramount with her. It was the last. The others were, in a sense, no more than means to it; though in themselves irresistible to her temperament, necessary to her happiness, and instinctively sought by her, yet in the combination they stood subsidiary to the masterstroke that was to crown her game and redeem the pledge which she had given to Leonard Octon as he lay dying. But doing the handsome thing by Margaret carried with it, or, rather, contained within itself, as Jenny conceived the position, another object to which in its turn it was, if not subsidiary, so closely related as to be inseparable. Fate had severed her life from Octon's; Jenny imperiously refused to accept the severance as complete. Octon, the man she loved, had been at odds with the neighborhood, had been scorned and rejected by it; she herself had openly disgraced him at its bidding; because she had not been able to resist his fascination, she had herself fallen into disgrace. She meant now to obliterate all that. For him she could directly do nothing; she would do everything for his name and for the girl whom he had left. She would vindicate—or avenge —his memory; she would even glorify it in the person of his daughter. That was the ultimate impulse which gave birth to her combination and dictated its moves; the achievement of that end was to be its consummation.

It was not a selfish impulse; it had indeed a touch of something quixotic and fanciful about it—this posthumous victory which she sought to win for Octon, this imposing of him in his death on a society which would have nothing of him while he lived, this proud refusal to court or to accept oblivion for him or for her friendship with him, this challenge thrown out to his detractors, in his name, as it were from his grave. Her personal restoration and aggrandizement, if welcome in themselves, were also necessary to this final object. The object itself was not self-seeking save in so far as she stood identified with the cause which she championed. Yet on the realization of it she did not scruple to bring to bear all the resources and all the arts which would have been appropriate to the most cold and calculating selfishness. Everything was pressed into the service—the resources of her own wealth, the opportunities afforded by the needs of her neighbors, Catsford's appetite for holidays and feasts, as well as its aspirations toward higher education; her own youth and attractiveness no less than Margaret's beauty; the wiles and the cunning by which she gained power over men. She spent herself as lavishly as she spent her money; she was as ready to sacrifice herself as she was eager to make use of others. She seized on every new ally and fitted him into her scheme. Dormer had appeared at the last moment—by happy chance. In a moment she saw where he could be of use, laid her hand on him, and pressed him into the service. He became a new piece on the board; he had his place in the combination.

Delicate and difficult is the game when it is played with living pieces. They may refuse to move—or may move in the wrong direction. There was one piece, of supreme importance in the scheme, which she must handle with rarest skill if he were to be induced to move at her bidding and in the direction that her combination required. He was to be the head and front of the final attack; at the head of the opposing forces stood his father! She must be very sure of her control over that piece before she tried to move it! Only when he had been brought wholly under her sway could the process of impelling him in the desired direction safely be begun.

Yes, Fillingford was the great enemy. Round him gathered all the opposition to her, her proceedings, and her pretensions; he lay right across her path, and must be conquered if her schemes were to win success. She was not bitter against him; she was ready to admit that he had the right to be bitter against her. She shared his pride too much not to appreciate his attitude. She respected him, in a way she liked him—but she was minded to fight him to the death if need be, and to use against him every weapon that she could find—even those that came from his own household. If he fell before her attack, the whole campaign would be won. But it was preposterous to suppose that he ever would? Jenny knew the difficulties, but neither did she underestimate her own resources. A long purse, a long head, and two remarkably attractive young women —these formed the nucleus of her forces; they represented a power by no means to be despised in whatever field they might be brought into action.

I was at the luncheon-party—" to talk to Chat," said Jenny; but in fact I had fallen into the habit of lunching at the Priory. Jenny had human weaknesses, and, from this time on, manifested a liking for a sympathetic audience—which she could find only in me. Chat was not, in her judgment, " safe "; she was too leaky a vessel to be trusted with the drops of confidence—carefully measured drops—which Jenny was pleased to let fall. Besides, she needed, now and then, a little help.

The young men arrived in high spirits, and Jenny, flanked by Chat and myself—Margaret was not down from changing after her riding lesson — received them gayly. They had a joke between themselves, and it was not long in coming out. They had been compelled to dodge Lady Sarah; only a bolt up a side road had prevented them from meeting her carriage face to face just outside Breysgate Park.

"You're playing truants, I'm afraid!" said Jenny, but with no air of rebuke.

Loft announced lunch; we went in without waiting for Margaret. She did not appear till we had been eating for ten minutes. By that time Jenny had both her guests well in hand. If her manner to Dormer was cordial, yet it lacked the touch of intimacy, of old-time friendliness, which she had for Lacey. But neither was she any longer so candidly Lacey's friend—and so definitely nothing else—as she had once thought it politic to become. She did not now hold her wiles in leash; she loosed them in pursuit of him, even as in the earliest days of their acquaintance.

The door opened. Jenny's eyes flew quickly to it; she stopped talking and seemed to wait for something. Margaret came running in, her hair bright in the summer sun, her eyes sparkling and her cheeks glowing — the very picture of radiant youth and beauty. Only a few feet separated me from Lacey. I heard him say "By Jove!" half under his breath.

Jenny heard, too. "Here's Margaret," she said. The girl ran to her, took her hand, and began to make a thousand excuses for being late.

"And, after all the rest, that nice clergyman stopped me on the road and talked to me!"

"You mean Mr. Alison? He stopped you?" Jenny looked interested. "What did he say?"

"Oh, nothing—only that he'd known my father, and that he hoped I was very happy. Of course I am —with you!"

"There's your place—between Mr. Dormer and Austin. Sit down, or Loft won't give you any lunch."

Between Dormer and me was opposite Jenny and Lacey—Chat and I each sitting at an end of the oblong table. Jenny showed no remission in her efforts to keep Lacey amused—indeed she rather engrossed him, and the other four of us talked together. But from time to time his eyes strayed across the table—and once he caught Miss Margaret studying his handsome face with evident interest. The girl blushed. Jenny was smiling contentedly as she regained her guest's attention.

Dormer made great play with the pretty girl. It did not take long to discover that this was Dormer's way. He had the gift—one enviable to slow-tongued folk like myself—of a perpetual flow of small talk; this he peppered copiously—I must confess to thinking that it needed seasoning—with flirtation, more or less obvious—generally more. He plied Margaret with the product, much to her apparent liking; she was at her prettiest in her timid fencing with his compliments, her shy enjoyment, her consciously daring little excursions into coquetry. But Dormer's eyes were not all for his own side of the table either; he made an effort or two to draw Jenny into conversation; he often looked her way. With those two in the room together, a man might well be puzzled to decide on which face to turn his eyes. Jenny assisted Dormer's choice. She would not be drawn by him —she was still for Lacey. The two couples talked, Chat and I falling out of the conversation; we could not condescend to call commonplaces across the space that divided us, and Chat and I seldom talked anything else to one another.

After lunch we all went into the garden—except Chat, who always took a siesta when she could. Here Jenny carried off Dormer, to see the hothouses—it was time to be civil to him. I fancied that she would not be vexed if I left Lacey and Margaret to a *tête-à-tête*, so, when they proposed strolling, I was firm for sitting, and we parted company. I could watch them as I sat. The two were getting on very well. For a little while I watched. My cigarette came to an end—I followed Chat's excellent example and fell asleep.

I awoke to find Jenny standing beside me. She was pulling a rose to pieces and smiling thoughtfully. Our guests had, it seemed, departed; Margaret was visible in a hammock under a tree at the other end of the lawn.

"I've really had to be quite shy with Mr. Dormer in the hothouses," she said. "He's such a ladies' man! And he's gone away with the impression that that's the sort of man I like. He has pointed out that Hingston is only fifteen miles off, and that he has a motor car and can do the distance in twenty-two—or was it twenty-seven?—minutes, so that lots can be seen of him, if desired. He has hinted that this is, after all, a lonely life for me—for a person of my gifts and attractions—and has congratulated me on the growing prosperity of Catsford. What do you make of all that, Austin?"

"Perhaps you told him that you wanted a bit of his land?"

"Mr. Cartmell would never have forgiven me if I'd let slip such a propitious opportunity. I did."

"It rather looks as if he wanted all of yours," I suggested.

"Then he communicated to me the impression that, in his opinion, Lord Lacey was considerably smitten with Eunice Aspenick and that the match might come off. In return for which I managed, I believe, to convey to him a sort of twofold impression—first, that I might possibly marry myself—some day; secondly, that, when I did, Margaret would be dismissed with a decent provision—a small addition to the little income which she has from her father. For reasons of my own I laid some stress on the latter half of that impression, Austin." She was looking over to where Margaret lay in the hammock. "She's very young," she said softly, "and of course, the man's glib and in a way good-looking."

"Are you beginning to feel a little responsible? It's easy work, marrying off other people!"

"But they make such a beautiful pair!" she pleaded. She did not mean Margaret and Dormer. "I love just to see them together. And the idea of it! How Leonard would have laughed! Can't you hear that great big outrageous guffaw of his breaking out over it? But you don't think I'd force her?"

"No. And he's a fine lad. You wouldn't be going far wrong."

"She's very young. She might—make a mistake. I thought Mr. Dormer had better understand her real situation."

"O mistress of many wiles, I understand! But is Lacey to share the impression?"

"I should like him to—up to the last possible minute. And then—the fairy godmother! It's all on the old-fashioned lines—but I like it." Her voice dropped "The old, mischievous, none-too-respectable fairy godmother, Austin!"

"Suppose the fairy godmother seemed not so very old herself—that mischief proved attractive—that——?"

"Impossible—with her here! Oh, you really think so, only you're always so polite. But anything short of—of that—would be quite within the four corners of the scheme." She laughed at me, at her schemes, at herself; yet about the two last she was in deadly earnest. So she grew grave again in a moment. "He'd have to get over so much to make that seem even possible."

Well, that was true enough. Fillingford's son—the accomplice of my evening expedition to Hatcham Ford! There was something to get over, certainly. But there was something to get over in the other plan, too.

"Still, I don't mind its seeming—just possible," said Jenny. She looked at me with an air of wondering how I should take what she was going to say. "It might just be made to seem—a danger!"

"This is walking on a razor's edge, isn't it?"

"Yes—it is rather. Mr. Dormer's got to help a little. I don't like him, Austin."

"No more do I—since you mention it. And you'd have no pity for him either?"

"I shall get his bit of land, but he won't get all mine," said Jenny, serenely pitiless. "He plays his game—I'll play mine. We neither of us stake our hearts, I think. You can't stake what you've never had—or what you've lost." She stood silent for a minute, looking down to where the smoke of busy Catsford rose in a blue mist between us and the horizon. " He's just ridiculous, but he serves my turn. No need to talk any more about him! "

Margaret tumbled herself out of the hammock with a grace which was entirely accidental and narrowly skirted a disaster to propriety. She came across the lawn, yawning and laughing. " I've been asleep, Jenny," she cried, " and having wonderful dreams! "

Jenny's face lit up with an extraordinary tenderness. She drew the girl to her and stroked her hair. " Why did you wake up? It's a pity to wake up when the dreams are wonderful."

" Oh, but waking up's great fun, too! Everything's great fun at Breysgate."

Stroking Margaret's hair, Jenny looked down at me in my wicker armchair. " I've been having fun, too—telling Austin secrets! "

" Tell me some."

" The day after to-morrow—or just about then! " laughed Jenny.

The ensuing days were full of triumph for Jenny. Her munificent donation was gratefully and enthusiastically accepted; a new Committee, composed of members of the Corporation, was appointed to take in hand the erection of the Institute immediately; there was no danger of this Committee's adjourning *sine die*! Her holiday and her feast went off in a blaze of success. She received a wonderful ovation from the town; there was no appearance of her being ostracized by the county. She came out to greet her guests, supported by the Aspenicks, by Dormer, even by Lacey; it was significant that the last-named should appear on so public an occasion. His presence compromised the attitude of Fillingford Manor; though its master was not there, though the lady who presided over the house was severely absent, the heir was there—and there, evidently, on terms of friendship and intimacy.

Lady Aspenick came, I think, not merely because she was committed to civility; she also desired to spy out the land, to get some light on the situation. Lacey's visits to Breysgate were becoming frequent; they had not passed unnoticed by vigilant eyes in the neighborhood, and the report of them had reached Overington Grange. Did Lacey brave the disapproval of his family for nothing? While Eunice joined the gay group which followed Jenny as she made a progress round the tables, Lady Aspenick fell to my share.

"All this is a great triumph for Jenny's friends," she remarked. "Those of us who have been her friends all through, I mean."

"It must be very gratifying to you, Lady Aspenick."

"I have been loyal," she said with candid pride, "and I am loyal still, although, as I told you, I can't approve of everything she does." Her eyes were on the group in front of us, where Lacey walked between Eunice and Margaret. Dormer was escorting Jenny, with the new Mayor of Breysgate on her other side.

"She has her own way of doing things," I murmured. "Sometimes they come off."

"Amyas Lacey here, too! How is that regarded at the Manor?"

"You ask me—but I shouldn't wonder if you knew better than I do," said I, smiling.

"Well, I admit I know Lady Sarah's views; she makes no secret of them. I was thinking of—well, of his father, you know. He doesn't share these visits!"

"If common gossip was right, there's an obvious explanation of that."

"Yes, but it seems to me to apply to the son almost as strongly." She turned her eyeglasses sharply round to my face. "Having jilted his father——"

"I didn't say I believed the common gossip; but even the fact of its having existed might make him shy of——"

"Oh, come, we both know a good deal more than that about it! However, let's hope they'll make it up—through Amyas. He can act as peacemaker, and then we may have the wedding after all!"

Lady Aspenick's voice failed to carry conviction. It was borne in upon me that she did not believe in her own forecast—that she knew very well, from information gleaned in the enemy's camp, that there was small chance of Lacey's effecting a reconciliation, and none at all of a marriage between Jenny and Fillingford coming off. She threw out the suggestion as a feeler; another possible alliance was really in her mind. She might elicit some hint about that; if people spoke truly, she was interested in the subject for her daughter's sake. Was it possible that

Jenny, having lost the father, would annex the son? That was in her mind. It would be rather a strong thing to do—but then, Lady Aspenick would retort, "Only look at the things she does!" The woman who brought Margaret Octon to Breysgate—would she hesitate at capturing young Lacey if she could?

"I can only say that in my opinion it's not at all likely, and has never entered Miss Driver's head."

"Then it's very funny that Amyas should come here so much!"

"Young men like young company," I remarked.

"It's not quite the only house in the neighborhood where there's young company," she retorted sharply. My remark had certainly rather overlooked the claims of Overington Grange.

She said no more, perhaps because her fish—my humble self—did not bite, perhaps merely because at that moment the Mayor of Catsford began to make a speech, highly eulogistic of Jenny and all her works. Lady Aspenick listened—or at least looked on (listening was not easy)—with an air which was distinctly critical.

Dormer was remarkably jubilant that day — perhaps as a result of his exchange of impressions with Jenny in the hothouses. He danced attendance on her constantly and was evidently only too glad to be seen in her train. Jenny received his homage with the utmost graciousness; he might well flatter himself that he stood high in her favor. There was a familiarity in his manner toward her which grated on my nerves; it had been there from his first meeting with her. It looked as though he thought that her past history gave him an advantage, and entitled him to consider himself a better match for her than he would have been held to be for another woman in her position. Perhaps Jenny would have had no right to resent such an idea; at any rate she showed no signs of resenting his behavior. She let him almost monopolize her—saving the Mayor's official rights—leaving Lacey to the care of Eunice Aspenick and of Margaret.

Lacey looked much less happy than might have been expected in such company. He appeared restless and ill at ease. When we were having a smoke together, while the ladies were getting ready for dinner (which was to be eaten hastily and followed by fireworks), I got some light on the cause of his discontent.

"It's curious," he observed over his cigar, "how disagreeable girls can manage to be to one another without saying a word that you can lay hold of."

"It is," said I. "Who's been exercising the gentle art this afternoon?"

"Why, Eunice Aspenick! You saw us three walking together? Well, we must have been walking like that—round the tables, you know—for the best part of an hour. Upon my honor, I don't believe she once addressed a remark directly to Miss Octon! And when Miss Octon spoke to her, she answered through me. And why?"

"The tandem whip, I suppose—hereditary feud and that sort of thing."

"It's not Miss Octon's fault; it's a shame to make her responsible."

"There doesn't seem to be any other reason."

He pulled his trim little fair mustache; I rather think that he blushed a little. "I don't like it, and I've a good mind to tell Eunice so. Miss Octon is Miss Driver's guest, just as we are, and on that ground anyhow entitled to civility."

I believe that he carried out his possibly chivalrous but certainly unwise purpose, and no doubt he got a snubbing for his pains. At any rate he had a short interview with Eunice just before we dined—and, afterwards, spoke to her no more that evening. While the fireworks blazed and the rockets roared, he placed himself between Jenny and Margaret. I managed to get near Margaret on the other side, just for the love of seeing the beauty of the girl's face as she watched the show with an intensity of excitement and delight. She clapped her hands, she laughed, she almost crowed in exultation. Once or twice she caught Lacey by the arm, as you see a child do with its father when the pleasure is really too much to hold all by itself. Jenny seemed to heed her very little—and to heed Amyas Lacey even less; she looked decidedly ruminative, gazing with a grave face at the spectacle, her clean-cut pallid profile standing out like a coin against the blaze of light. Amyas glanced at her now and again, but he was not proof against the living, exuberant, ebullient joy that bubbled and gurgled on his other side. Presently he abandoned himself altogether to the charm of it, fell under its sway, and became partaker of its mood. Now they were two children together, their shouts of laughter, of applause, of simulated alarm, filling the air. Grim looked the Aspenick ladies, very scornful that elegant gentleman Mr. Dormer! Margaret had never a thought for them; if Lacey had, he cast it away.

Thus they were when the show ended—but its ending did not check their talk and their laughter. Jenny rose, refreshments were spread within; to call Lacey's attention to her, she touched his shoulder. He turned round suddenly—with a start.

"Oh, I say, I beg your pardon! I—I didn't know you were still there, Miss Driver."

"There's something to eat indoors," said Jenny. "If you want it!"

"Oh, no, Jenny, dear, it's much nicer here. I'm sure Lord Lacey isn't hungry!"

He was not. Jenny turned away. As she passed me, she gave me an odd sort of smile, amused, satisfied, just a trifle—the least trifle—scornful. "Success number one!" she whispered. "But it's just as well that I'm not a vain woman, Austin!"

"You could undo it all in ten minutes if you liked."

Jenny's smile broadened a little — and her eyes confessed.

CHAPTER XXI

NATHAN AND DAVID

THE state of affairs at Fillingford Manor must have been profoundly uncomfortable. The father and his sister banned and boycotted Breysgate; the son spent there every hour of his leisure—he had much now, for the Parliament session was over—and made small secret of the fact that he cared very little to be anywhere else. Yet care came with him; he had more than a lover's proverbial moodiness. He never spoke of his home; it was the silence of conscious guilt; at Fillingford Manor, no doubt, he avoided all mention of us. More than once he took refuge at Hingston and paid his visits from there in company with his host; it is not probable that Fillingford Manor was deceived by this maneuver, but the daily strain of awkwardness was avoided. Dormer was complaisant. That young man had sharp eyes; he soon began to be at least very doubtful whether he need fear Lacey as a rival; when the two were at Breysgate together, it was Dormer's society now that Jenny sought. She would pair off with him, leaving Margaret and Lacey together. He took from this some encouragement, but he had also a lurking fear that Jenny was angling for Fillingford again, hoping some day to get at him through his son. He would make allusions, in Lacey's absence, to Fillingford's notorious obstinacy in all matters—how that he never changed his mind, was never open to reason, never forgot nor forgave. The more open hints were bestowed on me—for transmission to Jenny; the more covert he risked conveying to her direct. She would agree with a smile of resignation, and redouble her graciousness to Dormer. Yet the graciousness had limits. She kept him at his distance—eager, yet hesitating, and fearful to take the plunge. She had need of him still for a while longer; under the cover he afforded she was gradually, dexterously, unobtrusively, sheering off from Lacey.

The operation needed skill and pertinacity; for at first the young man resisted it vigorously. The more delicately she worked, the less conscious was he that she was working at all. Her avoidance of him seemed to him like his neglect of her; when he had, by her maneuvers, been kept out of her company for an hour together, his loyalty accused him of a lack of attention and of gratitude. He would come back penitent from Margaret's side, and turn again his chivalrous devotion to Jenny; he was remorseful at finding how happy he had been with another—at beginning to find that he was even happier. He did not impute to her any jealousy, or resentment at the fickleness of a lover, but he feared that she would be hurt by any falling-off in the affectionate homage which he had been wont to pay. Insensibly he was courting Margaret—but always by Jenny's permission. If it had been her will to summon him back to her side by his allegiance, he would have come; but, as day followed day, more and more reluctantly. Margaret's spell was gaining in power.

It could not well be otherwise. Youth turned to youth, the fresh heart to the fresh. Over Margaret hung no shadow; she was unspotted from the world. In her there was no calculation, and no scheming; all was instinctive and spontaneous. Her love leaped forth unashamed because it was unconscious of its very self. The fresh strange joy that painted life in new colors was unanalyzed. She was just so much happier, so much more gay, finding the days so much better. She did not ask why, but gave herself wholeheartedly to the new delight. With Jenny effaced by her own choice, this unmeant challenge fired Lacey to response; their fleet-footed feelings raced against one another, still neck and neck as they drew near the goal. A little further, and they would find themselves at it. It would then be time for Jenny to act.

The world misjudged her—which was just what she wished. Opinion was clear and well-nigh unanimous; for Jenny rehabilitation lay in marrying and could not be complete without it: then she meant to marry—Lacey if she could, Dormer if she must. There lay the explanation of the two young men being always at Breysgate! Lacey was the object of Jenny's spring; if she missed the mark, she would fall back on Dormer. But would she miss it? Gossip was rife, eager, interested, over this, and over this opinions varied; much is forgiven to sixty thousand a year, said some; there was one thing which Fillingford Manor would never overlook, said others. But on the whole it was admitted that there was great danger of her success; it was speculated on with the fearful joy that the prospect of a social disaster has the power to excite. Nobody thought of Margaret, or that she had any part to play in the matter, All eyes were on Jenny; it could not be many days before news came! There had hardly been more excitement over the flight itself.

Besides all the gossipers and watchers, there was one man who acted—according to his lights, whether they were right or wrong. I have hinted that Alison took a view of his office and its responsibilities which was at least fully adequate—and seemed to a good many people more than that. He was not content to stand by and see what he thought wrong done without a protest. It was nothing to him that he might be told to mind his own business: he would very confidently challenge your definition of his business and your idea of its limits; he would be very sure what his orders were and where they came from. Moreover he had seen the affair from the other side. He was intimate at Fillingford Manor.

He wrote to Jenny asking if he might call on her; he wanted to have a few words with her on a matter of importance relating to herself. He added that he was acting entirely on his own responsibility and in no way at the suggestion of any other person.

Jenny twisted his letter in her hands with an air of irresolution, almost of shrinking.

"I don't want to see him," she said to me plaintively. "It won't be—comfortable. He's let me severely alone up to now. Can't he let me alone still?

I suppose he'll lecture me horribly! If there were anything to be got by it! But there isn't."

"He sent you a pleasant message about Margaret," I reminded her.

"Yes, so he did. And I don't want him to think me afraid. I'll see him. But I'm afraid of him. Austin, you must be there."

"I don't think he'll expect that."

Never mind what he expects. If I see him, it's on my own conditions. I want you there. It's cowardly, but I do. Tell him he can come, but that I propose to see him in your presence."

So she would have it, being obviously disturbed at the idea of the interview. Was he coming to her as Nathan came to David—to denounce her sin? He was no doubt wrong about her intentions for the future, but he was fatally right in his opinion about what she had done in the past. He had a *locus standi*, too, or so he would conceive—a professional right to tell her the truth.

"I'm spoiled. I haven't had half enough of the disagreeables," she said with a woeful smile.

There was truth in that—so far as external things went, visible and palpable pains and penalties. She had not paid full toll. Luck had been with her and had afforded her a case—not a good one, but good enough to give her courage a handle. Her other advantages — her attractiveness, her position, her wealth, she had used with dexterity and without scruple to protect her from punishment. She had cajoled and she had bribed—both successfully; only the irreconcilables remained unreconciled. To no small extent she had jockeyed outraged morality—in externals. Many people did it even more successfully—by not being even half found out, and therefore not put on their defense at all. But for one who had been at least half found out, against whom circumstantial evidence was terribly strong although direct proof might be lacking, she had come off very cheaply. Nobody about her told her so; we spoiled her. She was afraid that Alison, in manner, very likely even in words, would tell her now, face to face. Being taken to task was terribly against the grain with her. Only Jenny might punish Jenny—and the blows must fall in secret.

Alison came to my house first a quarter of an hour before the time of his appointment with Jenny. He was grave and silent; in the spirit, though naturally not in the flesh, he wore full canonicals; the consciousness of his office was about him. I had grown—and I may as well confess it—into an intellectual hostility to all this, a skepticism which prompted rebellion. But he was doing what he disliked very much in obedience to his view of duty. It is churlish to show disrespect to a man acting in that way, simply because one may consider his view incorrect or exaggerated. I had once charged him with wanting to burn people; let me not fall into the temptation of wanting to burn him—or where stood my boasted liberality of thought?

"I'm not sorry that you're to be with us, Austin," he said, as we walked up to the Priory. "Interfere if I show any signs of growing hot."

"If she tells you the truth, you won't grow hot.

But if you grow hot, she won't tell you the truth," I answered.

"I don't go in my own strength," he reminded me with gentle gravity.

On the terrace, by the door, Margaret lay on a long wicker chair. She sprang up when we came near, blushing in her artless fashion at the encounter. Alison's stern-set face flashed out into a tender delighted smile. "God bless the pretty child!" he murmured as he went forward and shook hands with her. She had her little pet dog with her, and they talked a minute or two about it. He was country-bred and had dog-lore; she listened with an interest almost reverential. "Now!" he said with a sigh, as he left her to go into the house. He had welcomed that little interlude of brightness.

Jenny received him with stately dignity; if Nathan came to David, still let him remember that David was a King! She rose for a moment from the high-backed elbow-chair in which she sat; she did not offer her hand but, with a slight inclination of her head, indicated a chair. Then, seated again, she awaited his opening with the stillness of a forced composure. She might be afraid; she would show no fear. She faced him full where he sat, and challenged the light that fell on her face from the big window. I stood leaning against the mantelpiece, a few paces from her on her left.

"In coming to you, Miss Driver," he said, "I'm doing an unconventional thing. The circumstances seem to me to call for it; it's the only thing left to do, and nothing will be gained unless I face it and do it plainly. I want to tell you something about a household which you have no opportunity of seeing—something about Fillingford Manor. I go there, you know; you don't."

"No—not now," said Jenny.

"I say nothing about Lady Sarah. She is not, perhaps, very wise or very generous. Yet even for her allowances are to be made."

"I make such allowance as consists in absolute indifference, Mr. Alison."

"That's beyond your right—but no matter. In that house there is a father who loves his son and who respects himself. The father is miserable and humiliated. Do you recognize any responsibility in yourself for that?"

"Lord Fillingford once wanted to marry me—for my money, I think."

"I think you do him less than justice. Never mind that. I answer by asking you why he doesn't want to marry you now—even with your money."

"A very palpable hit!" said Jenny with a slight smile. "But did you come here only to say things like that? I know you think you have a right to say them—but what's the good?"

"The good is if they make you think—and I have a right to say them, though I fear your bitterness made me put them too harshly. If so, I beg your pardon. In whatever way I put them, the facts are there. Father and son are strangers in heart already; very soon they will be enemies if you persist in what you are doing."

"What am I doing?" asked Jenny, smiling again.

"Evil," he replied uncompromisingly. "Wanton evil if you don't mean to marry this young man—deliberate evil if you do."

"Why deliberate evil if I do?"

"You have no right to marry the son of that man. It would create a position unnatural, cruel, hideous."

"Alison, Alison!" I murmured. I thought that he was now "growing hot." But he took no notice of me—nor did Jenny.

"An inevitable and perpetual quarrel between father and son, a perpetual humiliation for a man who trusted you—and was wrong in doing it! Dare you do that—with what there is lying between you and Lord Fillingford?"

"What is there?"

"At least deceit, broken faith, trust betrayed, honor threatened. Is there no more?"

Jenny looked at him now with somber thoughtfulness.

"We're not children," he went on. "If there is no more, what was easier than to say so, to lay scandal to rest, to give an account of yourself? Wasn't that easy?"

"Lying is generally pretty easy," said Jenny.

He raised his hands in the air and let them fall in a despairing gesture. "You yourself have said it!"

"Yes, I have said it, Mr. Alison. You've always believed it. Now you know it. We're face to face."

"Then face to face I say to you that you're no fit wife for that young man."

"No fit companion either, perhaps?"

"I'll say no more than I need say. A sinner who

repents is a fit companion for the angels, and joyfully welcomed. Haven't you read it? I am on your duty, not to God—I pray Him that He may teach you that —but to the honorable man whom you deceived and humiliated. You charge him with having wanted to marry you for your money. Take it on that basis, if you will. What did you want to marry him for? Was it love? No; his title, his position. Was the exchange unfair? The bargain was fair, if not very pretty. Even to that bargain you were grossly false. If I'm wrong in my facts, say so: but if my facts are right, in very decency let his house—let his son—alone."

"Your facts are right," she said. "I was false to the bargain. Have you said all you have to say, Mr. Alison?"

"I have done—save to say that what I have said to you I have said to nobody else. I am no chatterer. What I've said to-day I've said in virtue of my office. What you have admitted to me I treat as told me in the confessional."

She bowed her head slightly, accepting his pledge. "I know that," she said. Then she turned to me, smiling sadly. "I'm afraid we must tell him our plans, Austin—in strict confidence?" She did not wait for an answer, but went on to him immediately: "I'll speak to you on the terms on which you have already heard me—as though I were in the confessional."

"What you are pleased to say is safe—but it's your deeds I want, not your words."

"My words will make my deeds plain to you," she answered, and then sat silent for a while, resting her cheek on her hand, looking very steadily in his face. At last she spoke in a low even voice:

"I don't admit your authority; and yet, as Austin knows, I shrank from this meeting. You claim the right to lay your hands on my very soul, to tear it out and look at it. I don't like that. I resent it. And what good does it do? We remain too far apart. I shall make to you no apology for what I have done; I don't desire to defend myself. The thing is very different to me, and you wouldn't even try to see the difference. Yet it is not less a great thing to me— as great as to you, though different. Yes, a great thing and a decisive one. I may look at it wrongly —I don't look at it lightly."

"I'm glad to be able to think that—at least," he remarked.

"I like you, and I want to work with you in the future. That's why I've listened to you, and why I now tell you what's in my mind—why I have come face to face with you. There was no obligation on me; my soul's my own, not yours, nor the world's. But I have chosen to do it. You came here, Mr. Alison, to tell me that I was not a fit wife for Lord Fillingford's son?"

He assented with a nod and a gentle motion of his hand.

"I agree with you there—with all you've said about that—but I go much farther. I don't think myself a fit wife for any man's son."

He looked up at her with a quick jerk of his head.

"I could go to no man as his wife without telling my story. And if I told it, what would he say? He might say, 'Go away!' Probably most men would, though there are some I know who, I think, would not. Or he might say, 'That's all over—forget all that. Be happy with me.' If he said that, what should I answer? I should have to say, 'It's not all over; it's not a wretched thing in the past that I've bitterly repented of and may now hope to be allowed to forget and to be forgiven for. It's not over and never will be. For me it's decisive; it will always be there. And it will always be there for you, too, and you will hate it.'" She spoke the last words with a strong intensity. "'Always something to be ashamed of, something to hide, something breeding a secret unconquerable grudge!' That's handicapping marriage very heavily—even though my husband were not son to Lord Fillingford! Do you know that it was only with the bitterest fear that I agreed to marry Leonard himself? Should I easily marry another man now?"

"Don't ask her to marry you—it only worries her." The words of Leonard Octon's letter came back; I could imagine the grimly humorous smile with which he penned that bit of advice to me.

She went on with a sudden suppressed passion: "I want none of it—none of it at all. I can make a happy life for myself. I can be useful—even if I have to lie—in deeds if not in words—before I can be allowed to be useful. Why am I to seek unhappiness, to seek fearfulness, to create misery? The burden I bear now my own shoulders are broad enough to carry. I had sooner carry it myself than have another groaning under it at my side!"

"Cast your burden upon God, and He will bear it. This is penitence, if only you would open the eyes of your heart!"

"Call it what you like," she said, a trifle impatiently. "Let it be pride—pride for Leonard and pride for myself; let it be calculation, precaution, fear, independence—what you will. You shall do your own name-giving, and you may give the name that satisfies your theories. But I have given you my names for it and my account of what I feel. Feeling that, am I eager to marry Amyas Lacey? I'm not eager, Mr. Alison."

There was a moment's pause. The sound of a horse trotting up to the house fell on my ears; Jenny gave me a quick glance. Alison seemed not to notice; he was looking down at the floor, deep in thought. Jenny's eyes returned to his face; she watched him with a smile as he sat pondering her explanation.

"I respect your conclusion," he said at last. "Even if there were nothing but the worldly point of view, I should say it was wise—as wise as it is severe. I hope you may find better reasons still for it, and new sources of strength to carry it out."

"You shall hope—and we shall see," she answered, not carelessly, but rather with an honest skepticism which was willing to respect his prepossessions, but would pay them no insincere homage.

"There is more for me to do than merely to hope —but enough of that just now." He smiled a little, for the first time in the interview. "I mustn't be too instant out of season. But if that is your conclusion, Miss Driver, how does it fit in with your conduct?"

"It fits in very well," she replied.

"That wouldn't be the general opinion. It's not the opinion at Fillingford Manor." He leaned back in his chair, looking rather weary and discouraged. "You're still minded to fence with me, I see," he said.

"No, I'll deal with you plainly—but I rely on your pledge. Nothing goes beyond these walls—neither to Fillingford Manor nor elsewhere?"

"I am bound to that: but pretenses are dangerous."

"It will soon be time to end this one."

As she spoke, merry voices floated into the room from the terrace outside. Jenny listened with a happy smile, and then went on, "You want to know what I mean by my conduct? Why I make Fillingford Manor unhappy, and all my neighbors mad with curiosity?" She laughed as she rose from her chair. "Come to the window here," she said to Alison.

They went to the window, and I followed. There, in the mellow sun of the late afternoon, Margaret lay on her long chair, her brown hair touched to gold, her merry laugh breaking out again, her face upturned to Lacey's. He stood beside her, his eyes set on her face, a smile of admiration plain to see on his lips. It was a fair picture of young lovers—and the complacent artist whose hand had designed it turned triumphantly to Alison.

"You ask what I mean. I mean that," she said.

Alison gave a violent start. "Miss Octon! And Amyas?" He looked for a moment at the pair, then turned back to Jenny, rather helplessly. "But that's pretty nearly as bad as the other!" he blurted out.

"Who speaks now?" she asked. "The priest in his office? Or Mr. Worldly Wiseman?"

CHAPTER XXII

THE ALTERNATIVE

ALISON watched the maid and the young man for half a minute, then drew back a little way into the room; Jenny followed as far as the piano and stood leaning her elbows on the top of it, smiling at him in mockery.

"That's a fair question, perhaps. But the idea is—staggering!"

Jenny raised her brows. "But why? Has she practiced deceit and betrayed trust? Has she broken faith or threatened anybody's honor? Or done worse things still? Is she no fit wife for a young man? What have you against her, Mr. Alison? Why is this pretty nearly as bad as the other?"

Alison was sadly put about and flustered. His confident air of authority vanished with the unimpeachable ground on which it had been founded. He had shifted his base; the new base failed him. "Surely you must see!" he protested.

"I see a dear beautiful girl and a charming handsome young man of high degree," answered Jenny in gay mischief, "and they look very much in love with one another. Is that dreadful?"

"It's quite a different case, of course—but really, really, just as hopeless!"

"You'd better not call this hopeless—neither you nor anybody else who has anything to say to it!"

"Octon's daughter!" He ejaculated the words in a low murmur, flinging his hands out wide.

"Yes, that's it!" said Jenny, her smile getting harder, and with a rather vicious look in her eyes. "That's why, isn't it? That's why she's not good enough for Amyas Lacey, not good enough to be mistress of Fillingford Manor! There's nothing else against her? Only—she's Leonard Octon's daughter! Well, now, I say to you that that shall not be against her. It shall be for her—mightily for her. To that she shall owe everything; that shall give her all she wants. If you have any influence, don't use it against her. Use it for her, back her up. It will be wiser in the interests of the friends whom you're so concerned for." She left the piano and came into the middle of the room, facing him. "Because it's the alternative to that unnatural hideous thing of which you came here to speak—and spoke so plainly. If I'm not much mistaken, I can turn this thing the way I choose. And I tell you that in spite of all you've said, and in spite of all I've said, your friends will be wise to accept the lesser evil. Margaret is better than me, at all events!"

She was on her high horse now. Very handsome she looked, with a glowing color in her cheeks; her voice was full of temper, hard-held. It was the turning point of the scheme which she was working out; through Alison she launched her ultimatum to Fillingford: "Margaret or myself—there is no other alternative."

THE ALTERNATIVE

Alison was recovering himself. He dropped into a chair and looked up at her commanding figure with a smile of kindness—with an admiration wrung from him by her *coup*.

"You're really wonderful," he told her. "I'll say that for you—and I'll be as worldly as you like for a minute."

"Yes, do try for once. There is such a thing as this world."

"Then—even setting aside the obvious objection, the objection our friends at the Manor are bound to feel—Lacey is Lacey, and will be Fillingford. The girl—I think her as charming as you do—comes from nowhere and has, I suppose, nothing?"

"She'll come from Breysgate Priory—and not empty-handed."

"Of course you'd behave kindly to her, but——"

Back to Octon's phrase went Jenny—back to the words in which he had bequeathed his "legacy" to her. Her face softened. "I shall do the handsome thing by her," she said in a low voice. "Can't you understand why I do this?" she asked him. "You were one of the few people who seemed to understand why I brought her here—to be with me. Can't you understand this?"

"Perhaps I can—a little. But is it fair to Lord Fillingford?"

"I can't think always and forever of Lord Fillingford," she told him impatiently. "He isn't all the world to me. I am thinking of Leonard—this is all I can do for him now. I'm thinking of the child—and of myself. I can give up for myself, but this is my compensation. What I could have she is to have —because she loves Amyas, and I love her—and because I loved her father. That's what I mean. I daresay you've some very hard names for it. They made me give up Leonard once—at any rate behave as if I was ashamed of him. Very well. They must take Leonard's daughter now—or that worse thing you and I know of."

"I'm still on the worldly plane," Alison said, smiling. "You can, of course, if you're so minded, abolish all objections except the sentimental. If it's a hundred thousand for an Institute, what mightn't it be for a whim, Miss Driver?"

"And what mightn't it be for my dear man who's dead?" said Jenny, very low.

He got up, went to her, and took her hands. She did not repel him. He whispered a word or two to her—of comfort or sympathy, as his manner indicated. Then he looked round at me. "You've had a hand in this mischief, I suppose, Austin?"

"Oh, we just take our orders in this house," said I.

"Heaven humble your heart!" he said to her, but now the rebuke was kindly, almost playful.

"The present question is of humbling Lord Fillingford's," retorted Jenny.

Alison walked back to the window. Jenny gave me a quick nod of satisfaction; the fight was going well. "Are they still there?" she asked.

"Oh, dear me, yes! He's sat down by her on the ground—looking up, you know!"

"Yes, I can imagine, Mr. Alison."

THE ALTERNATIVE

"A fine pair!" He turned round with a sigh. "And very fond of one another! And yet you think you could—? Well, perhaps you could—who knows?" He seemed to study her thoughtfully.

"I don't want to, you know—unless I'm driven," said Jenny.

"You mustn't do it," he told her, with some return of his authority. He softened the next moment; "I don't believe you would."

"Run no risks—advise your friends to run none. You've seen enough of me now to know that it's not safe to conclude I shan't do a thing just because I think it's wrong—or even because I don't at this moment mean to do it. I have to reckon with a temper; others had better reckon with it, too."

Alison looked at me, pursing up his lips. "I think that she points out a real danger."

"I'm sure she does," I rejoined. "And you must reckon with it."

"Yes," he murmured, his eyes again searching her face. She nodded her head ever so slightly at him with a defiant smile. "But losing your temper oughtn't to be relied on as a resource. Reckon with it if you like—not on it, Miss Driver."

Jenny laughed outright at that. "He hits me hard —but it makes no difference," she said to me. "The plan stands." She turned quickly on him: "In the end, what do you make of it?" She stretched out her right hand. "Are even good things soiled if they are taken from that hand?"

"The pity of it!" he murmured, with a soft intonation of profound sorrow.

"The child's a pearl. Let her be happy! Is the beauty of it nothing to you?"

"Yes, it's much—and your love for her is much." He paused a' moment. "And perhaps I should be overbold to speak against that other love of yours—now. Maybe it lies beyond the jurisdiction committed to us here on earth."

Jenny was, I fear, entirely devoted to earth and, at that moment, to arranging her own bit of earth as she wanted to have it. She gave him no thanks for what was, from him, a very considerable concession. Rather she fastened on his softer mood as affording her an opportunity.

"Then you oughtn't to be against me," she urged.

"I'm not against you. This is not my ground—not my business."

"You might even help me." He looked doubtful at that. "Simply in one way. There's one little thing you can do easily, though it's difficult for me. For all the rest, I leave you to do anything or nothing, just as you think proper."

"What's the one little thing?" he asked.

"Bring Lord Fillingford and Margaret together. It's very easy—except for me—and it commits you to nothing. Give her her chance. Anyhow, none of the trouble's her fault, is it?"

"There doesn't seem much harm in that."

"Give him no hint of what I've said. It would be so much better if the idea could come from himself."

"Impossible!" he cried.

"I don't know," she said thoughtfully. "He seems to be very frightened. How about some idea of—the lesser evil? He'd still be shocked—but his mind might be a little prepared."

"You're altogether too—well, shall I say diplomatic?—for me."

"Come, come," I interposed, "don't do the Church injustice!"

"Let's go out," said Jenny. "Wait a minute—I'll get a hat, and join you on the terrace. I expect Margaret and Amyas are still there." She walked out of the room with a light buoyant tread. Alison turned to me with a bewildered gesture of his arms, yet with a reluctant smile on his face.

"What am I to work on? I don't believe the woman has any conception of what sin means!"

"She has a considerable conception of the consequences of her actions."

"My dear fellow, as if that was at all the same thing! And what's her new game? What's she taking me on the terrace for?"

"To have a cup of tea, I suppose. It's nearly half-past five."

"I'll never give her credit for being as simple as that!" He was disapproving, but good-natured—and altogether occupied with Jenny in his mind. "I shall never get hold of her—I once thought I should. A pagan—a mere pagan!" He paused again and added with a reluctant admiration, "A splendid pagan!"

"There are fifty roads to town—and rather more to heaven," I quoted.

"Who said that?"

"William Mackworth Praed—and you ought to have known it."

"I daresay he knew the roads to town, Austin."

"In both cases the criticism is obvious—much depends on where you start from."

We were on the terrace now. At the other end of it we saw Margaret and Lacey walking up and down together. The tea table was deserted, and probably the tea was cold; we were neither of us thinking about it. Alison had put on his hat, but now he bared his head again to the evening breeze.

"Phew, that was a fight!" he said. "And I suppose I'm beaten! But if she yields to that temper of hers, I'll have no more to do with her."

"But if she doesn't—if she needn't?" I suggested.

He made no answer. I saw his eyes wander to the shapely couple that walked up and down.

"Why shouldn't the child have her chance?"

"You're tempters all in this house!" he declared.

Margaret and Lacey suddenly came toward us—no, toward Jenny, who had just come out of the house. She stood there, near the door, quite quietly—with all her gift of serene immobility brought into play. There was no signing to them, no beckoning: but at once, out of the midst of their delighted preoccupation, they came. I permitted myself a discreet glance at Alison; he was watching. I wondered whether he were any nearer to a theory of why Jenny had proposed that we should come out on the terrace.

Margaret Octon ran on ahead of her companion and caught hold of Jenny's arm. Lacey came up a second later. I saw Jenny give him a smile of the fullest understanding. The young man flushed suddenly, then laughed in an embarrassed way.

"I know I've been here an awful time. I thought you were never coming out," he said.

"The time seemed so long till I came, did it?" asked Jenny. She stooped and kissed Margaret on the forehead. The girl laughed—very gently, very happily. Jenny looked at Alison across the few feet that divided the two small groups. Her look was an appeal — an appeal from the shy happiness on the girl's face to the natural man that was beneath Alison's canonicals. "Shan't the girl have her chance?" asked Jenny's eyes.

Suddenly Alison left my side and walked up to her.

"I must go now," he said, rather hastily, rather (to tell the truth) as though he were ashamed of himself. "I think I can manage that little commission."

She moved one step forward to meet him. "I shall be very grateful," she told him in her low, rich, steady tones. "The other way wouldn't have been nearly so—convenient." Her bright eyes were triumphant. "Soon?" she asked.

"I can manage it in a day or two at longest. And now good-by. I fear I've tired you with all my business."

The young people listened, all innocent of the covert meanings.

"Let's not be tired till our work's done!" said Jenny.

She risked that "our" and challenged his dissent. He stood swaying between reprobation and admiration, between forswearing and alliance, between sympathy and repulsion. She had so much—yet not that without which, in his eyes, all else was in the end worthless.

But she had brought him—of her subtlety she had brought him—on to the terrace. For no cup of tea tolerably stale! For nothing stale—but that the imploring, aye, the commanding, unconscious desire, the unmeditated appeal, the unmeant urgency, of Margaret's heart might work. " Are you human? " asked Jenny's eyes, traveling with a slow meaning from his face to Margaret's.

The cunning of the serpent—the simplicity of the dove! Ah, dear serpent, what had you in your heart save to make your dove happy? Another thing—yes! The dove must triumph—for she bore Leonard's escutcheon, and must bear it victorious against his enemies. The serpent bade the dove wing her happy way!

Might not the dove be made bearer also of an olive branch, made a harbinger of peace? That was the idea which Jenny sought to put in Alison's mind when she brought him on to the terrace. Could not all that grace and joy avail to blot out the name she bore? It was only a name—a thing intangible—a name, if Jenny's plan prospered, soon to be deleted, buried under a new and newly significant designation. She must bring memories with her—of old wrong and old humiliation? Could she not herself destroy even what she brought? She seemed made to do it. Who could bear a grudge against that simple joyfulness, who resist that unconscious pleading for oblivion? Alison was to go from the terrace with a new zeal for the commission that he had undertaken, to go with his cause much closer to his heart.

While he was still there, Dormer whizzed up the drive in his motor car. He had come to meet Lacey at Breysgate, and drive him over to Hingston to dine and sleep. Lacey affected Hingston for his night quarters more than ever now—and Dormer generally fetched him from Breysgate; it was an arrangement convenient to both parties.

Jenny had told so much truth that she was inclined for a little mischief. She greeted the newcomer with coquettish demureness, marking, with a smile and a glance at me, Dormer's ill-concealed surprise at Alison's presence, and at the good terms on which he seemed to be with his hostess. Dormer asked for whisky and soda, and I went with him to minister to his wants.

"Did Lacey bring the parson?" he asked, after a first eager gulp.

"Oh, no. Alison came of his own accord—came to call, you know," I answered.

"Did he?" He would obviously have liked to ask more questions. "That's being neighborly, at all events," he ventured to comment, with a covert leer. "We shall be seeing Fillingford—or even Lady Sarah—here next!"

"More unlikely things than that have happened."

"That's what I always remember," he remarked, nodding sagaciously over his long tumbler. "What I say is—try your luck, even if it does need a bit of cheek."

I had a notion that Dormer was inclining toward the confidential.

"If it doesn't come off, you're no worse than you were before. If it does, there you are, by Jove!"

"I should think that must be every successful man's philosophy. But what, may I ask, makes this call on your reserve of cheek, Dormer?—which will, I make no doubt, be equal to it."

"Wait and see," he answered, with a pronounced wink. Having executed this operation, his eye turned to Lacey, visible through the window of the smoking room where we were. "There'll be a row at Fillingford Manor some day soon—that's my opinion."

"Let's wait and see about that, too," I suggested mildly. Now he was trying to make me confidential.

He winked again. "You're a pretty safe old chap, Austin," he was good enough to tell me.

When we returned to the terrace, Lacey was ready to start and, with a look at his watch, Dormer went up to Jenny to say good-by. During our brief absence Alison had departed—to set about his commission, as I hoped.

"I say, may I come over the day after to-morrow? Shall you be here?" Dormer asked.

"The day after to-morrow? Thursday? Yes, I shall be delighted to see you. I want to know how you're getting on in those negotiations with Mr. Cartmell, you know." This referred to those farms of his—she had by now settled on three—which she wanted to round off her frontier.

Dormer smiled slyly at her. "All right, we'll talk about that, too."

"Have we any other business?" she asked, lifting her brows in feigned surprise.

"Something may crop up," he answered with a laugh. "Till then, Miss Driver!"

The young men got in and drove off, Margaret watching and waving her hand as they went—a salutation copiously acknowledged by Lacey; Dormer was busy with his handles.

"If Mr. Alison is prompt with his commission, Thursday may be a busy day," Jenny remarked, as she sat down in a low chair and lay back in it with an air of energy relaxed. Sitting down by her, I began to smoke my pipe. Margaret passed us, smiling, and went into the house.

"That was a fight," said Jenny presently, "rather a stiff one—but we've got our stiffest still to come. Lord Fillingford will fight; I must move all my battalions against him. I shall bribe—perhaps I shall still have to bully." She sighed. For the moment, the afternoon's struggle done, a weariness was upon her. She sat silent again for a long while, her brows knit in meditation or in sorrow.

"I won't tell anybody else," at last she said. "I have told you, because I wouldn't have you live here on false pretenses—because you're my friend. I told Mr. Alison to-day for the reason you heard. I'll tell nobody else. The old attitude toward the rest! It's really no use telling—I can't tell it right; I can't put it into words. For myself even I can't recover the past—can't quite see how I did it—what woman I was then, or how that woman stands to the woman I am now. A mist has come between the two."

"For Heaven's sake, vex yourself no more! Let the dead bury its dead. Alison has upset you."

"I'm in the mist—but Leonard isn't. He grows clearer and clearer, and" (she smiled faintly) "larger and larger. His great kind loving-roughness fills all my vision. I suppose it filled all my vision then, and so—it happened!" She turned to me with a quick question. "Do you think I'm right in the determination I've come to about myself?"

"I should be far from holding it obligatory either on you or on anyone else. Good things pass by—and things indifferent—and things bad. The disturbance passes off the face of life's stream; the stream pursues its course. There's no duty on you, in my opinion. Yet I think that for yourself you're right."

"I'm glad you do," she told me. "At that we'll leave it—a fixed point!"

"Unless Lord Fillingford is very obstinate?"

As she looked at me, a smile broke slowly over her face. "From the way you say that, I think you suspect me of having indulged in a little bluff this afternoon. But I think I was honest. I don't mean to do it, I should hate doing it—but they might make me angry enough."

"I don't believe you'd ever go through with it. We should have flight again!"

"Too awful!" sighed Jenny, frowning, yet almost smiling. She smiled frankly the next moment, as she turned to me and laid her hand on my arm. "Do let's agree—you and I—that I'm quite incapable of it and was bluffing most audaciously!"

"We'll agree to that with all my heart."

"So you spoil me—so you go on spoiling me!" she said very gently.

I went down the hill to my own house, leaving her still sitting there, a stately solitary figure, revolving many thoughts in the depths of her mind.

CHAPTER XXIII

ON ALL GROUNDS—RIDICULOUS!

ALISON was prompt as could be wished. The next morning we received our orders. Margaret was to go to tea with him at the Church House, escorted either by Chat or by me, as Jenny preferred. He expected that some business would bring Fillingford there about five—and so the encounter; for the result of it, he added, he took no sort of responsibility.

"You must go, of course," Jenny decided. "Chat wouldn't be able to tell me anything about what really happened."

I had to see Cartmell earlier in the afternoon, so arranged to meet Margaret at the appointed place. She knew nothing of Fillingford's being expected, but she had taken a strong liking to Alison and was greatly pleased with her invitation—only surprised that Jenny should not be going, too.

"Oh, I told him I couldn't," said Jenny. Let us call that a diplomatic evasion.

Sir John Aspenick came into Cartmell's office while I was there. He had heard rumors of the proposed sale of Oxley Lodge and its estate by Bertram Ware—and to Jenny. Here was legitimate matter of inquiry and interest for the county. Aspenick was much interested; but he did not seem particularly pleased.

"The thing is hardly public property yet," said old Cartmell, "but I'm sure Miss Driver wouldn't mind its being mentioned to such an old friend as you are, Sir John. Yes, it's settled. Ware sells and she buys—the whole thing, lock, stock, and barrel, and at a pretty stiff price, too—to say nothing of an extra five hundred for early possession."

"Why does she do it?" demanded Aspenick, sitting on the office table and smoking a cigar.

"Ah! I can sometimes see what a woman is doing by using my eyes, and I can sometimes see what she's going to do by using my head; but why she does it or why she's going to do it—that's quite beyond me," said Cartmell.

"It's a pretty place," I urged. "Good house—nice sized sort of place, too."

"But who's going to live in it—unless you are, Austin?"

I modestly disclaimed any pretensions—and any desire — to be housed so handsomely. Sir John frowned in perplexity. "Seems to me she wants the whole county!" he observed.

"Old Nicholas Driver did, anyhow," said Cartmell with a laugh. "Oxley wasn't enough for him! He wanted Fillingford Manor—you remember, Sir John?"

"Well, that didn't come off," said Aspenick dryly; I fancied that he hinted it had not "come off" with old Nicholas's daughter either—so far. "Does she mean to let the house?"

"I really don't know anything about it."

"Well, she'll be a good neighbor, I suppose. She can afford to keep her fences in order, and she won't put up wire. More than I can say for Ware! His fences were a disgrace, and he's been threatening us with wire—that's only since we wouldn't have him as candidate, I admit."

"We'll answer for the fences and the wire," Cartmell promised him cheerfully.

" But, in spite of his being reassured as to these vital matters, Aspenick's brow was still clouded.

"You're her man, of course, Cartmell, but I don't mind saying to you that these new people coming in and buying up everything give me a sort of feeling of being crowded. Do you know what I mean?"

"Can't keep things just as they were six hundred years ago, Sir John," said Cartmell.

Aspenick was not mollified by this tactful reference to his long descent. "Hustling, I call it! I suppose you'll be wanting Overington next?"

We both repudiated the idea of laying profane hands on Overington's ancient glories. "We'll leave you in possession, Sir John. But we may take just a slice off Hingston, if Mr. Dormer's agreeable."

"Everybody knows that Dormer's outrunning the constable, and I daresay you'll get all you want from him—but not an acre of mine, mind you!"

"Don't cry out before you're hurt, Sir John," Cartmell advised him good-humoredly. But when he was gone he said to me with a shrewd nod, "Well, we all know why he's so precious sulky!"

Aspenick's want of warmth about our new acquisitions (Cartmell and I always said "our" when we meant Jenny's) no doubt had a personal cause—though it was not hard to appreciate also his class-feeling. The property of Oxley lay full between Overington and Fillingford Manor; but since her return Jenny had severed Aspenick's house from Fillingford's in another way than that. No more was heard about Lacey and Eunice.

Cartmell was no gossip and a man of few questions unless about a horse; yet now he turned his rubicund face toward me with an air of humorous puzzle. "Any news from the house?"

"Nothing particular—just at present," I answered.

"I've looked at it this way, and I've looked at it that way, and I'm flummoxed. Why early possession—and five hundred paid for it? She can't want the house—and as business it's ridiculous. But you know her way—'My wish, Mr. Cartmell, and please no words about it!'"

"She generally has a purpose—she doesn't act at random," I remarked.

"A purpose! Lord love you, half a dozen! And, what's more, I believe you generally know them. But, as she knows, you're devilish safe. There it is! I could make her a really rich woman if she'd let me—but with money thrown away like that, and her Institute, and what not—!" He looked as gloomy as if Jenny were on the verge of bankruptcy and all our livelihoods taking wings.

"I'll tell you one thing. I think you'll have to open the purse-strings wider still before many days are out."

He looked at me very sharply. "The marriage coming off? And a big settlement? Well, that'd be right enough. All the same, I can't say I like it, Austin. Fillingford's son! Doesn't it stick in your throat a bit?"

"I said I'd tell you one thing. I didn't say I'd tell you two or three more."

"All the town says it. My word, you should hear Mrs. Jepps! My wife says it's something terrible." He twinkled in amusement again. "Lord, it's sometimes worth being a bit staggered yourself just to see how much worse the thing takes other people!"

"Mrs. Jepps and the rest of the town had better wait a little. It's a pity to waste good indignation."

"Aye, and folks hate being cheated of a scandal they've made up their minds to."

"Scandal's a hard word in the case that you're thinking of."

"I've no great stock of words outside of a conveyance of land—there I can use as many as any man except counsel. But, to tell the truth, it goes against my stomach."

"It sticks in your throat! And it goes against your stomach! And all this before you've been even asked to swallow it! Aren't you considerably premature?"

"You think there's a chance she won't—?" His manner was openly eager.

"Yes—but hold your tongue, and pay up your five hundred for early possession."

"Upon my soul, Austin, I never more than half believed it. But when everybody buzzes a thing into

a man's ears—and his own wife first among them—
and he sees no other meaning of things, why——"

"The best of us are likely to give in—yes! Well,
I've got another appointment—at Alison's."

"Alison's? What have you got to do with Alison
these days?"

"Come now, does your position interfere with
your friendships? What have you to do with Mrs.
Jepps?"

"It was my wife. I never see the old witch."

"I've no wife—so I have to face the devil on my
own account."

From my talk with Cartmell I was the more anxious for the success of my other appointment. That
might help to free Jenny from the danger of being
made so angry as to do what she hated to do, and
what faithful old Cartmell could not stomach. If anything could drive her to it, it would be a slight, a
harshness, a rudeness, toward Margaret. How she
had flared up at Alison's objections! If Margaret
were spurned, to Jenny's mind Octon also was again
spurned. Then the temper would still have to be
reckoned with—the temper under disappointment as
well as wrath; for Jenny built upon this interview.

Margaret was punctual at Alison's—she came
spanking up in the carriage with the big gray horses
the moment after I had reached the door—and we
went together into the sparely furnished room where
he lived and did his work. He was no bookman—his
walls looked bare; his very chairs meant labor rather
than rest. And he was no student—"My convictions
from God, my orders from the Bishop, my time to

the ministry," he had once said to me—adding then, with the touch of humor that so often softened his rigorous zeal—" I sometimes think one's Bishop is the final trial of faith, Austin." Our Bishop was a moderate man, highly diplomatic, given to quoting St. Paul as an example of adaptability. "All things to all men if by chance—" So far as the chance lay there, his lordship never missed it.

But to see Alison with Margaret obliterated any criticism left possible by his affectionate nature and (may I add?) his ingenuous consciousness of possessing absolute and exclusive truth. He had so tender a reverence for her youth and receptivity—and with it such a high gentlemanly purpose that she should not think that he held her either too young for courtesy or too receptive for intellectual respect. He had great manners, born of a loving heart. Why, after all, should he worry about reading books? Guesses about appearances—that's books—from novels up to philosophy. But how pleasant is the guessing!

She became to him at once a delighted disciple. Here was no such discrepancy of heart and head as divided him from Jenny—no appeal to another standard—no obstinate defense against his attacks behind the ramparts of her nature. Margaret's nature was his to mold—small blame to him if the thought crossed his mind that it would be to the good if she were set in a high place—if such a light burned under no bushel of obscurity!

Fillingford was announced. Alison gave me a quick glance, as though to say "Now for it!"—and the grave stern man stood on the threshold of the room. I had not seen him without his hat for a long while; he had grown gray: his figure, too, was more set; he was indisputably, even emphatically, middle-aged. His face was more lined and looked careworn. His eyes fell first on me, and there was hesitation in his manner. Alison went quickly to him and greeted him.

"We've been having a little tea-party, but I shall soon be ready for business. Austin you know. This is my friend Miss Octon."

Fillingford came forward—slowly, but with no change of expression. He bowed gravely to Margaret, and gave me his hand with a limp pressure. "I hope you're well, Mr. Austin? We've met very little of late."

Margaret was regarding him with curiosity complicated by alarm. This was Amyas Lacey's father—and Amyas had given the impression that his father was formidable; there was a knowledge in her own heart which might well make him seem formidable to her, even had his bearing been far more cordial.

"I'm afraid I've come too soon," he said. "I interrupt your party."

"Sit down with us and have a cup of tea—Miss Octon will give you one."

He did not refuse the invitation, and sat down opposite Margaret. She ministered to him with a graceful assiduity, offering her timid services with smiles that begged a welcome for them. He remained gravely courteous, watching her with apparent interest.

"I hope Miss Driver is well?" he said to me with a carefully measured civility.

Very wisely Alison did not leave the pair he had brought together to entertain one another. Plunging again into the description of his work which had so won Margaret's interest before, he enabled Fillingford to see the gay charm which he himself could not elicit. Then, branching off to herself, he got her to describe the wonderful delights of her new existence—her horse, her dog, the little room that Jenny had given her for her own snuggery at the top of the house. "I can see your chimneys from the window!" she told Fillingford with a sudden turn toward him, followed by a lively blush—how came her interest in those chimneys to be so great? Fear kept her from Lacey's name; some instinct, I think, from more than casual reference to the donor of all the fine gifts which she catalogued and praised; little reference used to be made to Fillingford at Breysgate, and perhaps she had caught the cue thus given.

"But I haven't got enough work to do," she complained gayly to Alison. "And if you would let me come and work for you——"

"I'll find you plenty of work to do," he promised. "Lots of wicked old women to visit!" He smiled at us. "I might try you on the wicked young men, too," he added. "There are lots of them about. But plenty of very good fellows, too, if only we could really get hold of them."

"Try her on Mrs. Jepps," Fillingford suggested dryly; yet the smallest unbending, the least hint of a joke, from him seemed something gained.

ON ALL GROUNDS—RIDICULOUS! 359

"That's the old lady with the fat horses, isn't it? She looks very kind and nice."

"Hum!" said Alison. Fillingford gave a wintry smile. "Mrs. Jepps and I are considered the two ogres of the neighborhood," he said.

Her little hand darted impulsively across the table toward him, and was as quickly drawn back—one of her ventures, followed by her merry confusion. "You! Oh, nonsense! I don't believe that!"

"Ah, you haven't heard all the stories about me!"

"I've only heard that you're very—really very kind and—and just." She was summoning all her courage; she was full of deprecation and appeal.

"Who told you that?"

She cast a look of dismay at me, and I came to her rescue. "Your son, of course, Lord Fillingford. We see him sometimes at Breysgate."

"I know you do." He shot out the words and shut his lips close after them.

She looked distressed and rather puzzled; after thawing a little, he had relapsed into frost at the first mention of his son. Alison seemed to think a diversion desirable.

"Before you go, I should like to show you our chapel. We have a little one of our own here. We use it in the early mornings sometimes, and for prayers after supper."

She jumped at the proposal, both for its own sake, I think, and for a refuge from her embarrassment.

"We'll be back directly," said Alison, as they left Fillingford and myself together.

Fillingford sat in silence for some moments. Then he said slowly, "I didn't know that your newcomer at Breysgate was so attractive."

Jenny had not reckoned on my being left alone with him. I had no instructions, and had to choose my own course. "I thought that perhaps Lacey would have told you about her?"

He looked me in the face with his heavy deliberate gaze. "We don't often speak of his visits to Breysgate." He paused and then added, with something of restrained vehemence in his tone, "I don't care to ask either the number or the object of his visits—and he hasn't volunteered any information to me on either point."

"His visits are frequent," I remarked. "As to their object——"

"I don't think we need discuss that—you and I, Mr. Austin."

"I was only going to say that we could neither of us do more than guess at it."

For a moment he lost his self-control. "I hope to Heaven my guess is wrong—that's all," he said hotly.

Surprised out of reserve, he leaned forward toward me, with a sudden look of eagerness in his eyes. "I should like to know what you mean by that—if you're at liberty to tell me."

"I'd sooner not. It would come better from your son, I think."

"I prefer not to talk to my son about the matter just now. I might wrong him. I have many worries just now—business and others—and I don't trust myself to discuss it with him with all the calmness which I should desire."

"I'm afraid I can do no more than venture to advise you not to come to any conclusion prematurely."

He broke out again; it was evident that he was living under a strain which taxed his endurance sorely. "But Amyas is always there! And she——!"

The sound of Alison's voice came from the hall. "Hush! They're just coming back. You must wait and see."

A light broke over his face. "You can't possibly mean that it's this girl?" There was undoubted relief in his tone—but utter surprise, too, and even contempt. "Oh, but that's on all grounds utterly ridiculous!"

They were in the room again. "Don't say so, don't say so," I had just time to whisper.

Margaret came in, laughing and merry, recovered from her confusion, delighted with the chapel, she and Alison one another's slaves. While she worshiped him, she had almost got to ordering him about; she laughed at her own airs, and he industriously humored them. They were a pretty sight together. The grave careworn man at my side watched them, as I thought, with a closer interest. But it was time for us to go—Lord Fillingford's business had been long awaiting—and Margaret began to make her farewells, extracting from Alison a promise that she should come again soon, and that he would come again soon to Breysgate. I think that this was the first Fillingford had heard of his having been at

Breysgate at all; his eyes looked wary at the news.

Margaret came to him. "Good-by, Lord Fillingford," she said with shy friendliness.

He looked intently at her. "I'm glad to have met a friend of my son's," he said gravely. She blushed again; he turned to me with brows knit and eyes full of brooding question.

On the way home Margaret was silent for a while; then she asked, "Did Lord Fillingford know my father?"

"Yes, he knew him slightly."

"Were they friends?"

"Well, no, I don't think they were, particularly. Not very congenial, I fancy."

"No, they wouldn't be," she agreed. "Father would have thought him dull and pompous, wouldn't he? But I think I should get to like him and "—she smiled audaciously—" I believe I could make him like me. He looks sad, though, poor man! Though I suppose he's got everything!"

"A good many worries included, I think, Margaret."

"He spoke of Lord Lacey as if he was fond of him." The smile lingered on her lips. I think that she was day-dreaming of how, if he were fond of Lacey, he would be fond of what Lacey loved, and that so she might soothe him over his worries and take the lines out of his painful brow. "Anyhow I'm very glad I've met him."

I was glad of that, too—on the whole. The interview had gone as well as could be expected. Mar-

ON ALL GROUNDS—RIDICULOUS!

garet had won no such sudden and complete victory as had attended the beginning of her acquaintance with Alison. Fillingford was not the man to yield a triumph like that; he was far too slow and wary in his feelings, too suspicious and afraid of efforts to approach him; he had, besides, a personal grudge against Breysgate that must needs go deeper than Alison's enforced but reluctant disapproval of the mistress of that house. His words had not been encouraging—" on all grounds utterly ridiculous!" Yet there had been kindness in his grave tones when he told her that he was glad to have met a friend of his son's. I wondered whether Jenny would be content with this somewhat mixed result—and what she would say to the share I had taken in the interview.

I got no chance of making my report to her till late at night, for Cartmell came to dinner—to talk business—and the two were busy discussing Oxley Lodge. Cartmell was still sore about the price, especially sore about that five hundred pounds to satisfy a mysterious whim for early possession. But Jenny was radiant over her new acquisition, and full of merriment at the story of Aspenick's sulky comments.

" Really I think they've every right to hate me—and I suppose they do. But I can't stand still just because the Aspenicks have stood still for six hundred years, can I? Anyhow I think he'll be quite safe about the wire. His new neighbors will probably be hunting people themselves."

Cartmell pricked up his ears. " Hunting people, will they? Well, that's good. I didn't know who——"

"No more do I yet—exactly," she laughed, obviously enjoying his baffled curiosity, and casting a glance across at me for my sympathy in the joke. "But I'll have people of a good class, Mr. Cartmell—no one to offend his high nobility! No tradesman's son at Oxley! Breysgate is bad enough!" Her eyes dwelt for a moment on Margaret. "And Margaret tells me that she's made a conquest of Mr. Alison, and, as a consequence, is going in for all manner of good works."

Cartmell did not follow the connection of her thoughts, and she laughed again at that.

"I'm quite serious about it, Jenny," Margaret protested.

"Of course you are, my dear, I'm very glad of it. And I believe it would appeal even to Lady Aspenick!"

At last we were alone together—just before I said good night.

"Margaret has told me some of her impressions. What are yours?" she asked.

"I think that, on the whole, we did fairly well. I also think that Margaret and I between us pretty well let the cat out of the bag."

"Oh, you did! How was the animal liked?"

"It was pronounced ridiculous—on all grounds ridiculous!"

"Was it? We shall see." Jenny looked dangerous.

"But all the same it was thought better than—the fox."

"Ah!" she cried eagerly. "Better than the fox!" Her eyes sparkled. "Tell me all you can remember."

I told her my tale, not forgetting what had passed between Fillingford and myself when we were alone.

"Not so bad! I think we'll go ahead now!" said Jenny.

CHAPTER XXIV

A CHANCE FOR THE ROMANTIC

ALL was as ready as all could be made. The plans were laid, the approaches prepared, the battalions marshaled. For so much a commander must wait—a good one waits no longer. We went ahead. The Thursday which Jenny had forecasted as likely to be busy turned out to be busy in fact. One thing happened for which she gave the word—another which, as I am persuaded, did not surprise her very much. It had to come—it had better be over and done with. In all likelihood she gave the word for this second thing also.

How were these words given? Ah, there I am out of my depth. In our relations to the other sex we men are naturally on the aggressive. The man pursued of woman exists no doubt—but as an abnormality—a queer by-product of a civilization intent on many things non-natural. The normal man is on the attack, and ignorant, by consequence, of the minutiæ of the science of defense. Whether the intent be surrender, or whether it be that the moment has come for a definitive repulse of the main attack, there are, no doubt, preliminary operations. Scouts are called in, pickets withdrawn, skirmishes retired;

all these have served their function—have given information, have foretold the attack, have felt the strength of the opposing forces, and held them in check while the counsels of the defense were taken and its measures perfected. The order is issued—Let them come on—and on they come, to their triumph or their overthrow. But all this is woman's campaigning—to be dimly understood in its outlines, vaguely grasped in its general principles; but how precisely those preliminary operations are performed man, when he has the best opportunity of discovering, is generally too flurried to observe nicely, too deeply engaged in developing his attack to see, more than half blindly, the maneuvers that allow him an open field for it.

Somehow then, on that Thursday, Jenny offered battle—and on two fronts. She threw her ally Margaret open to Lacey's assault; she accepted, on her own account, a direct attack from Dormer. She wished the offensive operations to be practically simultaneous, and substantially achieved the object. One took place before four in the afternoon—the other not later than nine o'clock at night.

Keenly recognizing the fact that I was not wanted at the Priory—I am not sure that Jenny's pointed remark that she would be glad to see me " after dinner " did not assist the recognition—I remained in my own quarters after returning from our couple of hours' morning work. I rather thought that I might be called into action again later on, but I was not concerned in the present operations.

At five in the afternoon Lacey came to me—in a

state of the greatest agitation. He just strode in, without asking any leave, and plumped himself down by my hearthstone. His eyes were very bright, his hands and legs seemed quite unable to keep still. Obviously something decisive had happened.

" I've done it, Austin! " he said. " I never thought I should be so happy in my life—and I never thought I should feel such a beast either."

" Congratulations! And explanations? It sounds a curious frame of mind."

" Margaret's accepted me—and I'm on my way to Fillingford to tell my father. Miss Driver insisted on my doing it at once—said it was the only square thing. Otherwise—By Jove, I'd rather charge a battery! "

He got up and began to walk about the room; its dimensions were far too small, whether for his long legs or for his explosive state of mind.

" By gad, Austin, you should have seen how she looked! "

" Miss Driver? "

" No, no, man, Margaret. I was awfully doubtful—well, a fellow doesn't want to talk about his feelings nor about—about what happens on that sort of occasion, you know. Only if it hadn't been for Miss Driver, I couldn't have bucked myself up to it, you know. Taking away her friend—leaving her all alone again, too! " he paused a moment. " I tell you I did think of that," he added rather vehemently.

" Most men wouldn't have thought about that at all—perhaps oughtn't to have."

A CHANCE FOR THE ROMANTIC

"Ah, but then what she is to both of us! Well, it went right, Austin, it went right, by Jove!"

His voice was exalted to the skies of triumph. In an instant it dropped to the pit of dismay. "And now I've got to tell the governor!"

"All this has happened thousands of times before," I ventured to remark urbanely, as I filled my pipe and watched his restless striding up and down.

That brought him to a stand—and cooled him into the bargain. "Not quite," he said. "Not quite, Austin." His voice had become more quiet. "You must see that there are elements in this case which—which make it a bit different? My father's been a good friend to me. Things aren't very flourishing with us, as I daresay you know. But I've always had everything—and I've spent all I had, too. The election was a squeeze for him; of course he wouldn't let me take any subscription—it was the honor of the family. He thought of putting things straight himself once—you know how. He'd sooner die than do that now. I'm doing what's pretty nearly as bad to his thinking—and not putting things straight at all! I daresay you don't sympathize with all this, but I've been brought up to think that there's such a thing as loyalty to the family—and not to be ashamed of it. Well, I've cut all that adrift. I couldn't help it. But I don't know whether we can go on. It may mean "—he threw out his hands—" a general break-up!"

"But you're set on it?" I asked.

"Isn't it a good deal too late to talk about that? When I've tried to make her love me—and—and she does?"

"Yes, it's late in the day now. You must go to your father."

"I think I'd sooner be taken home to him with a bullet in my head."

"You'll find it won't be quite so bad as you think. Bad, but not quite so bad, you know."

"Ah, you don't allow for——" He stopped. "Well, you remember Hatcham Ford?"

"It seems rather long ago, Lacey."

"Not to him: he broods. If only she wasn't——!"

"'Romeo, Romeo, wherefore art thou Romeo!'"

"That didn't end so deuced happily, did it?"

"Only because Romeo got back at the wrong moment! Miss Driver, you say, was pleased?"

"Yes—oh, more than that! But for her I don't believe I could have done it. Still it's my own job—and I'm ready to face it. These things must be meant to come, Austin."

I glanced at the clock. He laughed reluctantly and nervously. "Give a fellow five minutes more!" he said.

"With pleasure. Spend it in thinking not of yourself, nor even of your father—but of Margaret."

"Yes, that's right," he said eagerly. "That's the thing to think about. That'll carry me through." He gave another unwilling laugh. "If he'd only be violent, or kick me out, or something of that sort—like the silly old fools in the plays! Not he! He'll behave perfectly, be very calm and very quiet—particularly civil about Margaret herself! He'll tell me I must judge for myself—just as he did about coming to Breysgate. And all the while he'll be breaking his

A CHANCE FOR THE ROMANTIC

heart." He smiled at me ruefully. " Aunt Sarah'll do the cursing—but who cares for that? "

" A good many people besides Lady Sarah will have a word to say, no doubt."

" I don't care a damn for the lot of them—except my father," he said—and I was glad to hear him say it. It expressed—vigorously—my own feelings in the matter. " And don't you think I'm the happiest man on earth? " he added a moment later.

" Earth's not heaven. Try to let Lord Fillingford see what you've shown me."

" What do you mean, Austin? "

" You don't mind my saying it? It's another of those things that one generally doesn't care to talk about. Try to show him that you love her very much, and that next in order—and not quite out of sight either—comes your father. Don't treat it casually—as if you were telling him you were going to dine out—though I daresay that's the etiquette. Try the open heart against the hidden one. You appreciate his case. Show him you do. That's my advice."

" It's good advice. I'll try." He came to me holding out his hand. " And wish me good luck! "

" You've had as fine a slice of luck to-day as happens to most men. Here's to another! "

He wrung my hand hard. " I've made an ass of myself, I suppose! " That was homage to the etiquette. " I'll remember what you've said. He has a case, by Jove, and a strong one! " He smiled again. " Somehow Margaret's case won, though," he ended.

He went his way—a straight lad and a simple gentleman. He had no idea that any schemes had been afoot, that any wires had been pulled, either for him or against his father—if to get this thing done were indeed against Fillingford. Nor had he any idea that his scruples about family loyalty were to be annihilated by the intervention of a fairy godmother. Jenny had stuck to the romantic color of her scheme. She sent him forth to meet his father with no plea in extenuation, with no proffer of gold wherewith to gild the hated name of Octon. His fight was to be single-handed. So she chose to prove his metal—with, perhaps, a side-thought that the fairy godmother's intervention, coming later, might be more effective—and would certainly gain in picturesqueness! That notion, unflattering maybe, one could not easily dismiss when the workings of her mind were in question. Yet it might be that a finer idea was there—that it was not only Lacey's metal which was to be proved that night. She had said that she was ready to bribe, that she might have to bully—and implied that she was prepared to do both at once, if need be. But had it come across her thoughts that, by divine chance, she might have to do neither? She knew Fillingford's love for his son; she had sent Margaret to met Fillingford that he might see her as she was. She might be minded now to prove if love alone would not serve the turn. The battalions might all be held in leash—and the God of Love himself sent forth as herald to a parley. If Fillingford surrendered to that pleading, the victory would not be so purely Jenny's: but she would, I believed, have the grace to like it better. That it was a less characteristic mode of proceeding had to be admitted: but to-day there would be an atmosphere at the Priory which might incline her to it. She would not force Fillingford, if she need not—neither by threats nor by bribes. Being myself, I suppose, somewhat touched by Amyas Lacey's exaltation, I found myself hoping that she would try—first—the appeal of heart to heart. That she would accept it as final—I knew too much to look for that.

The case could not, in its nature, be so simple. With the appeal of love must come that relief from a greater fear which she had carefully implanted, on which she certainly reckoned. That was in the very marrow of her plan; no romantic fancies could get rid of it. The best excuse for it lay in the fact that it would certainly be useful, and was probably necessary. When things are certainly useful and probably necessary, the world is apt to exhibit toward them a certain leniency of judgment. Jenny did not set herself above the world in moral matters.

I went up to the Priory after dinner, availing myself of Jenny's strictly defined invitation. But up there I made a blunder. I blundered into a room where one person at least did not want me—I am not so sure about the other. Dormer had gone clean out of my head; more serious matters were to the front. Heedlessly I charged into the library; there were he and Jenny! Luckily I seemed to have arrived only at the tail-end of their conversation. " Quite final," were the words I heard from her lips as I opened the door. She was standing opposite Dormer, looking demurely resolute, but quite gentle and friendly. He was looking not much distressed, but most remarkably sulky.

I tried to back out, but she called me in. "Come in, Austin. You're just in time to bid Mr. Dormer good night."

He shrugged his shoulders. "I suppose I'd better be off. I'll pick up the car at the stables."

"Good night. We shall see you again some day soon?"

"I don't know about that. I may go away for a bit—and anyhow I expect to be pretty busy."

"Oh, yes, we shall see you again some day soon!" she said very kindly and persuasively. "You won't let it be too long, will you? And you will see Mr. Cartmell about that business, won't you?"

He nodded in an offhand surly fashion—but he might be excused for being a little out of temper. Evidently he was not going to get Jenny's land; apparently she was still to get what she wanted of his. "You'll have to pay for them!" he reminded her, almost threateningly.

"A fancy price for my fancy? Well, I'm always ready to pay that," said Jenny. "Good night and, mind you, quite soon!" Her tone implied real anxiety to see her friend again; under its influence he gave a half-unwilling nod of assent.

I escorted him as far as the hall door—further than that he declined my company. I held a match for him to light his cigar and gave him a stirrup-cup. "Good night, Austin!" Then his irritation got the better of him. "Damn it, does she want Lacey for herself, after all?" Evidently the great event of the day—

from our point of view—had not been confided to him.

"Oh, no, you may be sure she doesn't."

"Then what the deuce she does want I don't know—and I don't believe she does!" With this parting grumble he slouched off sulkily toward the stable.

As a humane man, I was sorry for his plight; Jenny was still serenely ruthless.

"Annoyed, isn't he?" she asked when I rejoined her. "Really I was rather glad when you came in. He had got as far as hinting that I—he put a good deal of emphasis on his 'you'—ought to have jumped at him! It's quite possible that he'd have become more explicit—though it wouldn't have come very well from him under the circumstances."

"You've deluded the young man, you know."

"Oh, it'll do him good," she declared impatiently. "Didn't he deserve to be deluded? He wanted me for what I had, not for myself. Well, I don't so much mind that, but I tell you, Austin, he patronized me! I may be a sinner, but I'm not going to be patronized by Gerald Dormer without hitting back."

"Did you quarrel?"

She smiled. "No. I'm never going to quarrel any more. He'll be back here in no time—and have another try most likely! You see, I'm going into training—a course of amiability, so as to be ready for Lady Sarah." She sprang to her feet. "Do you know that this is a most exciting evening?"

"Oh, yes, I can imagine that. I've had a long talk with Lacey."

"Have you? Isn't he splendid, poor boy? You

should have seen his face when I sent him to her! He thought of nothing but her then—but I like him for thinking of his father now. And I've brought it off, Austin! He thinks there may be just a pretty wedding present — a trousseau check, perhaps!" She came up to me. " This is a good thing I've done—to set against the rest."

" I think it is. But the boy feels horribly guilty."

She nodded. " I know—and so does poor Margaret. I'm afraid she's crying up in her own den—and that's not right for to-night, is it? "

" Love's joy and woe can be simultaneous as well as alternate, I'm afraid."

" I can't stand it much longer." She looked at the clock. " He's to send word over to-night, if he can—by a groom—how he's got on—breaking the news, you know. Let's go out into the garden and wait for this important messenger. But, whatever he says, I believe I shall have to put my oar in to-morrow. I can't have my poor Margaret like this much longer. She knows now why she was taken to Mr. Alison's, and does nothing but declare that she behaved atrociously! "

We were a silent pair of watchers. Jenny's whole soul seemed absorbed in waiting. She spoke only once—in words which betrayed the line of her thoughts. " If I'd thought it would be as bad as this —for her, I mean—I believe I'd have brought her here under another name, in spite of everything, and perpetrated a fraud! I could have told them after the wedding! "

I was afraid that she would have been quite capable

A CHANCE FOR THE ROMANTIC

of such villainy where Margaret was in question, and not altogether averse from a *dénoûment* so dramatic.

"Either Lacey's shirked the interview—or it's been a very long one," I remarked, as the clock over the stables struck half-past ten. "Poor Dormer's home by now—to solitude!"

"Oh, bother Mr. Dormer and his solitude! Listen, do you hear hoofs?"

"I can't say I do," I rejoined, lighting my pipe.

"How you can smoke!" she exclaimed scornfully. Really I could not do anything else—in view of the tension.

A voice came from above our heads: "Jenny, are there any signs?"

"Not yet, dear," called Jenny, and waved her arms despairingly. "Ah!" She held up her hand and rose quickly to her feet. Now we heard the distant sound of hoofs. "I wonder if he's written to me or to her!" She started walking toward the drive.

"To you, I'll be bound!" I answered as I followed.

In a few moments the groom rode up. Jenny was waiting for him, took the letter from him, and opened it.

"No answer," she said. "Thank you. You'll ask them to give you a glass of beer, won't you?"

The man thanked her, touched his hat, and rode off to the servants' quarters.

"In old days the bearer of bad tidings wouldn't have got a glass of beer," I suggested.

"The tidings are doubtful." She gave me the letter: "He is terribly cut up. He promises me an answer to-morrow. I haven't told him yet that I must stick to it *anyhow*. That's for to-morrow, too, if it must come. My love to her.—AMYAS."

"It'd be so much better if he never had to say that," Jenny reflected thoughtfully.

Certainly it would. If the thing could be managed without a rupture, without defiance on the one side or an unyielding posture on the other, it would be much more comfortable for everybody afterwards.

"Still, you know, he's ready to do it if he must." Her pride in her romantic handiwork spoke again.

Suddenly Margaret was with us, out of breath from her run downstairs, gasping out a prayer for the letter. Jenny gave it to her, and she read it. She looked up to Jenny with terrified eyes.

"He mustn't do it for me. I must give him up, Jenny," she murmured, woefully forlorn.

Very gently, just the least scornfully, Jenny answered, "We don't give things up at Breysgate." She stooped and kissed her. "Go and dream that it's all right. It will be by this time to-morrow. Austin and I have a little business to talk over."

Having thus dismissed Margaret (who carried off the precious distressful letter with her), Jenny led me back into the library, bidding me to go on smoking if I really must. She sat down, very thoughtful.

"It's delicate," she said. "Of course I'm trying to bribe him, but I don't want to seem to do it. If I make my offer before he decides, that looks like bribing. If he decides against us, and we make it then —bribery still! But in addition to bribery, there'll be the bad feeling between Amyas and him. No, we must do it before he decides! Only you'll have to be very diplomatic—very careful how you do it."

"I shall have to be?" I exclaimed fairly startled. "I——!"

"Well, I can't go to him, can I?" she asked. "That really would be too awkward!" She smiled at the thought of the suggested interview.

"Pens, ink, and paper!" I suggested, waving a hand toward the writing-table.

"No, no—I want the way felt. If you see he's going to give in without—without the bribe—of course you say nothing about it till he's consented. That'd be best of all; then there's no bribe really. But if he looks like deciding against us, then you tactfully offer the bribe. You must be feeling his mind all the time, Austin."

"And if he has already decided against us?"

She looked at me resolutely. "Remind him that it's not as bad as it might be."

"Bribe—and bully?"

"Yes." She met my eyes for a minute, then turned her head away, with a rather peevish twist of her lips.

"This is a pleasant errand to send a respectable man on! Do you want me to go to him at the Manor?"

"Yes—the very first thing after breakfast, so as to catch him, if you can, before he has had time to pronounce against us, if that's what he's going to do. A man surely wouldn't do a thing like that before breakfast! You'll go for me, Austin?"

"Of course I'll go for you if you want me to."

"Then I'll give you your instructions."

She gave them to me clearly, concisely, and with complete decision. I heard her in a silence broken only once—then by a low whistle from me. She ended and lay back in her chair, her eyes asking my views.

"You're in for another big row if you do this, you know," I remarked to her.

"Another row? With whom?"

"Why, with Cartmell, to be sure! It's so much more than's necessary."

"No, it's not," she declared rather hotly. "It may be more than's necessary for her, or perhaps for Lord Fillingford. It's not more than is necessary for me—nor for Leonard."

I shrugged my shoulders. She laughed rather impatiently. "One's friends always want one to be a niggard!" She leaned forward to me, breaking into a coaxing smile, "Remember 'the handsome thing,' dear Austin."

I came to her and patted her hand. "I'm with you right through. And, after all, you'll still have a roof over your head."

She looked at me with eyes merry, yet foreseeing. "I shan't be in at all a bad position." She laughed. "No harm in that—so long as it doesn't interfere with Margaret?"

"No harm in the world. I was only afraid that you'd lost sight of it."

Jenny sighed and smiled. "You needn't be afraid of such a complete transformation as that," she said.

CHAPTER XXV

A FRESH COAT OF PAINT

IT was all very well to tell me that I must feel Fillingford's mind, but that possession of his had always seemed to me to achieve a high degree of intangibility. His words were not in the habit of disclosing more of it than was necessary for his purpose—without any regard for his interlocutor's—while his face reduced expression to a minimum. For all you got from looking at him, you might pretty nearly as well have talked with your eyes shut. That sudden stroke of surprise and relief at Alison's stood out in my memory as unique—the only real revelation of his feelings which I had seen reflected on his countenance. High demands were being made on me as an amateur diplomatist!

My arrival at the Manor was early—untimely probably, and certainly unexpected. The very butler showed surprise, and left me standing in the hall while he went to discover whether Fillingford could see me. Before this he had suggested that it was Lacey whom I really wanted and that, since Lacey had gone out riding directly after breakfast, my errand was vain. When I insisted that I knew whom I wanted, he gave way, still reluctantly; several minutes passed before he returned with the message that his lordship would receive me. He led me along a corridor, toward a door at the far end of it. To my consternation, as we approached that door, Lady Sarah came out of it—and came out with a good deal of meaning. She flounced out; and she passed me with angry eyes and her head erect. I felt quite sure that Lady Sarah had been against my being received at all that morning.

During previous visits to the Manor, I had not enjoyed the privilege of being shown Fillingford's study, in which I now found myself (not without qualms). It was a large room which mere neglect would have left beautiful; but, unlike the rest of the house, it appeared to have been methodically rendered depressing. His dour personality had—in his own sanctum—overpowered the native beauty of his house. Even the charming view of the old park was more than half hidden by blinds of an indescribably gloomy brown, which challenged to a match the melancholy of a drab carpet. Two or three good portraits were killed by their surroundings—but Fillingford himself seemed in a deadly harmony with his room. His thin gray face and whitening hair, his dull weary eyes, and his rounded shoulders, made him and his room rather suggestive of a funeral card—broad-edged in black, with a photograph of the late lamented in the middle—looking as dead as the intimation told one that unfortunately he was.

He rose for a moment to shake hands, indicating a chair for me close by the table at which he sat. The table was covered with papers and bundles, very neatly arranged; everything in the room was in its place to an inch.

"I'm glad to see you, Mr. Austin," he said in reply to my apology for so early a visit, "and if you come on business, as you say, the hour isn't at all too early for me." He was perfectly courteous—but dry as dust.

"I come on Miss Driver's behalf. As you are probably aware, your son Lord Lacey has done Miss Margaret Octon the honor of making her a proposal of marriage. Miss Octon is in the position of being under Miss Driver's care—I may perhaps call her her ward—and Miss Driver is anxious to know whether Lord Lacey's proposal has your approval."

"Has it Miss Driver's approval?" he asked.

"Most cordially—provided it has yours. Further than that she wouldn't wish to go without knowing your views."

He spoke slowly and deliberately. "You and I have approached this subject before — incidentally, Mr. Austin. I have little doubt that you gathered from that conversation that I had had another idea in my mind?"

"Yes, I rather understood that—from what you let fall."

"That idea was entirely erroneous, I suppose? Or, at all events, if ever entertained, is abandoned now?"

We had already got on to delicate ground. "The situation seems to speak for itself, Lord Fillingford. And I'm sure that the arrangement now proposed has always been desired by Miss Driver."

"Miss Driver has a very great influence over my son, I think," he remarked.

"I don't think she would wish to deny that she has favored this arrangement so far as she properly and legitimately could. She was naturally desirous of promoting Miss Octon's happiness. If in other respects the marriage was a very desirable one—well, she was entitled to think of that also."

"You consider that Miss Octon's feelings are deeply engaged in this matter?"

"If you ask me, I think the two young people are as much in love as any young couple could be."

"I know my son's feelings; he has made me aware of them. And Miss Driver thinks this marriage desirable?"

"She charged me to express the great pleasure she would take in it, if it met with your approval."

He sat silent for a moment, his hand up to his mouth as he bit his finger nail. For reasons I have given, to follow the trend of his thoughts was quite beyond my powers of discernment.

"I suppose I seem to her—and perhaps to you—a very ineffectual person?" he went on in his even voice, with his dull eyes (like a gas jet turned low to save the light!)—"I have the bad luck to stand halfway between two schools—two generations—of ideas. When I was born, men of my order still had fortunes; nowadays many of them have to set out to make fortunes—or at least careers—like other people. I've been stranded halfway. The fortunes of my house are gone; I've neither the power nor the taste to try to retrieve them; and I'm too old. Public life used to be the thing, but I've not the manners for that." His chilly smile came again. "So I sit on, watching the ruins falling into more utter ruin still."

It was not for me to say anything to that. But I had a new sympathy for him. His room, again, seemed to add a silent confirmation of all he said.

"Once I did try to retrieve the situation. You know how—and how the attempt ended. It served me right—and I've learned the lesson. Now the same woman asks me for my son."

"Not for herself!"

"No, thank God!"

He said that very deliberately—not carried away, meaning to let me have it for all it was worth. Well, my diplomacy failed—or I fear so. I did not like to hear him thank God for being quit of Jenny.

"She might have," I declared impulsively.

"I think you're right. She's a very clever woman. Young men are wax in hands like that."

"Shall we get back from what isn't in question to what is, Lord Fillingford?"

"I don't think that the digression was due to me—not wholly anyhow. If it were, I must seek excuse in the fact that I have lived a month under that nightmare." I must have given some sign of protest or indignation. "Well, I beg your pardon—under that impression."

"From that, at least, you're relieved—by the present arrangement."

"The proposed arrangement"—I noticed that he corrected my epithet—"has not my approval, Mr.

Austin. The other day I called it ridiculous. That was perhaps too strong. But it is profoundly distasteful to me, and not at all to my son's interest. I wish to say plainly that I am doing and shall do my best to dissuade him from it."

" If he won't be dissuaded? "

" I venture to hope that we needn't discuss that eventuality. Time enough, if it should occur."

" Miss Octon's feelings———"

" What Miss Driver has—properly and legitimately as you maintain—used her efforts to promote, she will probably be able, with a little more trouble, to undo. That seems to me not my affair."

His defense was very quiet, very stubborn. He told me no more than suited him. But I was entitled to lay hold of the two grounds of objection which he had advanced; the arrangement was distasteful to him—and not at all to his son's interest.

" I thank you for your candor in putting me in possession of your views. Miss Driver would wish me to be equally frank with you. She has anticipated your objections."

" She could hardly do otherwise," he remarked, smiling faintly.

" As regards the first, her position is that this girl can't be held responsible for anything in the past. She, at least, is blameless."

" I occupy the position of my parents—and bear their burdens, Mr. Austin. So do you of yours. It's the way of the world, I'm afraid, and Miss Driver can't alter it."

" She regards this sentimental objection———"

A FRESH COAT OF PAINT

"You would apply that term to my objection to allying my family with the late Mr. Octon's?"

I was not quite sure of my epithet myself. "I didn't say your objection wasn't natural."

"Perhaps you might go so far as to admit that it is inevitable? I on my part will admit that the girl herself appears to be unexceptionable. Indeed, I liked her very much, when I met her at our friend Alison's. That, however, doesn't in my view alter the case."

"I understand. Will you permit me to pass to the other point you mentioned—that of your son's interest?"

"If you please," he said, with a slight inclination of his head, as he leaned back in his chair. I could see that I had made no way with him. The best that we had hoped for was not coming to pass. There was to be no triumph of pure romance; even relief from the "nightmare" would not, by itself, serve the turn.

"Having placed Miss Octon in the position which she now occupies, Miss Driver naturally charges herself with Miss Octon's future."

"Miss Driver is well known to be generous. I had anticipated, in my turn, that she would propose to make some provision for Miss Octon who, as I understand, has only a very small income of her own."

"Miss Driver has recently concluded negotiations for the purchase of Oxley Lodge, together with the whole of Mr. Bertram Ware's estate. It is estimated that, freed from encumbrances, that estate will produce a net rental of three thousand pounds a year. Miss Driver will present the house and estate to Miss Octon on her marriage."

He raised his brows slightly, but made no other comment than, " I had heard that she was in treaty for Ware's place. Aspenick told me."

" She will settle on Miss Octon a sum of money sufficient to make up this income to the sum of ten thousand pounds a year. This income she will increase to twenty thousand on Lord Lacey's succession to the title. She will also present Miss Octon, on her marriage, with a lump sum of fifty thousand pounds. She will execute a settlement of funds sufficient to raise the income to thirty thousand on her death—this income to be settled on Miss Octon for life, with remainder among her children as she and her husband shall jointly appoint. I am also to inform you that, without undertaking any further legal obligation, it is Miss Driver's present intention to leave to Miss Octon, or (if Miss Octon predeceases her) to any son of hers who is heir to your title, the estate of Breysgate and the greater part of her Catsford property. I need not tell you that that property is of great and growing value. In short, subject to public claims and certain comparatively small private ones, Miss Octon is to be regarded as her natural heir no less absolutely and completely than if she were her own and her only child."

He heard me all through with an impassive face— even his brows had returned to their natural level. " Miss Driver is a young woman herself. She will probably marry."

" It is possible, and therefore she limits her legal obligation to the amount I have mentioned—approximately one half of her present income. I am, however, to inform you in confidence that it is her fixed intention not to marry, and that it is practically certain that she will not depart from that resolution—in which case the ultimate arrangement which I have indicated will come into effect."

The bribe was out—and fewest possible words spent over it! Now—how would he take it?

His manner showed nothing. He sat silent for a minute or two. Then he said, " It's certainly princely." He smiled slightly again. " I think I must apologize for my word ' provision.' This is a very large fortune, Mr. Austin—or seems like it to poor folks like the Laceys."

" It's a very considerable fortune. As I have said, Miss Driver regards Margaret Octon as in the place of her own daughter. Miss Driver thought it only right that these circumstances should be placed before you as possibly bearing on the decision you felt it your duty to make yourself, or to recommend to your son."

" Why does she do it? " he asked abruptly.

" I've just given you the reason which I was directed to give. I wasn't commissioned to give any other. She regards Miss Octon in the light of an only child—the natural object of her bounty and, in due course of time, her natural successor."

" We met once at Hatcham Ford, Mr. Austin," he said abruptly. " You remember? I think you knew pretty well the state of things then existing between Miss Driver and myself? I've charged you with possessing that knowledge before. That piece of knowledge may enable you to understand how the present proposition affects me. This isn't all love for Margaret Octon."

"No, not all love for Margaret. But now you're asking me for my opinion, not for my message."

"I didn't mean it as a question. But I see that you agree with me. Then you may understand that I can feel no gratitude for this offer. It—and consequently the arrangement of which it is a part—would transform everything here. It would accomplish the task which I haven't even had the courage to try to accomplish. It would blot out my great failure. But, coming whence it does and why it does, I can feel no gratitude for it."

"It would be very far from Miss Driver's thoughts to expect anything of the kind."

Suddenly he pushed back his chair, rose to his feet, and went to the window, impatiently letting one of the ugly brown blinds fly up to the ceiling by a tug at its cord. He stood there two or three minutes. His back was still toward me when he spoke again.

"I've been a steward more than an owner—a caretaker, I should rather say. This would make my son and his son after him owners again. It's the restoration of our house." His voice sank a little. "And it would come through her and Leonard Octon!" Silence came again for a while; then he turned round and faced me. "I've no right to decide this question. She has taken the decision out of my hand by this. I have memories, resentments, what I think to be wrongs and humiliations. Perhaps I have cause for thinking so."

"I wasn't sent here to deny that, Lord Fillingford.

A FRESH COAT OF PAINT

If that hadn't been so, not I should have been here, but she who sent me."

"And so," he went on slowly, "I'm no judge. I should sin against my conscience if I were to judge. The question is not for me—let her go to Amyas himself."

I was glad at heart—we had escaped bullying; only in one moment of temper had I hinted at it, and that moment seemed now far away. It was easy to see the defects of this man, and easier still to feel them as a vaguely chilling influence. His virtues were harder to see and to appreciate—his justice, his candor of mind, his rectitude, the humility beneath his pride.

"Lord Lacey attaches enormous importance to your opinion. I know that as well as you do. Can't you go a little further?"

"I thought I had gone about as far as could be expected."

"Not quite. Won't you tell your son what you would do if you were in his place?"

"I think you'd better not ask me to do that. I'm less sure of what I should do than I am of what he will do. What he'll do will, I think, content you—I might think too much of who his father is, and of who her father was, and from whose hand these splendid benefits come. I think I'd better not advise Amyas."

"But you'll accept his decision? You'll not dissuade him?"

"I daren't dissuade him," he answered briefly and turned his back on me again. He added in a tone that at least strove to be lighter, "My grandchildren might rise up and call me cursed! But if she looks for thanks—not from this generation!"

For the first time—though I sacrifice finally my character for morality by that confession—I was genuinely, in my heart and not in my pretenses or professions, inclined to regret the night at Hatcham Ford—the discovery and the flight. All said, he was a man. After much conflict they might have come together. If she had known then that it was man against man—not man against name, title, position, respectability — why, the case might have seemed changed, the issue have been different. But he was so seldom able to show what he was. He had no spontaneous power of expressing himself; the revelation had to be wrung out by force—*peine forte et dure*; he had to be pressed almost to death before he would plead for himself, for his case, for what he felt deep down within him. All that was too late to think about—unless some day, in the future, it might avail to make them decently friendly—avail against the deep wound to pride on one side, against the obstinate championship of the dead on the other.

But to-day he had opened himself frankly enough to absolve me from formalities.

"Gratitude isn't asked. I imagine that the proper forms would be."

He turned to me very quickly. "I'm on terms of acquaintance with a lady, or I'm not. If I am, I hope that I omit no courtesy."

"Nor give it grudgingly?"

"She told you to say that?"

"No—nor some other things I've said. But I

know how she'd take any paring down of what is requisite." I ventured a smile at him. " You would have to call, I think, to-morrow." I let that sink in. " And Lady Sarah a few days afterwards."

He gave a short laugh. " You're speaking of matters of course, if this thing is decided as it looks like being."

I got up from my chair. " I go back with the promise of your neutrality? " I asked.

" Neutrality is surrender," he said.

" Yes, I think so. Young blood is in the question. Besides—as you see yourself—the prospect may to a young man seem—rather dazzling."

" Let me alone, Mr. Austin, let me alone, for God's sake! "

" I go the moment you wish me to, Lord Fillingford. I carry my answer with me—isn't it so? "

Wonderfully recovering himself—with the most rapid transition to an orderly self-composure—he came and sat down at his table again.

" I shall see my son on this matter directly after lunch. It will be proper to convey immediate news of our decision to Breysgate Priory. I shouldn't like —in the event we both contemplate—to appear tardy in paying my respects to Miss Driver. At what hour to-morrow afternoon do you suppose that it would be convenient to her to receive me? "

" I should think that about four o'clock would be quite convenient," I answered.

With that, I rose to my feet—my mission was ended. Neither quite as we had hoped, nor quite as we had feared. We had not bullied—we had hardly threatened. If we had bribed, we had not bribed the man himself. He—he himself—would have had none of us; for him—himself—the betrayal at Hatcham Ford governed the situation and his feelings about it. But he saw himself as a trustee—a trustee for unborn generations of men, born to inherit—yet, as things stood, born more than half disinherited! There was no telling what Jenny thought of. Very likely she had thought of that, when she made her bribe no mere provision—nor even merely that "handsome thing"—but the new bestowal of a lost ancestral heritage. Amid profound incompatibilities, they both had broad views, long outlooks—a large conception of the bearings of what men do. Jenny had not been so wrong in thinking of him—nor he in thinking that he could take her with what she brought. Powerfully had Octon, in his rude irresistible natural force, and its natural appeal, broken the current, real if subtle, between them.

I went up to him, holding out my hand. We had won the victory; I did not feel very triumphant.

"Mr. Austin," he said, as he shook hands, "we make a mistake if we expect not to have done to us as we do to others. I learn that as I grow older. Do you understand what I'm at, when I say this?"

"Not very well, I confess, Lord Fillingford."

"Once I went to Miss Driver, holding what I have —my old name, my old place, my position, my title —I can't think of anything they've given me except care and a hopeless sense of my own inadequacy— holding those in my hand and asking for her money. I see now the opposite thing—she comes holding the

"*A fresh coat of paint wanted!*"

money, and asks for what I have. I didn't have my way. She'll have hers."

"There are the young people." It was all I had to say.

"Ask her to leave me a little of my son. Because there's no doubt. You've taken away all my weapons, Mr. Austin."

"I wish you'd had this conversation with her—you two together."

He relapsed into his formal propriety of demeanor. "I shall, I trust, give Miss Driver no reason to complain of any want of courtesy—if Amyas persists."

"You've accepted it that he will."

"Yes—that's truth," he said. "I may be expected at Breysgate to-morrow at four."

"Then try to make it happy!"

He gave me a slow pondering look. "There is much between me and her—not all against her nor for me. I've come to see that. I'll do my best, Mr. Austin."

He escorted me to the door, and walked in silence with me down a broad walk, bordered on either side by stately trees, till we came to his gates. He looked up at the venerable trees, then pointed to the tarnished coronets that crowned the ironwork, itself rather rusty.

"A fresh coat of paint wanted!" he observed with his chilly smile—and I really did not know whether his remark involved a reference to our previous conversation or not.

CHAPTER XXVI

PEDIGREE AND BIOGRAPHY

THE forms were observed most punctiliously; but before the forms began came Lacey, hot from his talk with Fillingford, amazed, almost bewildered, protesting against Jenny's excessive munificence, passionately anxious that she should be sure that he had not foreseen it.

"And how can you believe I never thought of it, when it's just what I ought to have thought of—just the sort of thing you would be sure to want to do?"

"I haven't forgotten your appalling misery, if you have," she retorted, smiling. "I was really afraid you'd kill yourself before Austin had time to get to the Manor. It was quite convincing as to your innocence of my wicked designs, believe me!"

"But I can't possibly accept it," he declared. "It's so overwhelming!"

"You're not asked to accept a farthing, so you needn't be the least overwhelmed. I give it to Margaret. No bride is to go from Breysgate without a dowry, Amyas. Come, you'd put up with ten times as much overwhelming for her sake." She threatened him playfully: "You can't have her with any less—so take your choice!"

"Well, we shall always know who it is that we owe everything to." He took her hand and kissed it. She looked at his handsome bowed head for a moment.

"If you ever do think of anybody in that sort of way, try not to think of me only."

Standing upright again, he looked at her gravely. "I know what you mean." He flushed a little and hesitated. "I hope you know that—that he and I parted—that day—in a—a friendly way?"

"I know it—and I'm very glad," she said. "That's all about the past, Amyas, in words at least. Keep your thoughts as kind as you can—and be very gentle to Margaret when she wants to talk about him. That's a good return to me, if you want to make any. And love my Margaret."

"My love is for her. My homage is for you always —and all the affection you'll take with it," he said soberly. "It's little she'd think of me if that wasn't so," he added with a smile.

Then came the forms, but the first of them—Fillingford's coming—was no mere form to Jenny. She was not afraid or perturbed, as she had been about meeting Alison—she had done with confession—but she was grave, and preoccupied with it. She bade me look out for him and bring him to her in the library. "You must leave us alone, and we'll join you at tea in the garden afterwards. Take care that Margaret is there when we come."

Nothing can be known of what words passed between them, but Jenny gave a general description of their conversation—it was not a long one, lasting perhaps fifteen minutes. "He met me as if he'd never met me before, he talked to me as if he'd never talked to me before. He was a most courteous new acquaintance, hoping that our common interest in the pair would be a bond of friendship between us. I followed the same line—and there we were! But I couldn't have done it of myself. I tried to thank him for that—that sort of message you gave me from him. The first word sent him straight back into the deepest recesses of his shell—and I said, ' Come and see Margaret.' "

"Oh, you'll make better friends than that some day." I had no strong hope of my words coming true.

"You seem to have got nearer to him than I ever could. His shield's up against—Eleanor Lacey! But he was kind to Margaret, wasn't he?"

Yes, he had been kind to Margaret. He took her hand and looked in her eyes, then gravely kissed her on the forehead. "We must be friends, Margaret," he said. "I know how much my boy loves you, and you are going to take his mother's place in my family." There was the same curious quality of careful deliberation as usual—the old absence of any touch of spontaneity—the same weighing, out of just the right measure; but he was obviously sincere. He looked on her young beauty with a kindly liking, and answered the appeal in her eyes by taking her hand between both his and pressing it gently. Margaret looked round to Jenny with a smile of glad shy triumph. Amyas came and put his arm through his father's.

"We three are going to be jolly good friends," he said.

Far more stately was the next ceremonial—the one that was, by my stipulation, to follow a few days later; yet I am afraid that we at Breysgate did not take Lady Sarah's coming half so seriously as she took it herself. She had disapproved of us so strongly before there was—to her knowledge at least—any good ground for disapproval that her later censures, however well-grounded, had lost weight. Sinners cannot take much to heart the blame of those who have always expected to see them do wrong and come to grief—and clapped themselves on the back as good prophets over the event!

Here was no private interview. The whole of her adherents surrounded Jenny in the big drawing-room. Lady Sarah was announced by Loft—himself highly conscious of the ceremonial nature of the occasion. With elaborate courtesy Jenny walked to the door to meet her, spoke her greeting, and led her to one of two large arm-chairs placed close to one another; it was really like the meeting of a pair of monarchs, lately at war but bound to appear unconscious of the disagreeable incidents of the strife. Now peace was to be patched up by marriage. Margaret was called from her place in the surrounding circle. She came—and with courage. We had, I fear, deliberately worked her up to the resolution of being, from the very beginning, not afraid of Lady Sarah—pointing out that any signs of fear now would foreshadow and entail slavery for life. " You'll get on much better if you stand up for yourself," Amyas himself assured her.

Margaret stood, awaiting welcome. Lady Sarah

put on her eyeglasses, made a careful inspection of her prospective niece, but offered no comment whatever on her appearance. She dropped the glasses from her nose again, and remarked, " I'm glad to become acquainted with you. I'm sure that you intend to make Amyas a good wife and to do your duty in your new station. Kiss me! " She turned her cheek to Margaret, who achieved the salute with grace but, it must be confessed, without enthusiasm. Lady Sarah did not return it.

" There will be a great deal to do and think of at Oxley," she pursued, " but I shall be very glad to assist you in every way."

" But there'll be nothing to do, Lady Sarah. Jenny's doing everything—every single thing."

" I'm going to give them a few sticks to start housekeeping on," said Jenny, with a lurking smile.

" Old houses have a style of their own; one learns it by living in one," Lady Sarah observed. Oxley was old—so was Fillingford Manor. Breysgate was hardly middle-aged in comparison. Lady Sarah cast a glance round its regrettable newness; Jenny's refurnishing had not availed to obliterate all traces of that.

" I'm not following this model," said Jenny. " I'm taking the best advice—though I'm sure Margaret will be very glad of anything you can tell her."

" Of course I shall, Lady Sarah. But the people Jenny's going to are really the best people in the trade—they know all about it."

" When you have seen the Manor—" Lady Sarah

began impressively, but Lacey—who had been, the moment before, in lamentable difficulties between a yawn and a smile—cut in:

"Ah, now when shall she come and see the Manor?"

Lady Sarah was prepared with an invitation for the next day: that was another of the forms, to be carried out precisely, as Fillingford had undertaken. She turned to Jenny. "You've seen it, of course, Miss Driver?"

Jenny nodded serenely. Aymas flushed again—his fair skin betrayed every passing feeling—as he said, "We shall be delighted if we can induce Miss Driver to come, all the same."

"Oh, very delighted, very, I'm sure," agreed Lady Sarah.

"You'll enjoy showing it to Margaret all by yourself much better," said Jenny to Amyas. "I'll come another day soon, and have tea with Lady Sarah, if she'll let me."

"Very delighted, very," Lady Sarah repeated.

She rose to take leave; this time she did herself kiss Margaret on the cheek. I think we were all waiting to see whether, in her opinion, the terms of the treaty demanded a kiss for Jenny also. Lady Sarah decided in the negative; Jenny's particularly erect head, as she held out her hand, may have aided—and certainly welcomed—the conclusion. We escorted her to her carriage with most honorable ceremony. Then we sighed relief—save Chat, who had been, from a modest background, an admiring spectator of the scene. "She's not very effusive," said Chat, "but she has the grand manner, hasn't she, Mr. Austin?"

"I never knew what it really meant till to-day, Miss Chatters."

"She probably never hated anything so much in her whole life," Jenny remarked to me, when we were next alone together," so it's really hardly fair to criticise her manner. But I rejoice from the bottom of my heart that she didn't think it necessary to kiss me."

"Since you escaped this time, I should think you might escape altogether."

"Well, the wedding day will be a point of danger," she reminded me, "but I'm pretty safe against its becoming habitual. We both hate the idea of it too much for that."

Then—a week later—came the public announcement, made duly and in due form in the *Times and Herald*: " Between Lord Lacey, son and heir of the Right Honorable the Earl of Fillingford, and Margaret, daughter of the late Leonard Octon, Esq." The sensation is not to be described. So many things were explained, so many mysteries cleared up! Folks knew now why Lacey had been so much at Breysgate, Sir John Aspenick learned for whom Oxley Lodge was wanted, and Cartmell understood why he had been forced to disburse that much grudged five hundred pounds for early possession. For, with the announcement, came an inspired leading article, revealing the main terms of the proposed settlement; a little discretion was exercised as to the exact figures, but enough was said to show that, besides the gift of the Oxley Grange estate as it stood, there were large sums to pass both now and in the future. Let the parties have been who they might, such a transaction would have commanded the universal attention of the countryside; when it took place between Lord Fillingford's heir and the late Mr. Octon's only daughter, people with memories recalled and retold their stories, and found newcomers ready indeed to listen. Once again Jenny filled all Catsford and all the neighborhood with gossip, speculation, and applause.

"I told you you'd have to undo the purse-strings to some style," I said to Cartmell. "What do you think of this, Mr. Chancellor of the Exchequer?"

He winked his eye at me solemnly. "It's great," he said. "What a mind she has! There she'll sit at Breysgate—with the town under one foot, and Fillingford and Oxley under the other!"

"Hardly that!" I smiled.

"Look what she's giving now! Aye, and, my boy, think of what she's still got left to give! If human nature goes on being what it's been ever since I remember, Miss Driver's word will be law in both those houses—if not now, in a few years at all events. It's a lot of money—but it's not ill-spent. It makes her the queen of the place, Austin!" He laughed in enjoyment. "I wish old Nick Driver could see this! He'd be proud of his daughter."

"However much or little that may be the result, I'm sure it was not her object."

He looked at me with a good-humored pity; he thought me a fool in practical matters. "Have that as you like," he said, " but she won't object to the result — nor waste it, either — I promise you." He chuckled again. " She's got back at them with a vengeance!"

It was true. Never even in the days before the flight did she make such a figure. The Aspenicks surrendered at discretion, Fillingford Manor was in forced alliance, Oxley Lodge was annexed; Hingston did not hold out long, and Dormer, placated by a big price for his farms, put his pride and his sulks where he had put the money. The town was at Jenny's feet, even if it were an exaggeration to say that it was under them. Timeservers bowed the knee to so much power; the charitable accepted so splendid an atonement. If any still had conscientious doubts, Alison's conduct was invoked as warrant and example. If he were enthusiastically for the mistress of Breysgate now, who had a right to criticise—who could arrogate to himself such merit as would entitle him to refuse to forgive—even though a certain feature in the arrangement made it forever impossible to forget?

The chorus of applause was loud—and almost unanimous; but it was broken by the voice of one sturdy dissenter—one to whom interest could not appeal and, even had she wanted anything of Jenny, would have appealed vainly—one on whom the sentimental side had no effect, since both her sentiment and her charity moved in the strait fetters of unbending rules. Mrs. Jepps was rigid and obstinate. She had not fallen to the temptation of using the park road, as Lady Aspenick had: she would not now bow the knee to Baal, however splendid and imposing a deity Baal might be. Many had a try at shaking her—and Alison among the rest. He told me about his effort, laughing as he confessed his failure.

"I was well snubbed. She told me that Romish practices led to Romish principles, and that where they led it was easy to see; but that she for her part had other principles and didn't palter with them. When it suited Miss Driver to explain, she was ready to listen. Till then—nothing to do with the woman!"

Jenny heard of this—her one signal failure (for she had extorted alliance, if not loyalty, from Lady Sarah) with composure, almost with pleasure, although pleasure of an unusual variety.

"Well, I respect Mrs. Jepps," she said, "and I wish very much that she wouldn't deprive herself of her drives in the park. I'd promise not to bow to her! Mrs. Jepps is good for me, Austin—a fat, benevolent, disapproving old skeleton at the feast—a skeleton with such fat horses!—crying out 'You did it, you did it!' That's rather useful to me, I expect. Still I should like "—she smiled mischievously—" to try her virtue a little higher—with an invitation to the laying of the foundation stone! I'm going to have that in four or five months, and Mr. Bindlecombe is angling for a prince to do it. If Mrs. Jepps holds out against the prince, she has my leave to hold out against me forever!"

Still it was her instinct to conquer opponents, even when her judgment indorsed their opposition and her feelings did not resent it.

"If she were a young woman, you'd get her at last," I said, "but she's very old. She'll go to heaven before you've time; I can only hope, for the sake of this household, that she won't be made a doorkeeper, or we may as well give up all hope and take what chances await us elsewhere."

"Let her be," said Jenny. "She only serves me as all the rest would have done, if I hadn't inherited Nick Driver's money. I've beaten them with that."

"That's not the way you beat Alison," I reminded her.

Her face had been hard as she referred to the power of her money; it softened at the mention of Alison's name. "It was more Margaret's victory than mine. I like best to fight with Margaret; that's a clean sword, Austin. When I'm fighting with and for her, then I'm right. But right or wrong, you wouldn't have me beaten?"

"You've no right to impute any such immoral doctrine to me."

"By now, I think I have," she laughed. "I wonder how soon Lady Sarah will tell Margaret all about me!"

"I don't think she will—and, if she did, you'd never know it."

Jenny smiled. "Yes, I should. Some day—for no apparent reason—Margaret would come and kiss me extraordinarily often." She gave a shake of her head. "I'd rather it didn't happen, though."

It is not to be supposed that, during her Fillingford campaign, Jenny had neglected her Institute,

No day had passed without talk or correspondence about it, and she had been in constant consultation with Bindlecombe, Chairman of the Committee of the Corporation in whose charge the scheme was. Fruits of the activity had now appeared. The gardens of Hatcham Ford had been laid waste. (O Bindlecombe, what of your deceitful promises to spare them?) Only the shrubberies in front (where Lacey had once hidden) remained of the old pleassure grounds. Everywhere else were excavations, or lines that marked foundations to be laid; already in some spots actual buildings poked their noses out of the earth, their raw red brick shamed by the mellow beauty of the old house which still stood and was to stand as the center of the architectural scheme. Like all things with which Jenny had to do, the plan had grown larger and larger as it progressed, took more ground, embraced more projects, swallowed more money. It spread across the road, absorbed the garden of Ivydene, and happily involved the destruction of that odious villa of unpleasant memories. It made inroads on Cartmell's money-bags till—what with it, and Margaret's great endowment, to say nothing of Dormer's fields—rich Miss Driver was for two or three months positively hard up for ready money! But the result was to be magnificent; with every fresh brick and every additional sovereign, Catsford grew more loyal, and the prospect of catching that prince more promising. " And I'm going to get Mr. Bindlecombe made Mayor again next year, and Amyas must pull all the wires in London town to get him a knighthood. With Margaret and Amyas married, the Institute opened, and Mr. Bindlecombe Sir John, I think I may sing *Nunc Dimittis*, Austin!"

"We might perhaps look forward to a short period of peace," I admitted cautiously.

"Come down and look at the old place once more, before it's changed quite out of recognition. Just you and I together!"

We went down together one evening in the dusk. Architects and surveyors, clerks, masons, and laborers had all gone home to their rest. The place was quiet for the night, though the rents in the ground and the rising walls spoke loud of the toils of the day. The old house stood unchanged in the middle of it all; unchanged, too, was the path down which Jenny had passed after she begged the loan of Lord Fillingford's carriage. She took a key from her purse and opened the door of the house. "Let's go in for a minute."

She led me into the room where once I had waited for her—where, another time, I had found her holding Powers's head, where Fillingford had come upon us in the very instant when I had hailed safety as in sight. The room was just as Octon had left it—his heavy dining table, his ugly dining chairs, the two old leather ones on each side of the fireplace, his spears and knives on the wall. And there, too, on the mantelpiece, was the picture of the beautiful child which I had marked as missing when I reached the house that night.

"You've been here before," I said to Jenny, pointing at the picture.

"I found it among his papers after he was at

peace," she answered, sitting down in one of the old leather chairs. " I knew this was its place; it has returned to it. And there it will stay, so long as I or Margaret have a voice here. Yes, I have been here before—and I shall be here often. This is to be my room—sacred to me. From here I shall pull the wires!" She smiled at me in a humorous sadness.

"Not the wires of memory too often!" I suggested.

"Two men have made me and my life—made me what I am and my life what it is and is to be. Here —in this place—they meet. This room is Leonard's —all the great thing that's coming into being outside is my father's. They appreciated one another, you've told me—and so has Leonard. They won't mind meeting here, Austin."

"They neither of them did justice to you!" I cried. "Was the Smalls and the Simpsons justice? And was what he—the other—let you do justice either?"

"I don't know—and I don't care," said Jenny. "They were both big men. They had their work, their views, their plans, their occupations. They had their big lives, their big selves, to look after. They couldn't spend all the time thinking whether they were doing justice to a woman!"

"That's a nice bit of special pleading!" I said. "But there, I'm not a great man—as both of your big men have, on occasion, plainly told me."

She smiled at me affectionately. "But one of them gave me—in the end—all he had, and for the other I—in the end—would have given all I had. Oh, yes, it's 'in the end' with us Drivers—because we must try to get everything first—before we are ready to give! But in the end all was given or ready to be given, and here they shall stay together. I have no pedigree, Austin, and I shall have no biography. Here stand both. At Hatcham Ford read my pedigree and my biography."

The room grew dark, but her pale face stood out against the gloom. She rose from her chair and came up to me.

"My big ghosts are very gentle to me now—gentler than one would have been in life, I think—gentler than the other was. You see, they're at rest—their warfare is accomplished. I think mine's accomplished, too, Austin, and I will rest."

"Not you! Rest indeed!"

"I may work, and yet be at peace in my heart. Come, my friend, let's go back home. Amyas dines with us to-night. Let's go back home, to the happiness which God—Allah the All-Merciful—has allowed me, sinner that I am, to make."

Through the soft evening we walked back to where Amyas and Margaret were.

CHAPTER XXVII

A MAN OF BUSINESS

BEHOLD us all engaged in laying the foundation stone of the Memorial Hall, which was to be the most imposing feature, if not the most useful part, of the great Driver Institute. At least—not quite all of us. Lady Sarah had begun, by now, her habit of making long sojourns at Bath, returning to Fillingford Manor from time to time on visits. These were usually arranged to coincide with Jenny's absences—in London or on the Riviera—but one had not been arranged to coincide with the laying of Jenny's foundation stone. And Mrs. Jepps was not there—although she had been invited to have the honor of meeting His Royal Highness. There Jenny had to accept defeat. But all the rest gathered round her from borough and from county—Fillingford stiff but friendly, the Aspenicks as friendly as if they had never been stiff, Dormer forgetful of his injuries, Alison to bless the undertaking, Lord and Lady Lacey, fresh back from their honeymoon, Cartmell—and Sir John Bindlecombe! He was not actually Sir John yet, but His Royal Highness—who did his part excellently, but confided wistfully to Cartmell that it was a splendid hunting morning—

was the bearer of a certain gracious intimation which made us give the Mayor and Chairman of the Reception Committee brevet rank at once. Sir John, then, held the mortar, while Jenny herself handed the silver-gilt trowel. His Royal Highness well and truly laid the stone, making thereafter a very pleasant little speech, concerning the interest which his Family took and had always taken in institutes, and the achievements and sterling British qualities of the man we were there to commemorate, the late Mr. Nicholas Driver of Breysgate Priory. It had been my privilege to coach His Royal Highness in the latter subject, and he did full justice to my tuition. That done, he added a few graceful words of his own concerning the munificent lady who stood by his side, and the men of Catsford cheered Jenny till they were hoarse. Amyas Lacey and Bindlecombe jumped forward to lead the cheers, and four or five eminent men of science, whom I had contrived to induce to come down, to add to the glory of the occasion, joined in with a will. After that—luncheon for us, dinner for half the population; and a brass band and a procession to conduct His Royal Highness back to the station. His way lay past Mrs. Jepps's window; so I hope that she saw him after all—without a stain on her principles!

"That's done, anyhow!" said Jenny. "Now the real work can go ahead!"

The next morning after this eventful day she dismissed me—summarily and without warning.

"You must go, Austin," she told me. "I've been very selfish, and I'm very ignorant. Of course I

A MAN OF BUSINESS

realized that your books are very clever, though I don't understand them, but till I heard what those great pundits you brought down said about you, I didn't know what I was doing. You mustn't waste your time writing notes and doing accounts for a provincial spinster."

"And are you going to write the notes and do the accounts yourself?" I asked. "Or is Chat?"

"I'm going to pension Chat; she's got a horrid cough, poor thing, and will do much better in a snug little villa at the seaside. I've got my eye on one for her. I shall get a smart young woman, who dresses nicely, looks pretty, and knows something about frocks and millinery—which last necessary accomplishment of a lady's private secretary you have never even tried to acquire."

"Dear me, no more I have! It never occurred to me before. I left it to Chat! Do you think I could learn it now?"

"I've the very greatest doubts about it," answered Jenny, deceitfully grave. "Go away, and write more books." She shook her head at me reproachfully. "To think you never told me what I was doing!"

"I suppose you're aware that you pay me four hundred pounds a year?"

"So did my father. I suppose he knew what the proper salary was."

"But you don't know perhaps how much I've made out of these marvelous books in the last four years? It amounts to the sum of twenty-seven pounds, four shillings, and twopence. Your new secretary will tell you in a minute how much that works out at per annum."

"Goodness!" murmured Jenny. "Oh, but, of course, I should——"

"Of course you'd do nothing of the kind! Time has consecrated my claim to be overpaid for inefficient services—but I won't be pensioned off into a villa with Chat! Here I stay—or out I go—to a garret and starvation!"

"And fame!"

"Oh, humbug! As for my work, you know I've more time here than I want."

"You really won't go? I shall have the clever girl, you know—for the notes and the accounts!"

"Have the girl, and be—satisfied with that!"

"You really refuse to leave me, Austin?"

"This is my home," I said. "Here I stay till I'm turned out."

She came to me and put her arm through mine. "If this is your home, nobody shall turn you out—neither before my death nor after it. As long as you live, the Old Priory is there for you. Even you can't refuse that?"

"No, I won't refuse that. Let me stop in the Old Priory and do the odd jobs."

She pressed my arm gently. "It would have been very curious to have nobody to talk to about things—especially about the old things." Her voice shook a little. "Very curious—and very desolate, Austin!"

It is now a good many years since we had that conversation—and we have never had another like it.

I must plead guilty to one or two books, but I manage to save a little of Jenny's work from the clutches of the clever girl, and old Cartmell is on the shelf—so I get some of his; and still I dwell in the little Old Priory under the shadow of big Breysgate on the hill above. Changes have come elsewhere. There are children at Oxley Lodge; the succession is prosperously—and indeed amply—secured. Mrs. Jepps has departed this life—stubborn to the last in her protest; a donor, who was, and insisted on remaining, anonymous, has founded a Jepps Scholarship at the Institute " as a mark of respect for her honorable life and consistent high principle "; I am inclined to hope that Mrs. Jepps is not permitted to know who that donor was. Lady Sarah is gone, too, and Alison has been promoted to a suffragan bishopric. But over us at Breysgate no change passes, save the gentle change of the revolving years—unless it be that with every year Jenny's sway increases. Down in Catsford they have nicknamed her " The Empress." The seat of empire is at Breysgate; by her proconsuls she governs the borough, Oxley, even Fillingford Manor; for though its rigid master has never become her friend, has no more passed than he has fallen short of the limits of punctilious courtesy which he accepted, yet in all business matters he leans more and more on her. So her power spreads, and will increase yet more when, in due course, Lacey and Margaret take possession of the Manor. The despotism is veiled; she is only First Citizen, like Augustus himself. She will grow no richer—" There is more than enough for them after I am gone "—and pours back into the town and the countryside all that she receives from them—*panem et circenses*—and better things than that. The Institute is even such a model to all institutes as Bindlecombe would have it; his dream of its broadening into a university is an openly avowed project now. No wonder that by public subscription they have placed a portrait of her in the Memorial Hall, facing the picture of Nicholas Driver which she herself presented. From where she hangs, she can see the old roof of Hatcham Ford, surrounded and dwarfed by the great buildings that she has erected. The painter of Jenny's portrait never saw the Eleanor Lacey at Fillingford Manor—indeed it has gone from its old place, and is to be found somewhere in a cupboard, as I suspect—but the likeness is indubitably there, all undesigned. You see it in the firm lips and jaw, in the straight brows on the pale face, above all in the hazel eyes, so bright and yet profound. Eleanor Lacey had little luck after her luckless flirtation. Fortune has been kinder to Jenny. She has a full life, a good life, a very useful one. The story has grown old; the name of Octon is merged; time has obliterated well-nigh all the tracks she made in her evening flight from Hatcham Ford.

Yet not in her heart; there is no obliteration there, but rather an indelible stamp; it may be covered up —it cannot be sponged or scratched out. For her, Leonard is not forgotten; he triumphs. He lives again in the son of Margaret his daughter; in the person of that son—his grandson—he is to reign where he was spurned. That is the triumph of the scheme she made—and to her it is Leonard's triumph. In her eyes her own triumphs are little beside that.

"My day is done," she said to me once. "Bad it was, I suppose, and God knows that it was short! But it was my day, and it is over." But she did not speak in sorrow. "I am content—and at peace." She broke into a smile. "Don't think of me as a woman any more. Think of me as just a man of business!"

A man of business she is—and a very fine one; tactful and conciliatory, daring and subtle. But not a woman? Never was there more a woman since the world began—never one who leaned more on her woman's power, nor turned the arts of woman more to practical account. She has had many wooers; Dormer returned to the charge three or four times, till at last he fell back—in a mood little above resignation—on Eunice Aspenick; we have had an ambitious young merchant from Catsford, a curate or two, and one splendid aspirant, a former brother-officer of Lacey's, a man of great name and station. All went away with the same answer—but all were sent away friends, praisers of Jenny, convinced, I think, that they had only just failed and that no other man could have come so near success. There lies her instinct, and she cannot help using it—sometimes for her purposes, sometimes for her instinctive pleasure, which is still to lose no adherent, and to make friends even in refusing to be more. She will not marry, but she is marriageable—eminently marriageable—and that is as much an asset now as when she threatened to use it against Lord Fillingford if he would not take her bribe. Not a woman? How little we know of ourselves, Jenny! Is not her great triumph—Leonard's triumph, for which she planned and wrought and risked—is it not a woman's triumph all over, and her satisfaction in it supremely feminine?

A woman—and, to my thinking, a great woman, too; full of what we call faults, full of what we hail as virtues—and quite with a mind of her own as to the value of these qualities—a mind by no means always moving on orthodox lines. Stubborn, self-willed, tortuous, jealous of domination, tenacious of liberty (at what cost and risk she had clung to that till the last moment!), not patient of opposition, suspicious of any claim to influence or to guide her; generous to magnificence, warm in affection, broad in mind, very farseeing, full of public spirit, never daunted, loyal to death, and beyond the grave—that is Jenny—and yet not all Jenny, for it leaves out the gracious puzzling woman in whom all these things are embodied; the woman with her bursts of temper, her fits of petulance, her joyous playfulness, her sudden looks and gestures of love or friendship; her smiles gay or mysterious, her eyes so full of fun or so full of thought, flashing while she scolds, mocking while she cheats, caressing when she cajoles, so straight and honest when suddenly, after all this, she lays her hand on your arm and says "Dear friend!" Such is "The Empress"—the great Miss Driver of Breysgate Priory. Such is my dear friend Jenny, whom I serve in freedom and love in comradeship. I would that she were what they call her! None fitter for the place since Great Elizabeth—whom, by the way, she seems to me to resemble in more than one point of character and temperament.

So we live side by side, and work and play together—with love—but with no love-making. There are obvious reasons on my side for that last proviso. I am her servant; the fourth part of twenty-seven pounds per annum represents, as I have hinted, the most I have earned save the salary she pays me. I should make a very poor Prince Consort—and Jenny would never trust me again as long as she lived—though it is equally certain that she would never tell me so. And there's another reason, accounting not for my not having done it, but for the odder fact—my not having wanted to do it. Humble man that I am, yet I was born free and am entitled not only to the pursuit of happiness, but to the retention of my liberty; the latter offers, in my judgment, the most favorable opportunity for the former. Jenny likes liberty—so do I. As we are, we can both enjoy it. If by any miraculous freak Jenny had made me her husband, she would have made me her slave also. Or would Jenny have been the slave? I fancy not. I know her—and myself—too well to cherish that idea; which is indeed, in the end, little more attractive.

For her decision is right for herself, as once I told her. She has found happiness—more happiness than would have come to her if she had never fled from Hatcham Ford, more happiness, I dare to think (though never to say!), than would in the end have been hers, had Octon never faced the Frenchman's pistol at Tours. She is not made for an equal partnership, no more than for a submission or surrender.

How hardly she accepted a partnership at all, even with the man whose love has altered all her life! It is her nature to be alone, and through a sore ordeal she came to that discovery. Once, I think, and in just one sentence she showed me her true heart, what her true and deepest instinct was—even about Leonard Octon.

We were sitting by the fire one evening alone. Talk dragged and she looked listless, tired after a busy day's work, thoughtful and brooding.

"What are you thinking of?" I asked.

"Oh, my thoughts had gone back to the early days here. I was thinking how pleasant it would be if we had Leonard back at Hatcham Ford, dropping in after dinner."

At Hatcham Ford, mind you! Dropping in after dinner! That was the time to which her wandering thoughts flew back—that the point on which their flight instinctively alighted. Not the heart-trying, heart-testing, perhaps heart-breaking, days of union and partnership, but the days of liberty and friendship.

I must have smiled to myself over her answer, for she said sadly, yet with a smile herself, "I can't help it! That was what I was thinking, Austin."

So think, dear mistress—and not on the harder days! Defiance, doubt, despair, are over. Abide in peace.

THE END

www.ingramcontent.com/pod-product-compliance
Lightning Source LLC
Chambersburg PA
CBHW030213170426
43201CB00006B/70